The Build-up

For David McDowell

By William Carlos Williams (in print)

The Autobiography
The Build-up
Collected Earlier Poems
Collected Later Poems
The Farmers' Daughters
I Wanted to Write a Poem*
In the American Grain
In the Money
Kora in Hell: Improvisations†
Many Loves and Other Plays
Paterson, Books 1-5
Pictures from Brueghel and Other Poems
The Selected Essays
Selected Poems
White Mule

Beacon Press
† City Lights Books

THE BUILD-UP

A NOVEL BY
WILLIAM CARLOS WILLIAMS

A NEW DIRECTIONS BOOK

Waiting, that's the most terrible word in the language.

Flossie was waiting to grow up. All the happiness of childhood is bordered in black by that crushing weight. For the time has passed while we are waiting. Falsehood is the natural flower of such a vine. Children lie naturally. Flossie did. To keep, to keep the "thing," the nameless thing that never waits, never, intact.

As they drove away in the livery coach from their last residence in Hackensack Flossie insisted on bringing along with her one prize possession, Pully, the cat. It wasn't Pussy, it was Pully, definitely and distinctly, and she clung to him as to the name, with desperation. Pully, in her lap, her hands sunk in his fur, she was secure. With Pully along, the trip was a sigh, a skip, nothing at all. Without him—death.

As they were going jogging along in the hack—*Hackensack*. That's funny. Jogging along in the hack along the Polifly Road they passed one of the brownstone farmhouses of the early settlers.

"Now, that's where I'd like to live," said Olga, the fat auntie.

"Is that so?"

"They're beautiful."

"You can have them," replied her sister Gurlie, Flossie's

mother. "They're damp in summer and—cold in winter. And what are you going to do with the second floor? They never have room enough there to stand up in."

"They had to have it that way to keep warm."

"And they were always cold or too hot."

"You can sleep better that way, with the snow drifted in over the blanket in the morning, over the coverlet."

"You can have that today in Vermont—if you want it. Not me."

George Washington (and his men!) came also along this road, so the sign said, on his retreat "from California."

"What?"

"I mean Fort Lee."

"But that was November. This is . . ."

"Listen to that little bird! I wonder what it is. He can sing." Clipeety clop, clip, clop, intoned the horse's feet. "A song sparrow, I think."

"Did you bring lunch?" said the fat auntie. She was always the prime mover in these situations—migrations might be the better word—she who was so little migratory.

"Hurry! Hurry!" It had begun to rain again. "Why did it have to rain today?" Gurlie grabbed the cloth strap and pulled up the window on her side just as the rain splashed against it in a sudden gust, the side toward the flat meadow land, the east. "Pull up your window!"

"It isn't coming in here," said Lottie, Gurlie's older daughter.

"Pull it up, I tell you. Haven't you any brains? We'll all be soaked." Thus the adult makes a fool of himself and children looked at him amazed. No rain was striking in from that side.

"But Gurlie, we'll suffocate in here," said Olga. "Let it down a little bit at the top. Look at those poor blossom trees."

The rain was pelting down heavily now as they passed an old Dutch house with a beautiful sloping lawn and at the side of the house, close to the wall, a peach tree in full blossom.

4

"Look at that box!" It was really impressive in its dark luxuriance against the house, by the front stoop, as they call it here.

"Nonsense," said Gurlie. "I can't see anything."

Neither could Flossie, nothing of the sort in sight. "A box? Where?" So she changed her interest as children will, trying to see what had happened to the coachman. He seemed not to notice the rain which rattled on the roof of the coach in slashes and lulls, the wind sometimes shaking the whole vehicle, which kept moving along, notwithstanding, steadily in its course.

"Didn't that come suddenly!" said the fat auntie. "Why, I thought the sun was coming out."

"It was out," said Gurlie. "I suppose everything we've got's being soaked." For they were being followed down by the van containing the furniture, not a very satisfactory-looking van as they saw it packed, with nothing but a tarpaulin strapped across the back for protection with assurances from the movers that everything would be all right.

The inside of the coach smelled stale, of dust and horsehair, and the violets, crushed on the seat now, to say nothing of the cat which little Flossie had insisted on bringing with her also as a last souvenir of the happy day she had spent, before leaving Hackensack, in Mrs. Waldron's garden. Mrs. Waldron had a back yard full of sweet violets, or so Flossie believed, acres of them, it seemed—in her small imagination—though this could not possibly have been the case in that small kitchen area. But the garden scented the mind of the little girl, who had one day discovered the flowers there—just yesterday, in fact. There they were, intense clusters of the low purple blossoms and, wonder of wonders, Mrs. Waldron had come out herself, while Flossie started shyly to move away, and told her she could have all she wanted of them.

"Pick all you want and take them home to your mother if you will pick some for me too, please. I have all I can ever use and there will be more tomorrow." So Flossie had bathed more than once in that sense of generous perfume which her own hands could touch and pluck to her heart's desire. Entranced, she had moved about with Mrs. Waldron standing there, picking the fragrance of that garden whose owner was a goddess. Now she was leaving that world to go into another, exciting in its vagueness and distance from all she had begun to love.

It was close to the May of the year. "You better take a coach," Joe had cautioned them. "Otherwise you'll have to go to Jersey City on the train, wait in that room, take another train, change cars with all that baggage."

"It isn't worth the difference."

"Take a coach. Spend the money."

"You better give me enough then," said Gurlie.

"How much have you got now?"

"I don't want to be short of money. You better give me a ten-dollar bill. And some change."

"I'll go down to the livery stable and arrange for it there myself."

"Come on," said Gurlie insisting. "Who do you think I am?" So Joe gave her a few bills and went off to the city.

The rain had stopped as quickly as it began and the sun came out. Gurlie was the first to let down her window. "Oh what a relief! *Es stinkt!*" The little girls giggled. The sweet air of the afterstorm earth blew in their faces. Pully struggled in the old shawl in which Flossie had wrapped him but she hung on for dear life, and he, puffing, with the tip of his pink tongue sticking out, subsided again, watchfully growling under his breath.

"You'll kill him," said Gurlie. "Why did you have to bring that stupid cat?" said she. "We could have left him there just as well as not."

"That would have been cruel," said the fat auntie.

"Agh, someone would have found him. He had plenty of homes he could have gone to. Open the door and let him go.

He'll be sick in here and mess us all up. I think he's done something already."

Flossie closed her ears, dreading what would come next. But she held on. Nothing happened. Her heart quieted again as the wobbly coach moved steadily ahead. It had a peculiar swing to it that you had to get a little used to. The back swung slightly from side to side as the old horse began to trot on the downhill into the town that was approaching, the small shop windows on either side seeming quaintly old-world as the two women and the little girls looked out curiously. Right, left, right, left, the coach swung, so that all the heads in it wobbled a little also adjusting themselves to the jostling.

Lottie noticed it first and thought it very funny. She said nothing but looked from one to the other amused to see all the heads jiggle joggle as they went along. "Whew! it's getting hot in here," said Gurlie. "I wish to God we'd get there. What is this on the seat?" She picked up the limp violets and threw them out the window. Flossie noticed that two of the flowers had escaped under the edges of the fat auntie's ample skirt. She said nothing.

"Have you got the keys?"

"What keys?"

"To the house. I hope so!" Gurlie started furiously to dig into the bottom of her handbag. "Yes."

"I hope they're the right ones."

"Whew! That old horse. Phew! Who was that? Was that the cat?" Nobody said a word. "You ought to be ashamed of yourself." Lottie looked at Flossie, Flossie looked at Lottie. They both shook their heads. Now they were going over cobblestones and the racket in the cab was intense, they felt as though their teeth were on edge. But they liked it. It was funny. Everything was funny at that moment for some reason and the two girls started giggling.

"Stop that nonsense."

"Oh, leave them alone," said the fat auntie. "Look,

7

there's a Catholic church," she said. Flossie and Lottie looked quickly to see what the fat auntie had so identified but they couldn't see a thing. They wondered how the auntie knew it was a Catholic church. Lottie even turned around after they had passed and stared out of the window at the back.

"Keep your dirty feet down," said Gurlie.

But she had seen the retreating street, still running with dirty brown water, and on one side a church with a tower and a cross on top. "But how can you tell it's Catholic?" she wondered. She gave it up, in fact she felt a little sick to her stomach. "I feel sick," she said to the occupants of the coach in general.

"*Ach Gott!* That too," said Gurlie. "Sit down. No wonder you're sick if you keep jiggling around like that. Sit down and put your feet where they belong."

She didn't know that her feet belonged any particular place—anyhow, why? But she sat down and the fat auntie, who had been fumbling in her *étui*, unexpectedly put a bottle of smelling salts under Lottie's nose, which made her jump back in surprise, her eyes watering.

"Smell it," said the fat auntie. "Gently. Gently. Come on. It will do you good." It was a green bottle. Lottie sniffed more gently, gingerly, this time and felt better. It smelled like violets.

Flossie knew better, leaning over to try it too. But it was nice. Only it wasn't violets. She chuckled to herself. She knew what violets smelled like! Pully began to struggle again.

"Give some to him," said Gurlie, chuckling to herself. "Maybe it'll fix him too. Here, let me smell it," and she grabbed the bottle of smelling salts from her sister and took two or three good whiffs. "Where did you get that?" she said. "It's stale. Pouff, cheap stuff."

"It is not cheap stuff," said her sister. "It's the best that can be bought. As a matter of fact, you can see where it came from. Paris."

"Agh, they always put that on the labels."

8

"Not this, I bought it myself on the Rue Royale last year."

"All right," said Gurlie. "Let me have another smell. Agh, they cheated you. It's no good."

"It's the finest you can buy," said Olga. "It's the same place all the millionaires go."

Gurlie laughed.

"Those people have cheap things, too, with the same labels on for the ones who don't know. Don't tell me. I know them. You should let me buy things for you when you want something good."

"You!" said her sister. "What do you know? Have you been to Paris in your dreams?"

"Huh, Paris. What's Paris? I'm going everywhere in a few years. Wherever I want to go. But I want to settle down first. I'm sick of moving around. I want to take it easy until these things"—pointing to the girls—"grow up. Then I'm going to see the world. I want to travel."

It was raining again, but the wind, now they were under the hill, was gone.

Flossie was still wondering about the boxes. She hadn't seen any, probably they were there, though. The coach stopped and they could hear the driver talking to his horse. "Git up! G'on y'old fool, haven't you ever seen a railroad train before? Git up!" The coach moved ahead, then backed a little. They all sensed danger.

"What's the matter?" said Gurlie, putting her head out the window in the rain.

"A train coming, he don't want to go under the viaduct. G'on there." But the horse wouldn't move. They heard the swish of the whip. The horse danced but wouldn't enter the archway under the tracks.

"He doesn't know how to drive," said Gurlie.

"Leave him alone," said the fat auntie.

Then a terrifying sound broke out almost over their heads, a clatter and bang topped by a deafening blast of a whistle as a heavy freight engine took the bridge over their heads and pounded heavily past.

"Whoa! whoa!" said the driver, sawing at the reins. "Stand still, you old fool. It ain't coming down here."

Bang, bang; bang, bang; bang, bang! The long freight began to follow the engine over the tracks. They could see it now, on both sides through the coach window, and the enormous new world it inhabited. Both the children trembled.

"What's the difference?" said Gurlie. "We'll just have to wait. We've got nothing to do." So she relaxed and waited.

And the cars, empties bound westward, kept pounding by, red and yellow following the engine now long past. Finally the pounding ceased, and they all saw the last of the freight, the small red caboose with a man leaning in the window as it wore past and was gone!

The silence after its passing was intimate and sweet. The children returned into their minds again, slowly, and picked up their thoughts after the intrusion of that foreign emissary. They looked at each other as much as to say, "I'm glad to be here, aren't you?"

"Come on, boy!" said the driver, and the horse started again, bolting in the underpass, jerking them all off balance, then turned right on the other side and proceeded on his way.

The adventure was past. They had been taken out of themselves, all ears, all eyes. Flossie had forgotten where she was, forgotten even . . .

"Look at that cat!" suddenly cried Olga, as Pully made a wild leap for the top of the partly open window. But the opening was too small and he fell back defeated. Flossie grabbed him around the belly. Why he didn't strike out at her would be hard to tell.

"The beast!" said Gurlie. "Why don't you let him go? Well, I suppose here we are. It looks like it, anyhow. Yes, this is it. Hey, where are you going?" she called to the cabby. "That's not the way!"

Strangely enough when they had passed through the

underpass the sun was shining. "That's impossible," said the fat auntie, "that just on the other side of the railroad track the sun should be shining and it was raining on the other side."

"Well, you can see it, can't you?" said Gurlie. "Open the windows." Which they did, and a big fly flew in buzzing all about the inside of the coach for a few moments, loudly, then disappeared again, out the same window, leaving a double silence now the train had passed.

"This is your new home," said Olga to the children. They were all eyes, but saw nothing but the embankment on one side, brownstone topped by cinders, and on the other some wooden buildings.

As they topped the incline and came into a little square by the railroad station, the coach stopped and the driver leaned his head around to ask directions. He had a long face, a long chin, a long nose and small, very pale blue eyes. He had been chewing a quid and coughed a little before he began to talk. The girls had never seen anything like it.

"Where are we headed for?"

"Pull up at the curb," said Gurlie. "Isn't that a grocery store over there? Go over there."

"Look, lady," said the man, "I'm not driving you around to no grocery store. I want to know where your house is at."

"Listen here," said Gurlie, "I have to buy staples, don't I? I can't just go up to a new house without anything in it. And I'd like a piece of ice. Do you know where I could get some ice?"

"I don't know anything about this burg. And I don't want to know nothin' about it. Where are we headed?"

"Now look," said Gurlie, "I'm paying you to drive us where I want to go."

"No, ma'am. I'm taking you to your place and I'm not hanging out in front of no grocery store." He looked as if he were going to get down from his seat—at least he started to unbutton the rubber storm shield that was about him. The little girls were frightened, thinking that he might come into the cab and fight them all.

"For heaven's sake, stop it," said Olga to her sister.

"All I want to know is the address," rumbled the man. The women were talking in Norwegian now, but Flossie and Lottie could understand them perfectly.

"Tell me what you want," said the older sister, "and I'll get it while you go on with the children."

"What do I want?" said Gurlie, and she laughed scornfully. "All sorts of things. I can't tell you. I'll get out."

"No," said Olga. "It's your house. The movers are coming. I don't know where you want to put things."

"Oh," said the younger sister, "you make me tired. You're not practical. What can you do? Here, here's the address and the key. Go on. I'll come in a few minutes, it isn't far."

"You should have your brains examined," said Olga.

"Here, do what I tell you. Here, here are the keys. I'm sick of sitting in this confined place. I want to stretch my legs. Take the children, that's what you're good for. Just put things anywhere. I don't care."

"I can imagine."

"Well," said the man outside, "make up your minds." With that Gurlie got down, straightened herself without looking back and walked away. The sun really had come out. Olga handed the man the little slip of paper with the address carefully written on it in Joe's engraver's script and in a moment they were rolling again, taking a left turn and out a long broad street with large drooping trees along it, all in new leaf.

"How are you, little spider? How are you, Lottie?" said Olga, leaning down and comforting the children. "Oh, and that old cat. I bet you love him." Flossie said she did. "That's good, that's very good," smiled the fat auntie, who wasn't so old after all at that time except in the minds of the children.

So the cab began to sway again at the back a little from side to side, and they saw people, strange new people, walking along the sidewalk. They were excited and tired, too. "It won't be long now," said Olga to the children.

And here they were. When they got out of the cab they felt very strange, their legs especially, but everything was strange. They walked around in circles stretching their legs, Flossie still holding Pully in her arms. The street was completely empty. Just nobody there. It felt odd. And there was the cab. They looked at it from the outside now. And the horse. It was a brown horse with black feet and a white nose. The driver got down, fastened a long strap with a heavy lump of iron on the end of it to the horse's bridle. He was very tall and stooped and just a young man.

All around the house there were trees full of white and pink blossoms. Lottie, especially, was entranced and began to walk around the house. Flossie stayed near her auntie. It seemed like the moon to her. She didn't know what to do with Pully.

"Well, take the cat in the house first," said Olga, "so he won't run away. Lottie, do you think you can unlock the front door? You're a big girl now. Here, try it while I pay the man—and he can bring up the bags. Look out for that box!" Olga cautioned. "That has our lunch in it."

"You got an awful lot of stuff here," said the man. But he finally got it all indoors, turned his rig around and drove off. Flossie especially watched the coach rolling off down the street. Now they were here, sure enough.

The cat had slunk, smelling along the wainscoting of the empty hall, starting back suddenly from time to time and disappeared finally upstairs. There was nothing to do. The place was empty, dreary and smelled queer. But as the fat auntie started to investigate the kitchen, finding the water turned on and the gas, too, she began to prepare a little lunch from the things they had brought with them.

Lottie wanted to go to the toilet.

"Well go, it's upstairs, I suppose."

But Flossie had already heard and was on her way before

Lottie started. Lottie came running behind her. Both rushed for the door, "I'm first."

"No."

"Get out of here."

"No," yelled Flossie.

"Children, stop that," called Olga from downstairs. "Shame on you."

There was a struggle. "Get out! I was here first."

"No."

"Auntie, Flossie won't let me in the toilet! I've got to go."

So Olga had to come up. "Why can't you both go in together and take turns?"

"No, I don't want her in here. Keep her out," said Lottie.

"Now Flossie, Lottie was the first to ask. Come here to me. You can wait."

"I got here first."

"But Lottie was first to ask. You can wait."

Flossie bit her teeth together and glared. Then, turning to her sister, she said, "You ought to have your brains examined." Olga laughed out loud. "Little spider," she said.

"Look outside at the pretty trees," said Olga, taking the child into the bare back room while Lottie was busy. "Look, aren't they lovely? Ugh! What dirty windows. Don't touch. There's a lot to be done here. I think this will be your bedroom. One of you anyhow." Then, hearing Lottie flush the toilet: "Now, now, you can go in. Go on. You see how simple it is?" And she went downstairs.

But Flossie was having difficulty with her clothes. Gurlie had made sure that there would be no accidents on this trip; the button at the back had been put twice through the hole in the waistband. She couldn't undo it.

"Auntie, I can't."

"Lottie, you go help her."

"No."

"Come down then to me."

"No."

"You must—or else you can stay there. I've got things to do."

So Spider came down but went to one of the moving men who had arrived and was sitting on the front step waiting for Gurlie. "Will you unbutton my drawers?" she said.

"What was that?" replied the man.

"I can't unbutton them. Will you help me?"

"No, ma'am," he said. "Not me." And wise he was too, for at that moment Gurlie came with her short chopping gait hurrying up the street. So Flossie waited for her.

"What?" said Gurlie. "Agh, don't bother me," and went into the house.

"Is that your Mommie? I'm glad she's here," said the moving man.

2

Summer is often a dull time for a child, especially in the suburbs. "There's no one to play with!" "I've got no one to play with." They were still too new in the place to have made any near friends.

"Why can't we go to Vermont?" wailed Lottie. "Vermonkey," chipped in the smaller girl. But it was amazing just the same what a difference just a few months, a few weeks you might almost say, were making in her. She was already beginning to grow up.

"I tell you what we'll do," said Gurlie, who was herself a bit bored, with everything closed, schools, churches, and nothing for the children to do. "I'll have your pictures taken," said Gurlie.

"You too?"

"No. Just you children. I want to send them to Grandma."

"Now?" said the children.

"Let's get dressed first." Which is always a sign of festivity for any little girl. "What shall I wear?" was Lottie's immediate thought.

Gurlie was a medium-sized woman in her early thirties then, round-bodied, with powerful, straight legs of which she was inordinately proud in a country that stressed the straightness of women's legs, but she had big rather ugly feet. Her arms, like her legs, were round and powerful, supporting broad, thick hands with blunt fingers. She wore no wedding ring. Joe had refused to accept one, so had she, though she occasionally wore an opal, her birthstone, on the third finger of her left hand, for all others unlucky but not for her.

The woman's whole appearance was purposeful, though far from seductive. But her face, as one might suspect, was the key to her nature: a broad, full face, smooth-skinned and of a good color, a firm though not a heavy chin, and a mouth which was never at rest. It was a good mouth, though narrow-lipped, which even at that age had begun to show vertical lines about its corners from the way she puckered it up very often for no reason whenever she was talking. But when she laughed you could see them. Her small eyes, well separated, were so seldom revealed that you scarcely knew their color—clear blue, with heavy lids, which Gurlie often kept completely closed when talking to a person, a disconcerting habit.

Her nose was small, too small, but turned up humorously at the tip under a low forehead, like a battering ram, mounting her small, round head on which the hair was blond but scanty and not very attractive or well cared for. Small ears, close to the head; a face you'd remember because of its insistence rather than its beauty.

Gurlie never listened to anybody—unless perhaps a gypsy or someone like that—or when getting ready to attack—when she'd nod her head up and down, purse her lips and signify her disagreement with whatever was being said, in no uncertain terms. Her mouth would pucker, her eyes close or flash out with a blue fire, like some angry lighthouse warning of danger, in primitive flashes of blind fury.

Generally, though, her manner was almost constantly bantering and her laughter disconcerting, loud and riotous. There was no reflective smile familiar to that face.

It was hot, terribly hot, that late July day, and Gurlie's hair was sticking to her forehead. "Go up and take a bath first, the two of you," said their mother.

"Wonderful!" said Lottie with enthusiasm; it was a word she had recently discovered and applied to almost everything.

And the two girls raced for the stairs. Flossie got pushed aside as usual.

"Hey, come here," said Gurlie. "Lottie, let your sister go first. I need you."

"Oh, she's such a pig," said the older girl. "Anyhow, she doesn't know how to fill the tub."

"I do so."

"Now don't spill any water on the floor. You can see how the ceiling in the kitchen is now. Be careful."

"Yes, I will."

"Yes, she will! She'll leave the floor all wet and use all the towels. She doesn't know anything. And the tub all greasy. I don't want to take a bath after her."

"Mind your own business," said Gurlie, "and go out in the kitchen and help Magna. She needs you."

"Can't I practice?"

"No. I don't want to hear that piano today. You need to be out in the fresh air. Look at you. Just bones."

"Oh, I wish you'd leave me alone."

Little Flossie was upstairs and had the water running by that time. She liked it deep!

Anger and derisive laughter were always just beneath the surface with Gurlie. People were afraid of her and her blunt speech, which could be rough enough without question, when she was stirred or furious. Terrifying in that unreasonableness that stops at absolutely nothing, *en eckte berserker* when aroused, she didn't have her five hundred years of unbroken Viking history behind her for nothing.

Upstairs Flossie had begun to undress. She was not a dreamer. Just turned seven in April, there was little for her to dream about—except her daddy, whose picture she kept on her bureau in her bedroom and kissed every night before she went to bed. She kissed it now, out of an excess of affection as she stood barefooted in her Ferris waist and drawers, a slender little girl with very lovely blond hair. She could hear the water running in the bathtub.

She didn't strip, but wore the last of her clothes into the bathroom itself before finally disrobing. She was not like her mother, though she had her mother's small eyes, blue, to be sure, but not the intense blue of the full Norwegian descent. Her eyes were more like those of her father and deep sunk, like his, not on the surface of her face like her mother's. A good little nose, a funny little v-shaped mouth, like her father, a small head with narrow brows and little, narrow shoulders.

What could be in a child's head, a little girl's head? Nothing. That is to say, everything. But she could run! Her legs were straight as arrows but awfully thin. She put one toe into the water and it was very cold—even if the day was so hot.

"Are you through yet?" yelled her sister from downstairs.

"No," she called back. "I haven't even started."

"Hurry up, you slowpoke."

Bough! The water was cold. But she was in. It sent thrills into the back of her head. "But don't get your hair wet!" her mother had cautioned. She must not get her hair wet. She was going to have her picture taken. Now the glow of the cold soothed her and she relaxed to it. She had no more thought of herself as a little girl than as a kitten. She looked at her feet and kicked the water.

All the future played in the sunlight about her really beautiful head of golden hair. Her little eyes would never be what they could never be, seductive and full of dreams. Dreams there were, like the day itself, clear and sweet-smelling. The long, narrow feet, like her father's, who always had to have shoes specially made for him, her feet were for dancing. The only thing she had ever wanted to do was dance. She was never tired. She was afraid of her mother.

Her long, narrow hands cupped the water and threw it into her face. Oh! But she had been careful, the hair wasn't wet. Her fingernails definitely were not clean.

19

Not that there wasn't meanness in her! Why did Lottie have to torment her? All right. She didn't want to play the piano. But *that* thing, with her piano. I could play the piano if I wanted to. I wish I had roller skates.

With that she got out of the tub and dried herself—a little. Oug! It felt good to be out of the water. How hot the air felt!

"Yes, you pest. You would!"

"All right, then get out." Lottie was already there. "You dope, look how you've left the bathroom. Go on, I'll fix it. Here, take your clothes!" and the older girl threw them out onto the hall. Flossie, naked, picked them up, towel in hand, and walked to her room.

Daddy! And she took up her daddy's photograph and kissed it and put it down carefully again. The erect head of a man in his middle thirties, the big moustache, the striking head of coal-black wavy hair, the high white forehead, the executive's eyes, but with something poetic, something protected by that air of almost bravado with which the head was held up—a man of great sensitivity, straight as an arrow. As straight as little Flossie's skinny legs. This was her father.

She sat on the bed and finished drying herself. She even lay back a moment and stretched herself out flat on her back as a little girl will sometimes do.

You could hear Lottie draining the water in the bathroom. *She* wouldn't let her little sister see her undressed. There was a reason. Lottie was over three years older than her sister and the change had begun. Poor child. But Lottie wasn't quite as moony as she might appear.

Flossie wanted to go back into the bathroom for her stockings, but her sister wouldn't let her. She swished her little tail—her big sister didn't cow her—and scampered across the floor back to her room.

"What are you doing up there?" said Gurlie from below. "Get in your room. Shame on you running around naked that way. Where's your sister?"

"She's in the bathroom taking a bath."

"Well, tell her to be quick."

"Can I wear my organdy dress—with the blue sash?"

"Don't let her wear that," said her sister opening the bathroom door a crack. "I want to wear mine and I don't want her to wear the same thing as I do. Let her wear . . ."

"Get in there and take your bath," said Gurlie, coming to the bottom of the stairs.

"Well, I don't care."

"Neither do I."

"Flossie, get your clothes on." Which was exactly what the little girl was doing. Now she was all dry.

"Do you want me to help you?"

"No, I can do it. Can I wear that dress?"

"Yes, it's clean. I looked at it."

"All right." And Gurlie went about her business.

So little Flossie sat down on the edge of the bed.

"Be sure to put a shirt on under your waist," Gurlie called from downstairs. "Do you hear me?"

"Yes," said Flossie.

So she pulled her shirt on over her head. And then she put on her Ferris waist with the long garters hanging down her bare skin. Then she put on long black stockings and clipped them to the garters. She already began to feel too hot in that oppressive room. "Oh!" she said, pretending adult annoyance —and put on her little lace drawers. Then her shoes. Then one petticoat, a plain one. Then the beautiful one with broad lace edges and then she sang out of tune:

> The little flowers came through the ground
>   At Easter time, at Easter time
> They raised their heads and looked around
>   At happy Easter time
> And every little bird did sing
>   —did say
> Good people bless this holy day
>   Christ is risen, the angels say
>   At happy Easter time.

She had learned it at Sunday school.

"Shut up!" said Lottie from the bathroom. She was trying to memorize a difficult passage from one of Bach's suites— tapping it out on the edge of the washstand.

Flossie had a high, clear little voice and loved to prattle, when excited—to amuse the Sunday school class, the family or whoever it might be, that is, when Gurlie cared to exhibit her. She was a typical second child, a complete extrovert, with the objective of all second children: to beat the firstborn. Except for two things. She had been intended to be a boy, so that she was a great disappointment to her mother. And she was not the "genius" of the family; there had to be a "genius" in any family Gurlie would have, but Lottie was that. The little one was always looked on by her mother as nothing much. Even a little unfortunate.

But on the good side, the favorable side, she had a quick sort of a little mind, a shrewd mind, which was lucky, for she needed friends, she would always need friends or a friend. And in September she was going into the first grade. The fourth drawback was that the family were "foreigners." That was a strange feeling that ran through the whole family and its relationships in the town where they had come to live or any town where they might live. It made for internal solidarity, but it was, for a child at least, something to live down. And they knew it. They all knew it.

There was a curious little accent that lingered in Gurlie's speech. Not that Gurlie didn't speak the language. In some ways she spoke it better than Joe, more colloquially at least, for, after all, Stecher was a man of ability of no mean order or he wouldn't have got where he was—and considerable skill: his work with the labor unions proved that—but still . . .

All this incited Gurlie to aggressive designs on the society about her, but, at the same time, with a scornful contempt. Joe didn't care. He had his garden which, when he permitted it to be so, was a great relaxation from the shop for him. His father had been a forester near Breslau. He had an instinct for trees and he loved them. There was a wildness in his mind which few suspected. And his culture. "All those things a European must lose to become an American, an American!" Gurlie would say, tilting her nose. Many things had to be left behind, and what Joe left behind was not the same as what Gurlie had left behind.

As she fussed about downstairs waiting for the girls—as a matter of fact she went outside to pick a few flowers, which she grabbed up in her heavy hands like artichokes—her mind was running in the old groove. Was not her ancestral home being recommended to the government as a national monument. Alverheim! They were not peasants, but wealthy farmers. The two old women who lived there could be brought around. If I went there, with a son!

None of her brothers or sisters was interested, though they had plenty of sons and daughters. "Agh! Fools. They were always fools. No ambition. But a son. Someday I'll go there and . . ." She knew it in fact. If in the next years she had a son and went with him to Norway, *he* would inherit Alverheim. There was no one else. Why hadn't it been a son the last time?

Meanwhile, in the bathroom, Charlotte stood, a tall, sad-looking eleven-year-old gazing at herself in the mirror. Dreaming. Her dark hair wound in a towel, her long, skinny arms and long, narrow hands resting on the edge of the wash basin. Her widely separated dark eyes seemed hardly to take in anything of her external surroundings.

The water was running into the tub. "There won't be any hot water left, I suppose."

She was very different from her sister. The dreamer—but covert. No one knew what she was thinking. No one ever would. She would be a big girl, a tall gypsy of a girl. She stood on tiptoe and looked at her beginning breasts. They didn't frighten her—she had been careful to lock the bathroom door. She threw out her chest—not much of a chest—as best she

23

could and took hold of her two nipples and pulled them out. No good. She looked down at her belly and shrugged her shoulders. Broad hips, a big pelvis, long legs—but nothing else —long feet.

The head was the whole thing and the hands. Somehow she'd get out into the world. She had no particular love for anyone in the family. They don't love me. She could see herself bowing to a great audience at a concert hall. She could see the whole thing. There she stood with one hand just touching the top of the grand piano and bowing, bowing. She lifted her chin and smiled—a smile, her big mouth grimacing condescendingly, her eyes beaming—or half-closed might be better!

She had a generous mouth, a good straight nose—and then! Then what? I suppose I'll have to be married and have children. Ugh. She might as well get into the tub.

There came a banging at the bathroom door.

"Who's that?"

"Open that door."

"All right, in a minute," came the child's voice from within.

"Open it at once," said Gurlie, fury in her voice. "Or I'll push it down!" She shook the knob violently.

There was a sudden splatter inside.

"Hurry up!" called out the mother, still rattling the lock.

"I'm hurrying," came the child's voice.

"Well, hurry more." The door opened a crack and the child's face showed, her head still in the turban made of the towel, her body kept out of sight.

Gurlie snatched the door into her own grasp and pushed it open, almost knocking the child off her feet as she stood there naked and dripping, her mouth open in amazement.

"Why did you lock that door?"

"I didn't want *her* to come in."

"Agh, nonsense. What could she do? What do you mean by doing such a thing as that?"

"But I've done nothing."

"You *know* you mustn't."

"You never told . . ."

"Shut up."

"But why?"

"Suppose you should faint?"

"I'm not going to faint."

"Suppose you should slip and fall and hit your head? You could drown and nobody would know it."

"But I could yell."

"I've told you never to lock the door when you go into the bathroom. Who wants to come in and see you in your bathtub, anyhow? Who do you think you are?"

Lottie didn't know.

"Look at you! You skinny thing. Turn around." Lottie turned around, showing her nakedness to her mother. "Stand up straight." One shoulder was a little higher than the other. "Put your shoulders straight. Agh, look at you. What's the mirror doing off the hook?"

"Oh!" said Lottie. "Oh . . ." She had to think quick this time. "I was just cutting my toenails."

"Is that so! Don't lie to me. You don't need a mirror to cut your toenails. I suppose you were admiring your beautiful legs."

"Oh, Mother!"

"Shame on you! Shame on you! Let me tell you one thing. If I ever catch you in this room again with the door locked, you dirty thing, I'll fix you so you won't sit down for a week."

The child thought, Now I'm going to get it. But she said, "What's so wrong . . . ?"

"You know what I'm talking about," said her mother. "Don't try to fool me. Look at your head in that towel!" Lottie undid it at once. "A beautiful lady! I suppose you think you're grown up. You—be a grand woman, a concert player, and you'll pose on the stage—I tell you what you'll be . . ." But her anger was beginning to wane a little, and she didn't continue. Instead she laughed, derisively. "Get your clothes on. You string bean!"

Now, that was the worst thing Gurlie could have said. The child was furious. "Anyhow," she said, "my legs are straight."

"Well, they'd better be, because that's about all you've got, with your flat chest."

I won't always be that way, thought Lottie.

"Your big head and your big eyes. I suppose you feel awful sorry for yourself. One thing, I'll say for you, you've always got an answer."

And Gurlie dismissed her—to the child's relief. "Now get out of here. And look at the floor."

"That's because I got out of the tub so fast."

"All right, get out. Get your clothes on and don't stand mooning around looking at yourself any more."

"But I haven't had my bath yet."

Flossie had heard it all, but she wanted someone to tie her sash for her. "Your sister will do it for you later," said Gurlie. "And keep yourselves clean, both of you, until I call you."

So in the intense heat of a July afternoon they walked downtown under the magnificent branching elms that met at their branch tips over this broad avenue, Gurlie in front with her short rigid steps and the girls, Flossie very proud and Lottie dragging behind, trying to balance her broad straw hat —keeping it from flopping into her eyes and . . .

"Stand up straight!" She straightened her shoulders. "What are you going to be with a back like that when you grow up?"

3

"You're lazy," said the little girl from across the street to Gurlie, who was lying in the hammock on the front porch. The little thing stood up there like a bump on a log and with expressionless face made her drastic comment. "Why don't you get up and make supper? Your husband's coming home!"

Gurlie, after a moment's astonishment, burst out laughing, not without sympathy, at the serious face for she had heard the story of the big German, the child's father. He was always the gentleman, dressed to perfection. But the poor woman at home, his wife, was like a crazy person running around in rags, terrified at his approach. Neighbors seldom even saw her.

In later years he had seized a young girl of high-school age, toward dusk, near his house, and kissed her obscenely, till she wanted to spit for a week afterward every time she thought of it, thinking, with horrid fixation of the witticism that had now got a terrifying meaning for her, a kiss without a moustache (he had a fierce moustache) is like an egg without salt. She spit again to think of it. She had already been raped, in her mind—though afterward, there must be more to it than *that*, she thought.

But when Gurlie told the family about the hammock incident at supper Joe laughed as loudly as she had. The occurrence took possession of all of them for years afterward: "You're lazy. Why don't you go get supper? Your husband's coming home."

"*Echt deutsch!*" said Gurlie. "Don't you ever try to do that to me. Not to a free Norwegian!"

Joe smiled good-humoredly.

"That's what you need," he said.

"Try it! Just try it!"

After his first guffaw he looked at his wife. That was enough.

"What kind of people do we have living around us here?" said Gurlie. "What kind of neighborhood did you get me into?"

"What kind of neighborhood did you get yourself into? You were the one to choose it. I didn't see the drunk again tonight." Coming home late the night before in the dark he had stepped over the bulk of a man prostrate on the sidewalk. "Where's supper? And where are the children?"

"Supper is late! I told you the children are out. Dutch!" she said to him. "It would do you good to get drunk yourself once in a while."

Joe looked at her, half-angry. "Did they bring the load of manure, at least?"

"Yes," said Gurlie. "They brought the manure. It doesn't look very good, half straw, but they brought it. Can't you smell it? I suppose now you want to go out and look at it. It's back by the chicken yard. Now are you satisfied?"

"Where did you have them dump it?"

"I told you."

"Which side of the chicken house?"

"Agh. Wherever they wanted to dump it. I don't care." Joe went upstairs to change his shoes. When he came down, he looked at his watch; Gurlie was glancing at the headlines of *The Sun* he had brought home.

"I'm going for the children. Where are they?"

"Leave the children alone. Do you want your supper now? We won't wait for them. Dutch! Everything must run like a machine. The children have to be in the house. Ha, when I was a girl they never knew where I was. It's not late. Sit down, read your paper. It's only seven o'clock—you must have come home earlier today than usual. Look at those people!"

Joe wouldn't move. But Gurlie went over to him, took him by the elbow and forced him to the window, where he stood, casually, in his shirt sleeves. He always wore sleeve garters and detachable cuffs.

"What are they?" said he. "Gypsies?" Gurlie merely stared. In front was a short, smiling woman with a Persian shawl around her head and with long skirts that dragged the ground behind her. Two small girls followed her, dressed in every color of the rainbow, or so it seemed.

"Who are they?" said Joe.

"I think they must be the people who have bought the new house back of us on the next corner."

"Ya," said Joe, "I understand. He was the United States consul at Manila."

"Huh," said Gurlie. "So the little Dutchie knows something. But why do they dress that way?"

"He's a Mohammedan and has come back to this country to do some missionary work here. I think he wants to convert people to the Prophet Mohammed. Why don't you try him?"

Gurlie turned away. "Where are those children?" she said.

"So now it's you," said Joe. "There she goes," he added looking out.

"Supper must be over across the street. The nut has just thrown the dishwater out the kitchen window. Now she'll fling the scraps to the chickens."

"Well, once school starts we've got to expect the children to make more friends. Where are they?" said Joe. "You haven't told me."

"At the Barrys', just next door."

"Oh," said Joe.

"That's her brother, Tom."

"Who's Tom?"

"The one you stepped on, the drunk."

"How do you know so much about it? Who told you?"

"Tom."

"The drunk?"

"Sure."

"For God's sake. When did he do that?"

"This morning. I gave him a cup of coffee. I felt sorry for him."

"Why didn't you send him home to his wife, across the street?"

"He wouldn't go. What's sauce for the goose is sauce for the gander!" Gurlie was a perfect monkey and imitated the voice of poor Myrna, the aggrieved wife. "How that woman works. You know," said Gurlie, with genuine admiration, "she's the finest dressmaker I've ever seen. She supports the whole family. And fresh! Nobody can put her down."

"Did you try?"

"She's got the brains."

"What relation is the milkman to them?"

"Cousin. They're all here in the neighborhood. All of them."

"They're honest people," said Joe, "aren't they?"

"They are real old-timers. But I like Mrs. Barry. She's the nicest."

"There she comes," said Joe, still looking out the window at the house next door from which a stylishly dressed woman had just emerged.

Gurlie chortled. "Ya, yes, just like a man! The floozie."

"Sure," said Joe. "Anybody that's better-looking than you and knows how to dress herself has to be a bad woman. It seems to me she's the only good-looking one in the neighborhood."

"Her legs aren't any better than mine. Look how she lifts

her skirts at the gutter. Oh my!" And Gurlie laughed. "Such a lady."

"What does she do?"

"They say she has a job in the lawyer's office downtown!"

"You can't say she isn't beautiful. She looks different from the rest of the frumps around here."

"Sure," said Gurlie. "It's her simple-minded sister and her poor mother that do all the work. And her brothers."

"Nobody ever does anything in that house as far as I can see," said Joe.

They could hear the children calling out, "See you tomorrow," and stamping excitedly up the front steps.

"Now don't say anything to them. Leave them alone."

The children came in, cowed, but immediately sensed the released atmosphere and started babbling happily about the wonderful party they had had and showing the beautiful little favors Mrs. Barry had given them. Joe was pleased in spite of himself.

"Now let's have supper."

Magna began to bring in the dishes. She was a beautiful thing, from the same village in Norway that Gurlie's father had come from, a descendant of one of the historic families.

"Um, yumm! Corn!" said the children simultaneously.

"You eat some of the good stew first," said Gurlie. But they made sour faces—they had had cake and ice cream in the afternoon—but there was always room for fresh corn on the cob.

"You eat it," said Gurlie to each of them in turn.

"Eat it," said Magna. "It's very good," in her careful *Gymnasium* English, and she smiled broadly. And it was delicious stew, veal in small chunks cooked with little carrots, a few onions—which Lottie, in particular, always put aside— the heart always tastes so bitter, she would say. The rest of the meal was the corn, a steaming stack which had caught the children's eyes, and a dish of sliced tomatoes.

"How much did you pay for that stuff?" asked Joe, referring to the corn.

"Ten cents a dozen. Well, aren't you going to eat it?"

"Sure, if you'll cut it off the cob for me," which she proceeded to do. That's one thing that he, stiff-necked, would not bow to, pick up an ear of corn and gnaw it from the cob, held in both hands with the butter running down over your chin. That was one concession to American manners, or lack of manners, he stuck at.

Gurlie cut the corn for him as always. "It's delicious," she said. "You and your peasant manners. Eat it! It won't kill you to hold it in your hands."

"How much are tomatoes?"

"Ten cents a basket," said Gurlie.

"From the farmer across the street?"

"Yes," said Gurlie.

"Put some of those on a separate plate, with some oil, and I'll fix them the way I want them."

"Magna!" called Gurlie.

"Yes, ma'am."

"Bring him some olive oil."

"Yes, ma'am."

"Oh, Magna," said Lottie. "May I have a glass of water?"

"No," said Gurlie. "Don't fill up on water. Eat your stew."

"But I can't swallow it. It's too dry!"

With that Joe, caught off his guard, let out his half-sardonic chuckling laugh. "Too dry, with all that soup in the dish. Magna, bring a pitcher of water. I want a drink myself."

"Agh, you," said Gurlie. "All right, give it to her. Look at her, there's no more meat on her than a starved chicken. And you let her. . . . Look at her face, is she ever going to fill out? She needs food. Good food. Look at Magna," who at the moment came in through the kitchen door with a pitcher of water. "Look at her."

"Oh, stop picking on me!" said Lottie.

Magna didn't know what was said. "What?" she said. Her lively round face, blond hair, all about her head, her arms, her hands, her firm young breasts bulging out her plain dress.

"Sure, look at her," said Joe chuckling.

"What?" said Magna again, putting down the water.

"Yes, you!" said Gurlie. "That's the man of it. But look at that thing!" pointing at Lottie with her long, sad face, deceptively sad! Her rather hollow eyes. "No," mocked Gurlie, puckering up her nose and whining, "no, I don't want any stew. Why when I was a child we were lucky to have such things—I ate like a pig."

The children made no comment.

"We had to eat everything we had before us and we grew up strong with good legs and healthy. Eat some of your supper." Lottie ate.

"Look at Magna." Magna's cheeks got crimson, beautiful as they always were.

But the girls didn't want to look like Magna, no matter how much their parents admired her. They were not Norwegian peasants and were foreign enough, anyway, compared to the American children living around them. Magna was all right, but Lottie didn't want any stew.

"All right then, eat your corn. But no dessert."

"What are you going to have?"

"Something nice," said Magna. "Fresh peaches, sliced with sugar."

"How much?" said Joe.

"Ten cents a basket."

"Ha," he laughed. "Did they throw in the basket, too? What do you think of the farmers around here?" said Joe unexpectedly to Magna, wanting to change the subject.

"I think they are very nice," said Magna, as she left for the kitchen.

Flossie had not spoken so far. She wasn't hungry, either, but she knew enough to keep quiet, watch her mother out of the corner of her eye and pick carefully.

Magna came back to remove the big plate of stew from before Gurlie. For that was another thing Joe would have nothing to do with, serving a meal. Not he. He didn't come to the table to work.

"What do you think of them?" he repeated to Magna. Gurlie didn't interfere, for she sensed something in her husband's voice that stopped her. Sometimes Joe liked to make an oblique point in his talk, and Gurlie knew when it was coming.

"What?" said the pretty maid. She had a dish of stew in her hands and was just about to go into the kitchen with it. As she half-turned, the dish raised, Joe somehow felt like keeping her there. At least he did. Her right foot kept the kitchen door partly open.

"What do you think of them?"

"Let her go," said Gurlie.

"I want to know what she thinks. I'm interested."

Magna came back for some of the other dishes.

"Do you ever talk to them?" asked Joe.

"No," said Magna. "The children are very nice. But the other people are strange to me. They seem such odd people."

Joe chuckled to himself.

"Shame on you," said Gurlie. "Leave the girl alone. What's the matter with you?"

"I thought she might like to have us introduce her to some of our friends!" he commented. "We really ought to make her get acquainted."

"Mommie," said little Flossie after a while, "can we go to dancing school?"

"There it comes," said Joe.

"Can we?" said Lottie. "They're going to have dancing school even for little children in September."

"Sure," said Joe, magniloquently. "Sure, let's hire a hall —maybe they could have it in old Tom's barn." Magna was

34

watching him, fascinated and puzzled. The children were crestfallen.

"How much do they want for a lesson, ten dollars?" The children looked at Gurlie. "What do we care? Buy 'em a private teacher."

Magna giggled to herself and left the room—but came back quickly to hear the rest of it.

"I don't see that there's anything funny about it," said Gurlie. "I think they ought to learn how to dance. Everybody does here." Magna agreed with her mistress, silently. The children's heads turned to Joe.

"Can we?"

"I suppose so," said Joe, taking a cigar from his pocket. "Ask your mother, she has all the money."

"Can we? Mother?"

"I don't know anything about it. I'll have to speak to Mrs. Barry."

"That's the sister of the drunk," said Joe. Magna snickered. "Why don't you call the ex-consul's wife, from Manila. Or the secretary to the president of the Erie Railroad up the street. He's a great Masonic muck-a-muck, ask him."

Joe hated all clubs and organizations.

"Dutch!" said Gurlie. "All right, Magna, you can clear up the table."

When the dishes had been cleared, and it being still light out of doors, the children had gone out again to play a little while, Gurlie went to the sideboard and took out a bottle.

"Take some *schnapps*, here." Gurlie never asked anybody what he wanted. Joe took it and sniffed it with a disgusted look on his face.

"What do you want, a new fur coat, or a trip to Norway?"

"You could afford it. We've got money now. We've got to move up in the world."

"Ya! I see. I knew it was something. You want two servant girls? We haven't room for one here."

"We got to get a bigger house, then."

"Ya, *Donnerwetter!* We hardly move into the place when you . . ." But Gurlie smothered him in her rough caresses, and I mean rough. She almost knocked him backward off his chair. He was half-alarmed at the fear of falling, half-angry at her.

"No, this house is good enough for now," she said surprisingly.

"What then?"

"These people around here aren't the only ones. There are other people in this town. I want you to meet them."

"Go ahead and leave me alone. I don't care."

"You."

"Me?"

"Yes, you."

"No."

"Drink up your glass." Joe had not touched it. "That's what you need."

"For someone to stumble over me in the dark, drunk? Ya."

"You should be more like me."

"Stupid enough to lie in my own vomit on a public sidewalk and have my neighbors stumble over me in the dark?"

Gurlie shouted in mock laughter. "You? There's lots worse things than that."

"What, for instance?"

"To be mean and stingy."

Joe looked at her hard.

"Not you, stupid! Not a man like you—but the rest of the pack he comes from. I feel sorry for him. Look at them, your 'honest citizens.' Peasants, Dutch peasants, gone to rot. Ignorant! But ignorant! Do you know what they think?"

"Don't bother me."

"You don't know! You think everyone is honest, ha! Even after what you just went through."

"What I went through. If it hadn't been for the honest men that helped me, I couldn't have done it."

"Well, it doesn't do any harm to know. I'll bet you I find out about this town."

"From a drunk, huh? That I kicked on the sidewalk."

"I'll find out. And I'll get to the top too, by jiminy. You wait and see."

"I'll wait and don't bother me about it."

"Have you got a dress coat any more?"

But this time Joe really let loose! Wow!

4

Nearly a year had passed. It was a March night; the room was cold. Joe was already in bed. But Gurlie, with an old wrapper around her shoulders over her nightgown, was sitting on the cane bench in front of the mirror braiding her blond pigtails. She tied the two ends with blue tapes, then, leaning her face nearer, examined her teeth, putting her finger in her mouth to pull back the lower lip on the left side.

"Put out the light and come to bed."

She didn't answer him, but went on surveying her back teeth. Her small bullet head, the skull close under the scanty blond hair pulled tight, had a round forehead to it. It wasn't pinched in at the temples like her sister Hilda's, but round there also. Her pale blue eyes were not deep-set but level with the rest of her face. She screwed them up not to stare at herself, a shrewd, silent study, taking in her small, blunt nose, her thin lips, her ears close to her head. It seemed a head meant for action, not dreams.

"You're lucky to have such a good-looking wife."

"Agh," said her husband, "don't make such a fool of yourself. Open the window and come to bed."

She started to rub some cold cream into her skin. "In this country," she said, "they don't know what it is to have a good complexion. Magna is already starting to lose hers. It must be the climate."

"Let her have what she has. She's better-looking than you ever were."

"Is that so? When you married me my skin was perfect."

She went to the window. "Look at it snow."

The flakes were sailing aslant around the street light on the pole in front of the house. "March is a horrible month. We've had enough. I think it's going to keep up all night."

"Um."

"Something funny happened today. Wake up, I want to talk to you."

"Well, don't talk so loud, then, you'll wake up the whole house." He spoke in German.

"I don't care if they wake up. Listen to me." She sat on the edge of the bed and, putting her left foot on the edge of a chair, began to pick at her toes. "Listen to me." She shook him.

"Agh, leave me alone."

"Annie across the street was out shoveling snow this morning in her husband's pants. What a stick! I suppose he was too drunk to do it himself. I was watching her—she's all right. All the women were out cleaning the sidewalks. She yelled across the street."

"Who yelled across the street?"

"Mrs. B. did. 'Oh, what I see!' she said. But Annie thought she was making fun of her because of the pants. She's quick. So she turned around, stopped shoveling and said, 'If you don't like it, you can turn the other way.'" Gurlie imitated the voice perfectly.

"Ho ho!" said Joe in spite of himself.

"Yes," said Gurlie. "She's a smart woman. We have to find another music teacher for Lottie."

"Isn't the one we got good enough for you?"

"He's moving out west."

"Well, then get somebody else. Now shut up and leave me alone." And he rolled over on his side. Gurlie went on working at her toenails. There was silence for awhile. She got the nail scissors, then as she worked she burst out laughing. "What people!" she said.

He was already asleep.

"Hey," she said to him. "Wake up. I want to talk to you."

He didn't stir.

She leaned across the bed and pushed roughly against his shoulder with her heavy hand. "What's the matter with you?"

"God damn it," he said, "can't you leave a man alone?"

"No, I don't intend to. This is the only time I have. You are in the city all day. When we are at meals the children are there, and I'm not going to tell all my business in front of the maid. I am not a servant you can order around. There are things I have to ask you and tell you. I don't like this house. This is not the part of town I want to live in. Get me another house—you're making lots of money now. I want to move up on the hill. You have two daughters—I want a place . . ."

"*Um Gotteswillen!*" he began . . . "*Du bist verrückt.*"

"Agh." She roughed his black hair and laughed her clown's open-mouthed, raucous cackle of a laugh. "Don't talk to me. I'm not one of your scared German wives you can frighten with a loud voice. Wake up while I tell you what I want to say."

He looked at her with fury in his eyes. "Well, talk then— if you've got something to say. What is it?"

"I didn't say I had anything to say. I'm not a piece of wood. I just want somebody to talk to. I'm sick and tired of sitting here dumb all day with the servant and the children. I want to get out of here. They have a club I'm going to join called the Literary Club."

"What's that, the Literary Club? What do you ever read?"

"The best women in town, those that have money, all belong to it. I have to have some clothes. And they all live in the other part of town."

"Well, if you can get somebody to propose your name,

join it. I can't help you. And get a teacher for the kid. And come to bed."

"The piano needs tuning."

"Well, get it tuned."

"What do you think happened today? I went to the woman up the street, you know the one I mean, and asked her if she didn't want to have the piano tuner. I thought it would save something, I went all around the neighborhood, it would save them money if two or three had him at the same time." Gurlie laughed. "Do you know what she told me? She said, 'No thanks' (imitating the woman's way of talk), because she has the kind of piano that doesn't need tuning. Wha!" And she laughed out loud. "Have you caught the man who's been stealing?"

"No."

"Well, isn't it about time you did something about it?"
Joe did not answer.

"You're too easy. You should notify the police. You're afraid to hurt someone. I'll bet he's that man you had trouble with before. Why didn't you fire him? You are too soft; you were sorry for his wife. What about your own wife?"

"Don't talk like a fool. Come to bed."

"*You* are the fool."

"Well, you've got a roof over your head, that's more than some people can boast."

"Dutch. So you think that's something. You are too timid. You think that ought to satisfy me. I don't like it here. After I have a house that I do like, I want to go to the theatre, I want to go to the opera. I want to have parties. I want to entertain my friends, give dinners. What can we do here? I want to go away in the summer."

"To Newport? You want a yacht? Do you want a butler and a lady's maid?"

"No, but I would like a farm with horses and cows and a big orchard and a nice stone house on a hill."

"Your sister has that in Vermont. Go up there with her. What else? Just ask for it and I'll give it to you."

"Is that so? Well, I'd like a new fur coat, right now. I'd like a diamond ring."

"Get half a dozen. Wouldn't you like a diamond dog collar like Mrs. Vanderbilt to go with them and a crescent to put in the front of your hair and diamond shoe buckles, and bracelets, and a string of them around your neck as big as walnuts?"

"Why not? I'd look good in them."

"What else?"

"I'd like to take an ocean voyage, to Norway once more while there is somebody there I know."

"Sure, let's all go. I'll give up my business and spend a year at Mannheim—for my health."

"The children should see the kind of people they come from. These people in this country think they are aristocratic. My ancestors were Vikings. We know what good things are. I was brought up on a rich estate. . . ."

"It was a farm, and they were broke."

"Not such a farm as you think. The buildings were some of the oldest in the country. I was used to horses and servants. We went to the best schools."

"Well, some day you can go and boast to your old friends back there. Provided I don't lose my money before you get the chance. Now I tell you I want to go to sleep. To-morrow . . ."

"Tomorrow is Sunday. You don't have to get up early."

"I have to shovel the sidewalk."

"Yah. Do you want to know something?"

"What is it now?"

"I'm going to have a baby. I bet you it will be a boy."

"Come to bed then. You need the rest."

"Is that all you're going to say to me?"

"What else is there to say? You'll have to put the maid in the attic."

"We won't be living here in this house by then."

Gurlie put out the light and crawled into bed beside her husband. There she lay for an hour or more looking up at the ceiling before she dropped off.

Asleep at last, the trolls romped in Gurlie's brain, triumphant. Roaring with glee. Boy! they kept repeating. It will be a boy! Joe swung at them with his fists, but he was too clumsy. They ran away a few steps and when he turned his back there they were again.

"It is indeed your own child," she kept telling him. "I swear it is yours." At that the trolls laughed louder than ever. Joe was furious at them. But Gurlie tried to stop him. She said it would bring bad luck on them all if he didn't act differently. It was his German blood! "You scientists! But I tell you it's a mistake to make the supernatural angry at us."

"Those are not spirits. That's all in your own mind. Get out of here," he shouted as the little men danced impudently around him. "Get out."

"You are the one that did it," she said to him. "You are the papa." And now it was snowing. She was alone in the snow and it was still coming down, a heavy fall just when they were expecting good weather. What would she do with a newborn baby in the snow?

She saw herself walking through it with the child in her arms. It was a heavily wooded place—where she had often hidden as a child with her dog—what was his name? She remembered the whole thing very well. . . . She remembered well how she had snuggled against the dog's hairy coat and fallen asleep. She had slept a long time. Because when she wakened it was dark and she heard them calling her. Gurlie! Gurlie! Far off . . . and . . .

Out of doors the street had disappeared. Annie, in the old house opposite, had locked her bedroom door to sleep without interruption and be the first up in the block in the morning, the first to get her sidewalk shoveled. Clean. Clean!

"I'd like to clean the whole place out." She'd attack the whole house every day with mop and broom. She'd push the chairs savagely about in all except the front room, which was kept locked from them all with their dirty feet. That, at least, no one was going to spoil, with its faded black walnut chairs and hair sofa. No one was going to ruin that.

All her life the snow had been falling, smothering her. No more. Not if she could help it. . . . She, too, fell asleep as the snow continued to fall, the anarchistic snow, blotting out all distinctions between river and swamp where the little town lay.

Magna, the maid, had heard from her room, that evening, a vague babble of voices, but could not make out what was being said. What of it? In a few months she hoped to be married. She didn't know who it would be, but it would be someone. She knew a girl who had married and gone out west and had written her. That was the place to be. It was the unmarried brother of that girl's husband who had sent her his picture and she had sent him hers. Who knows, perhaps it would be he—someone, at any rate.

Lottie, on going to bed that night, had lain awake a long time, thinking. She had never wanted to be a man; men had to work. Little boys were all afraid of her, at least they left her alone. She was tall and skinny and she looked at them in a way, out of her big brown eyes, as if she knew something that they did not know. She had skinny legs, too, and she wasn't afraid of them. She walked right past them as if they weren't there. She just didn't see them.

She didn't notice her father much, either. He was a man. She was a woman. When he spoke to her she had learned the trick of guessing what he wanted and saying yes. It didn't matter what it was, her answer was yes. After that you began to think how you would get out of it. There were a hundred ways of doing it. You could be sick; sometimes you had to pretend to be sick. Or you could say it was Flossie's turn. Or you could say you had to practice, or just disappear when you were wanted, or not hear. Once in a while you really didn't hear.

Women had all the best of it—if they were any good. She knew that. Men, at least all the men that she knew, were ugly and common. She wanted to be loved and have nice presents. There were many men, of course, in books, men still too old for her, who were beautiful, and when she had become a great artist one would appear and rescue her, some beautiful young man who would give her all she desired. I won't ask for too much—not at first. Until then no one shall know what I am thinking. No one.

"Oh," said little Flossie to her sister, in the morning, going to her room to waken her. "Look!" It was a new world.

"Go away," was all she got for her pains, as her sister snuggled tighter into her covers. "It's cold. I thought we were through with winter. I hate it."

There had been no wind, so that the snow clung to each last twig of the trees; there was a double .tree, one dark, in the early morning light, one, a complete other tree in white, outlined on the pale sky, awaiting the first breath of a breeze which was sure sooner or later to come and ruin it all. Sure enough, the sidewalk across the street had already been shoveled. Otherwise nothing had been disturbed. But as Flossie stood at the window now in the spell of the stillness, afraid to breathe, there was the faintest movement in the maples before the house, and in the silence, which was intense, a cloud of powdery snow was released.

The child went to her own room and plunged into bed again. From where she lay she could watch the rising of the sun, for the day was cloudless. Late in March the snow could not last. As a matter of fact, when she woke again the trees were already bare. The fields which you could see between the houses across the street were sparkling in the light.

That spotless world of enchantment was not to last. Snow

always reminded Joe of his childhood in Silesia and of his brothers and his sisters. His feet were always cold and wet when he took his thick shoes off in the evenings. He remembered when he would go to the small Catholic church with his mother. He always enjoyed the candles and the images in the little chapel. Once a month his father made them go with their mother. The children were not Catholics, but since the mother had been brought up in that religion, their father made them go. He himself never went. It was very amusing to little Joe, like a circus, but he didn't want to go unless he had to go to accompany his mother. In winter the church was gloomy and cold. The candles flickered in the draught that played about the altar while the old priest was saying mass. At least it was a little warmth. That was long ago. What changes he had witnessed.

He had been the careful one. All the others—well, all except Ida—all the others had had too much of the mother in them for their own good. That was the French of it. He didn't remember his mother—Armande, or was that his father's mother's name? Oswald, who had run off with his regimental commander's wife and come to America—he was the youngest. Good for nothings. Mathilda, on the stage. What a thing to do! Served her right. Dead having her first baby. Ida had lost her only baby at birth, and never tried again. Rudolph, the wildest of them all, never married, as Oswald had never married. Rudolph, teaching violin at the conservatory in Prague. Joe had lost track of him completely. "That's where Lottie got her music, I guess."

He shoveled away at the snow on the front steps, down the front walk to the street. Flossie came out with her little shovel to help him. "That's right," he said. "Somebody has to do the work around here."

She kept at it and didn't quit. He watched her with a smile. It was getting warm. This snow wouldn't last. Flossie wanted her coat unbuttoned from around her neck. Gurlie banged on the window and shook her head, but after she had disappeared he took pity on the child, seeing how uncomfortable she was, and undid the button. Some boys, finding the snow good and packy, had already begun to throw snowballs.

He had been the only one to repress all that foolishness that possessed the family. Somebody had to work, somebody always has to work and make a living. Someone had to be careful and get ahead. Pay strict attention to business, to honesty, to routine, especially in this rich country, and you would get ahead.

Flossie had made a snowball and was eating it.

"Na, na!" cautioned her father. "That's not good for you." She made no objection, but threw the stuff away and went on with her work.

The secret Gurlie had told her husband in the night had put him in a comfortable mood. She was his only extravagance. Seeing her straight legs on which she stood like a mountain, so firm and so well-footed, had first given him the sense of stability he lacked. Good strong legs.

Her blue eyes had looked right through him in one glance, sizing him up from his wide forehead, his black curly hair, his delicate violinist's hands, but especially his deep-set eyes, as her man. The cleft chin, the moustache hiding his sensitive mouth. He was a comer. He was serious, balanced, intelligent. She had determined to marry him. Let the others go ahead. Her little Dutchie would beat them all and she'd damn well see to it that he did.

Maybe it would be a boy this time. Who would have thought that he, of all the five children, would be the one to carry on the name?

"There," he said to little Flossie, "you've done the job. Now let's go in and have breakfast." She smiled up at him with her one blue eye, one half-blue and half-brown. He noticed it in the brilliant light of the snowy morning. Another would have leaned down and kissed her out of an inner satisfaction and gaiety; she had always been *his* girl. But he merely took her little shovel from her hand and made her stamp her feet clear of snow as he led her indoors.

5

The custom at that time was for the grocer to send a wagon around in the morning to take orders, perhaps to leave bread and a few staples, then to make the principal deliveries in the afternoon. So that when the driver, John Dempster, found out that there was a new family in the block, he pulled up in front of the house, threw the weight to the ground to keep the horse from wandering, and went to make himself known. He looked so much like Gurlie's youngest brother that as soon as the girls caught sight of him they let out a cry, "Einar!" and rushed into his arms.

"No, I'm not Einar," he said, laughing. They were taken aback. He patted their heads, said he was sorry. But they still kept looking at him as Magna went to get her mistress. "Glad to make your acquaintance," he said. "Do you like it out here in the country?"

Flossie assured him that they did. So he became her friend.

It was her birthday, the eighteenth of April—hardly a man is now alive, as her father had recited it to her. And she had been given her first bicycle. But there it stood. She did not know how to ride it. She had carefully examined it, but was afraid to take it out and let the other children know. That evening or maybe not until Saturday when her daddy was there would she get to ride. John Dempster must come and look.

"A beauty!" he said. That made her feel fine. "But why aren't you out riding?" She hung her head. "Let's take it out and try it." Her heart leaped at the idea.

"Can I?" she asked her mother.

"You can't give the time to teach a child to ride a bicycle."

"Sure I can. Come on," he said. So the wonderful bicycle was trundled down the front steps into the middle of the street. Flossie was put on the leather seat which had to be adjusted with the little wrench which John took out of the tool case which hung just under it.

"Now take hold of the handles. Push down on the pedals. That's the way. Now steer! Here we go." And for fifteen minutes he pushed the child up and down the street until she began to get the hang of it.

Two days later she could manage it alone and rode down the street two blocks to meet the grocer and wait for him as he stopped here and there to show him what she could do.

Her special friend, Martha, who lived in the old house down on Meadow Road, was now within easy reach. Life was beginning to open out.

After the talk with his wife four weeks ago—it didn't seem possible that these fine days of April could have followed that storm—Joe had stopped in at the real estate office of E. S. Brown, and secured an option on a piece of real estate, a hundred-foot front, one of the best among the many still vacant lots in the better part of town. They had joined the Presbyterian church, since there was no Lutheran church in Riverdale proper, taken a pew, received their envelopes for their regular Sunday contributions.

"Now you're a church member in good standing: that means you pay your money regularly," was Joe's remark. The girls were enrolled in the Sunday school. Lottie didn't want to go. But Joe insisted and himself became much interested.

"Who was there this morning?" asked Gurlie, who had stayed in bed late that day. "Was it a good sermon?"

Joe was engrossed by then in the Sunday paper. He didn't hear her. She grabbed it out of his hand. That infuriated him. "Don't do a thing like that."

"Well, then, listen to me," she replied.

"What do you want to know?" and he picked up the paper again and straightened it out.

"Who was there?"

"Where?"

"In church this morning."

"Well, who do you think was there? I don't know. A lot of women dressed up to kill and men making up at one-half of one per cent for the money they've been stealing from their customers all week."

"Did you talk to anyone afterwards?"

"Yes, I met the minister and he introduced me to some of the men who guarantee his salary."

"Wasn't there anything else?"

"Yes, he preached a sermon."

"What about?"

"About paying your debts to God Almighty. He's a Scotsman, probably wants a raise." At that moment Lottie came into the room from play.

"Is it true," she said, "that a man was shot and killed last night in Riverdale?"

"What's that?" said Gurlie.

"Nonsense," said her father. "Who's been telling you such stuff? Run along and play."

"What is this?" asked Gurlie, when the child had gone.

"One of the members of the congregation. It was an accident."

The first inkling of it was that morning when he had gone down for the papers. "Whiskey?" he had heard a man say. Riverdale was a local-option town. "I can get all you want of it." He had seen the man standing bleary-eyed in the sun often before, weatherbeaten, his nose crooked on his face. The town philosopher he was called; he never worked. "How much do you want of it?"

"I didn't know George was that good a shot. Right through the heart."

"What'll they do to him?"

"What can they do to him?"

"What can they do to him? He was doing no more than his duty."

It seems that the town had been pestered by burglars, as it very often was when the good weather began and the big-city vagrants began to take the road. Several of the better houses had been entered and clothing and a certain amount of silverware removed. The cops had been blamed for their laxness, as usual. So that after dusk when George, the officer on the beat, saw a man coming out of a dark ground-floor window behind some shrubbery, he yelled to him to halt, pulled out his gun and ran forward to make the arrest, thinking that at last he had come upon a marauder.

Half-expecting to see the flash of a pistol and to hear the whistle of a bullet from the fugitive, George saw the man make a run for it to get out of sight around the corner of the house. "No you don't," said the policeman. "Halt or I'll fire." But when the man kept running, he was as good as his word. He fired and the man dropped. The cop ran up to him. He was dead. Right through the heart.

George almost fainted, though he had been a soldier in the Spanish-American War. He had only meant to wing him. A well-dressed, respectable-looking man somewhere in his forties, he looked familiar, but George didn't know who he was or where he'd seen him.

By that time the neighbors had been aroused. Officer George was trying to revive the man when young Bannister ran up. "You got him all right, didn't you? That's the stuff."

"Yes, I got him all right. But I guess I was too God-damn good a shot."

"Is he dead?"

"Dead as a doornail. Help me roll him over. I don't know who he is." And as the young man leaned to help the officer, "My God," he said, "it's Mr. Blamford."

"Who?"

"He's one of our neighbors. You've killed one of our own people."

The officer turned pale, "Well, I saw him coming out that window, I called to him to halt. He kept on running, so I fired. We have strict orders to shoot to kill."

"What window?"

"That window there."

By then Mrs. Brewster, in a dressing gown, had come out of the front door, attracted by the crowd of neighbors that had begun to gather. Her husband was on a trip to St. Louis. She approached young Bannister, "What's going on, Dwight?" she said, confused by the darkness and the excitement which had been aroused.

"A burglar has been shot and killed. You'd better go in."

But her curiosity got the better of her. Something drove her to see for herself, with the hope that her first impression had been wrong—when she first heard the single shot and silence following it, then the sound of people walking through the shrubbery. She staggered when she saw her lover's face, but managed to control herself, turn and walk into the house where she immediately began to throw some clothes into a traveling case. She dressed and, locking the house, walked unobserved the half-mile to the railroad station for the midnight train to New York.

"She's gone," said Joe. "I hope he got his money's worth. And that's what happened to two members of your congregation."

"The poor man. What's to happen to his wife and children?"

"They can't prove anything," said Joe. "One of the chief witnesses is dead."

"They ought to punish such a policeman. Any man who kills a person for just a little burglary is dangerous to have on the force. Anyone could be killed. Anybody who is outside his house, closing the windows. Or suppose she had forgotten her key and asked him to open the door for her. How do you know he came out of the window? He may have been just closing it. You men always want to blame the woman. Maybe she is innocent."

"Maybe he's the burglar? 'Society thief caught trying to enter suburban home.' He thought she was out, he was losing money in the market, his friend was away, nobody would suspect him. He knew she had some jewelry worth thousands. So he forced his way in. Why, if he had known she was in he'd have gone in by the front door."

"You think it's funny," said Gurlie. "But you always want to believe the worst. I don't believe Mrs. Brewster was immoral. She is a very nice woman."

"And damned good-looking," said Joe. "Leaving a woman alone like that in the house, she needs some protection."

"Ha, you," said his wife. "You could never do anything like that. You have to be a sport like your brother Oswald, to run off with your captain's wife. Like all these men who haven't got the nerve to carry on a romance, all you want to do is talk about a woman."

"Well, he's dead," said Joe, "and that ends it. You asked me what I heard—now you can go with your women and get the details. They'll have to have a coroner's inquest and they'll fire the cop. He shoots too straight."

The parties to the tragedy being so prominent in the church and in the town didn't prevent the men on the eight-

eighteen Monday-morning train from saying their say. Girardy, though, the town philosopher, standing in front of the bank in the morning sun, had no comment. He didn't let it spoil his whiskey-bred contentment, took it for what it was. "Yes, I heard it," he said. "Doc, could you let me have a quarter of a dollar this morning? I'll pay it back by the end of the week."

"All right, Emile," said his friend, and he took out a little crimson leather-covered book which he kept in his vest pocket. And he wrote it down on the page under the heading, "Emile Girardy." "Twenty-five cents."

"Thank you."

"Any time you hear any interesting news about the people in town that you think I ought to know about, keep it for me, my friend. Your little account has mounted up quite a bit since the first of the year."

"You know more about this one than I do. What's the inside story?" asked Girardy.

"All on the surface," said his friend.

"They won't do anything about it, will they?"

"No. What can they do?"

"You're not going to let them fire George off the force, are you?"

"We'll find him a job. Don't worry about George."

Girardy, with the quarter in his hand in his pocket, looked up at the sun, silently scrutinized the young women hurrying by two's, in their long skirts, talking excitedly together past him, shying slightly away toward the gutter. "That man!" His expression never changed. He squinted up at the sun, saw it halfway toward noon.

By a hardly noticed movement, as if without intention, stretching, moving his feet, he began to drift toward the nearby tracks. The train had long departed bearing the ladies away to their shopping in the big city. No one ever saw him go. He would stand at the gates a moment, then gradually he'd flow across the tracks to a less arid province on the other

55

side. You'd hardly have noticed him first standing by the bank, as his more prosperous admirers passed on their rush to the train. You'd hardly see him leave his official post. He seldom spoke, the look never changing on his weatherbeaten face, winter and summer. But by mid-morning he'd be at the bar, just across the track, quiet, his first pony of whiskey before him, his manners perfect, slow-moving, silent.

"Do you smoke, Girardy?"

"No, but I drink whiskey," he would say.

"Can I ride my bicycle down to Martha's this afternoon after school? Can I?" said Flossie to her mother.

Martha was her first friend in the neighborhood. Lottie, being nearly three years older, wouldn't play with her younger sister. "All she wants to do is bang the piano," Flossie would say, and seek out her new acquaintance, one of the youngest of nine children, with brothers on all sides of her. She lived in the big old house down the hill at the edge of the low land stretching away to the east for miles—ditches and waving cattails—to the Hackensack River and "the city" beyond.

Captain Ellice, of the local militia, lived there in a semi-squirelike isolation from the rest of the town. There were fields and orchards all around him, the remnants of old Dutch ownership in the neighborhood, brown sandstone farmhouses now going to decay along what was the old highway along the bottom of the hill to Newark. They were still occupied by the Van Ripers, the Alyeas, the Vreelands. There he raised his numerous family. As a young lawyer he had married a local schoolteacher and had taken a job as school principal in the last years of the past century to piece out a scanty income. From there he more or less defied the town, living, and thriving, by his wits—keeping a farm besides.

Real estate is something a long-headed man knows how to prize. He was a crafty man to deal with; he knew his law. He was a Democrat while the rest of the town was on the other side of the fence, an almost unbeatable majority. Captain Ellice was still a Democrat; so was Stecher. That brought them together.

So as soon as school was out little Flossie rode her bike down the lane, bordered by the white board fence, slowly, with her friend running beside her. The apple trees of the orchard were beginning to be in bloom. But as soon as they got to the back door of the old house, four or five of the boys gathered round.

"Look at the new bike. Gimme ride, will you?" They were a little older than the girls and a good deal stronger. "Now, don't you do it," said Martha.

"Come on, we won't hurt your old bike, lemme see how it feels. Lookit," they laughed. "Look how you get on. It's a girl's bike. Let's see it," and one of the boys tried to take it out of Flossie's hands. But she held grimly and would not let go.

"Give it to me."

"No!"

"Mama!" yelled Martha. "The boys are trying to take Flossie's bike."

Mrs. Ellice came to the back door and the boys walked off. "We weren't going to hurt her old bike, it's a girl's bike anyway. What do we want with it?" And they went off toward the barn.

"Better put it in here," said the mother. "I'll watch it."

The girls went across the road to pick violets, the large purple ones, and, where it was wet from the springs at the bottom of the sloping fields, the tiny, white ones—the only American violets that are sweet-scented.

When they returned to the yard, the boys asked them if they wanted to see the new kittens.

"We haven't any kittens," Martha told them.

"Yes we have. We found them up in the barn."

"I don't believe it."

"All right."

They had an old ladder up the front of the hay loft. One

of Martha's brothers even went up a few rungs to show them how easy it was.

"What color are they?"

"Go up and look."

"It's a trick. Don't go," said Martha.

"Do you want one?"

Flossie had a kitty, but she wanted to see. So she started to climb the ladder while the boys clustered around the foot of it looking up. When she got to the top and found that there were no kittens there, the boys let out a yell and danced around like Indians laughing and rolling on the ground.

"You dirty things," said Martha slapping one of her brothers, but he merely punched her in the stomach, and by that time Flossie was down.

"We got square on you," they said. "Serves you right."

6

The first thing that had attracted Stecher to Riverdale was the river. When he was a young man, just over from Germany to escape military service, he used to come from the city out to the quiet stream to fish. There were still bass to be caught from its banks. But now the pollution from the Paterson factories had long since ended that. It was a great disappointment to him when he discovered it.

On their trips to see the house Gurlie had the man drive them around to see the lay of the land. It was a pretty place, so near New York and very respectable—even showing some evidence of wealth in a restrained sort of way. Or was it the veritable castle, as it was called, which had arrested Gurlie's gaze and her thoughts? It capped the hill in the new part of town, formerly a pine grove with an old nondescript stone mansion in the center, a transformation at the cost of a million dollars or more into a positive mediaeval French château. A six-foot iron picket fence surrounded its lawns and gardens. It was indeed impressive.

But the real center of the town still was a farm, where a descendant of the original Dutch grantee, a bachelor, tilled his rye, corn and potato fields, living in his colonial farmstead, rather primitive, but with a huge wisteria vine twisted about its latticed well house. He still had his old wood lot, limited

59

though it was by small newly built houses on the recently cut through streets. And at the edge of his apple orchard, on the short cut through the fields, stood two hay racks of the old kind, their pyramidal roofs held up by pegs in the four corner posts. They were quite near the street, quite unprotected, and had a reputation among the young lads of the town as a good place to take a girl.

Gurlie admired the farm and the castle. "They must have money," she said. "What they should do is to combine those two places, the farm and the castle. Do the same people own them?" she asked the hack driver.

"No, they got nothing to do with each other."

"In Europe that would be part of the same estate."

"Do you want to buy it?" said her husband.

"I would, if I had enough money," she said. "I bet I could make it pay. Give me the money and I'll show you." The hack driver looked at her, but hardly seemed to waken from the trance he was in.

"Well, have you seen enough?" said her husband. "Now you can go back and look at the place you're going to live in."

The driver gave a collapsing sort of half-laugh and spoke to his horse. "Gid ap," he said and the carriage rattled off over the macadam.

"Your streets need paving," said Joe.

"It's not the only thing the place needs," said the hack driver. "It isn't what it was before all these newcomers have come into the town. There used to be money here, but the old-timers are dying out. What they need is to build a decent hotel and put a good restaurant in it where you can get a drink with your meals."

"You can't buy a drink here?" asked Gurlie.

"No, it's as dry as a bone."

"I heard it was a temperance town."

"If you can call it that, from the drunks I take home every Saturday night, women and men. Everything goes on here just like everywhere else. But it's getting too congested."

Joe was satisfied to be far over on the east side, but Gurlie felt under a cloud from the first. She hadn't bargained on that.

"Well, how did you make out today?" said he at supper a few weeks later, watching his wife carve the roast. "Did you go to the Club?" His intonation was mocking.

"Yes, and I saw a lot of women."

"Well, what did you think you were going to find? A lot of horses and hyenas?"

"They're smart-looking—some of them."

"Do they look as if their husbands make any money?"

"They got brains, I tell you."

"Why don't they stay home, then, and use them? They haven't enough to do. What did they read?"

"A poem by Browning."

"Ho, ho, ho!"

"He's an English poet."

"They must be a lot of schoolteachers who got married too late to have any kids."

Magna came in from the kitchen at that moment with the mashed potatoes and the peas. "Shall I bring in the salad now?"

"Yes, bring it all in," said Joe. "A lot of idle women who haven't got anything else to do."

"We found some violets today," little Flossie broke in. "Sweet ones."

"Violets don't smell sweet in this country," Joe said. "They're all show, like a lot of other things here. They want to have something to talk about."

"These are sweet little white ones—where it was wet, near the edge of the meadows. Do you want to smell them? I brought some home." And she got up and went into the other room.

"By God, they are sweet," said Joe. "You didn't lie to me. I didn't know that." There was silence while everyone was eating. Magna came in and whispered to her mistress.

"Sure, go on. I don't care what you do."

"What does she want?" said Joe, after she had gone back to the kitchen.

"She wants the evening off. A friend is waiting for her. The children will do the dishes."

"Who were some of these poetic women you met today?"

"I can't remember their names. There was a Mrs. Coburn or Hoburn. Her husband is a music teacher in some school."

"That sounds like it. Who else?"

"Somebody by the name of Foster or Hoster. She's the president. And a Mrs. Blackwell—I didn't pay much attention—and about twenty others. They had a man . . ."

"That's it. I knew it," said Joe. "They had a man."

"Don't be so stupid," said Gurlie. The children leaned over their plates. "You want to ridicule something you don't know anything about."

"Do *you?*"

"No, but I want to see what is going on. I want to know who is who in this town and you have to go out and look if you want to get on. All you want to do is stick in your own back yard and smoke a cigar. You never go anywhere. But I am different."

"Why do we always have to fight at meals?" said Lottie.

"We're not fighting."

"I don't want anything to eat."

"I know the kind of women that go to such meetings to read poetry," said Joe. "Women who have to meddle into everybody else's business. They probably haven't any children, keep dirty houses—or they want to show off their hats and their fur coats and jewels, if they have any. Disappointed women and vain women without a smatter of brains in their heads. And that's the kind of creatures you think are great."

"Don't talk like a fool," Gurlie came back at him. "I don't say they're anything wonderful, but they are interested in getting out of the house and seeing what there is in the world."

"Well, what is there? Not reading poetry."

"It's cultural."

"Somebody has been teaching you already. It improves your mind. Fake. Any excuse to keep from doing your job as a woman. That's the kind that runs up a bill at the grocer and the butcher. I've already heard about the people in this town, the reputation they have. A lot of fourflushers."

"That's not true. Every town has that kind of people, but that's no reason for saying they all are. They are simply not going to rot in their own houses and say, 'Yes sir' to a lot of men who want to dominate them. They are forming a club to be called the Town Improvement Association. . . ."

"Are they sick of their poetry already?"

"I think that's more of a place for me. I'm not literary," said Gurlie, with a good deal of sense.

"If it isn't one thing it's another. Anything to get out of doing your job."

"I tell you I'm not going to stay home and sew up holes in your socks, no matter what you say. What do you suppose it is makes this town more attractive than some of the towns around it?"

"Because the people here make more money," said Joe.

"Because the women here are more cultured," said Gurlie. "They want to know more and that's why they have these clubs. The women in the old days in Norway were equal with the men. They had their place in the councils; they were queens and did what they pleased."

"That's the reason they wrecked the place. Not until they got put in their places by the men did they ever amount to anything.

"May I be excused?" said Lottie.

"Where are you going?"

"I'm going to practice."

"No, not tonight. Go upstairs and do your lessons. Don't you want any dessert?"

"What is it?"

"Tapioca pudding."

"No, I don't want any."

"Can I be excused, too?" said Flossie.

"Yes."

The children left.

Magna had left, too, so Gurlie went into the kitchen and brought their dessert in herself. Joe looked at it dubiously.

"If they had any husbands that were worth anything or children to take care of, they wouldn't have to run off busying themselves with gossip. That's all they have their 'meetings' for—to find out what somebody else is saying. They're afraid they might miss something."

"Dutchie!" said his wife. "You can't discourage me. I met the women of some of the best families in town today. It's their last meeting of the season. But I tell you I'm not going to take a back seat for anybody, for them or for you. I'm my own boss. I don't know much, but I'm going to find out. There was a woman from the South, an aristocrat."

"Did she try to borrow any money from you?"

"We didn't talk about such things. She told me about her family."

"Lost their money after the Civil War?"

"Yes."

Joe snorted.

"But they have a big estate there—or what is left of it."

"And you fell for that? Sucker. She'll get you yet. Did you tell her your ancestors were Vikings? That you have an estate in Norway? Or did have it before your father went broke?"

"She was very nice and is going to call on me."

"Here it comes. What's her name?"

"Moore."

"Don't let me hear of her again or her of me. Or, yes, tell her I make a million dollars a year cheating the Government like the rest of the crooks in Wall Street. They'll make you president of the club."

"She's very nice to talk to."

"What does her husband do?"

"I think she said he's out of a job just now."

"So we've got the wife of a music teacher, a Southern aristocrat whose husband is out of a job, and who else? Somebody by the name of Foster or Hoster and a man to tell you about some English poet. I'll bet if you find out who the husbands are, you'll find a lot of henpecked good for nothings."

"Agh, you make me tired," said Gurlie. "Go back to Germany." And she went out of the room. Joe lit his cigar and went into the front room to look at the evening paper. Little Flossie was there looking out of the window, Pully, the cat, beside her, its front paws on the lower sill. Joe leaned down to smell the little bunch of white violets in a small glass which stood in the center of the parlor table with its doily neatly centered.

"I suppose that's what you think the women should be doing," said Gurlie coming after a few minutes from the kitchen.

"What's that?" said Joe. Seeing her full length in her long flowing wrapper called to his mind the fact that she was pregnant and that for that reason had to be especially protected. He was sorry for her, though he had no need to be.

"How do you feel?" he said.

"There's nothing the matter with me," she replied. "I feel fine."

"Shouldn't you be taking it a little easy?"

"What for? The women in the fields in my country used to work up to the last day, then go behind a haystack to have the baby, wrap it in a shawl and go home with it. They never felt sick."

"You're not a peasant."

That made no impression on Gurlie. "At least I'll be carrying it through the summer. It won't get heavy till the cool weather."

"When will it be born?"

"About the middle of December, I think. Before Christmas. I hope I can nurse it this time. I was talking to one of the ladies this afternoon."

"So you told them?"

"Why not? I say what I please. Nobody can stop me. She had no children. She had one but she lost it when it was an infant. She nursed it two years."

"Was it from reading Browning?"

"Bouff!" said Gurlie, sitting in an easy chair and stretching her sturdy legs out in front of her, her arms hung down out of the loose sleeves of her gown. "I'm tired."

"Why don't you go up and lie on the bed then?"

She closed her eyes for a moment. "It's my back. If it weren't for my back . . ."

"It's from sitting in those hard wooden chairs they had there this afternoon that gave you the backache. You've got a comfortable house. Why don't you stay in it?"

Gurlie didn't open her eyes.

After a moment, though, she asked her husband if he had gotten an option on the lot they had looked at.

"Yes, they want two thousand dollars for it, just the lot itself. I could get a lot four times its size in Kronstadt, up the hill."

"You could, could you, and who wants to buy a lot in Kronstadt?" asked Gurlie.

"Well, you could do worse."

"*Mein Gott in Himmel!* Then you would be fixed. You have two daughters, they'd have to go to the schools there."

"What's the matter with the schools there?" Joe demanded. "I'll bet they've got just as smart children as they have in Riverdale. The girls could go to the *Turnverein.*"

Gurlie was wide awake and fighting by now.

Kronstadt was an old German-speaking community, a freethinking town founded by a Carl Weiss, a German Swiss, in the middle of the last century. It was independent, believed

66

in small enterprises and stayed conservative, with no church allowed in its precincts—but for the past fifty years good beer to be had on nearly every corner. It was one of the first towns, an entirely psychological opposite from commuter Riverdale. It had remained stable, going its own commonplace way.

Sunday mornings when Joe went for his long early morning walks, covering the entire local territory, he had stumbled into Kronstadt. It surprised and fascinated him. Here, if his eyes did not deceive him, was a part of old Germany. At one place, holding up the hillside where the main road to Hackensack passed—so familiar to him, so different in spirit from anything in this country—was a section of old wall that looked like mediaeval embattlements. It looked for all the world like the remains of an old crumbled castle. The street that led down from it was called Lilac Lane. It awaked strange memories in Joe. He shook his head and walked on.

"I've been thinking of moving my printing plant," he went on to Gurlie. "There are a lot of thriving businesses in this region so near New York. There are going to be more. The ink company I deal with is located there. Rents in New York are getting to be exorbitant. If I could find the right sort of factory building I'd move out, the whole business. I think it would pay me."

"And live in Kronstadt?"

"We could save a lot of money." He probably didn't mean it. He probably was moved by something he could not have analyzed, but he said it and went on. "Lottie could keep on with her piano lessons. We could have an *Obstgarten*. It's a nice place."

"I'm not a German. Why didn't you marry a nice, obedient little *Hausfrau* who would cook sauerbraten for you and make her own children's dresses? She'd never go out of the house and not even talk to the neighbors. I came to this country to be something else. If you move to a place like that, you can go alone."

Joe had lost his battle long before this and knew it. Gurlie knew it too. "Where is that daughter of yours?" he said.

Lottie was upstairs, in the fading light, in the library—Gurlie always insisted on a library—her great brown eyes full of tears. In her hands, as she stared into the growing light, half-falling from her fingers, was a well-worn copy of her favorite romance, the immortal *Thelma*, Marie Corelli's masterpiece. Whenever she was unhappy and felt alone and cheated in the world, she identified herself with that sad Norwegian maid. She had been forbidden by her mother to read the book. Why? She never could figure it. Nothing so pure and so tragic had ever been imagined as far as she could see.

What could be wrong with a young Englishman being in love with a pure Norwegian girl? Englishmen are great travelers and frequently went to the far north, to be alone, to fish, and to escape the world of cities. And what could be more natural than that in that isolated subarctic land near the North Cape, where the supernatural spirits of the past still live in faded glory—what could you expect else than that just there should grow up in all her blue-eyed loveliness and purity of thought such a one as Thelma, the Viking's daughter, and that he should discover her there, love her and carry her away, his wife, to the world of English life?

Gurlie didn't want her to be reading about what took place from that point on, the deceitful woman of the world, who had seduced her beloved, thrown Thelma into neglect, and sent her back at last to her northern haven, where she arrived only to witness a ship burning at sea and to hear of her father's final illness and death.

Lottie was so far lost in her thoughts that she did not hear her mother come up the stairs and just had time to slip the forbidden book under her knee, without changing her position, when Gurlie stood at the door.

"What are you doing here?"

"Looking out the window."

"Go downstairs and dry the dishes and put them away."

"Yes."

And Gurlie went to her room.

7

"Who does she think she is," said Mrs. Jacobsen, "a princess of the royal family? She came over here the same as we did. On a little ship. Her brother has a delicatessen shop in Brooklyn."

Magna didn't dare answer. They were drinking their afternoon tea in the kitchen behind closed doors. Lottie was playing the piano, arpeggios up and down the scale. Gurlie was supposed to be asleep.

"How much do they pay you?" said Mrs. Jacobsen, whose breath smelled strangely sweet. "Oh, you musn't mind me, it's my own stuff. I haven't been touching anything in the house. How much do you get?"

"Sixteen dollars a month," said Magna modestly.

"In this place, here in the country? You should get more to come out here. In Brooklyn you could get more."

"No," said Magna. "I tried. I like it here."

"What part of Norway does she come from?"—nodding toward the second floor.

"Sarpsborg, I think."

"That's to the south, the farm country. They have big farms there. She was a farmer's daughter. So."

"No, her father had a lot of money, I heard. But he lost it. They lived in a big house, old, old. It was an old family. An aristocratic family."

"There are no aristocratic families in Norway except the royal family."

Magna looked down, but did not reply. Mrs. Jacobsen leaned back in her chair and yawned. "I think I'll go up and lie down myself. *Tak for café*. That tasted good, just what I needed." She was a well set-up, full-breasted woman with muscular calves and strong hands. In her white nurse's uniform she made the boards creak as she mounted the stairs.

But after a moment she was down again. "I haven't been out of the house for two days. I think I'll take a walk. Which way is the downtown part?"

"That way," said Magna.

"I'll see what the place looks like."

She had no more than reached the street when Magna heard Gurlie calling her. "Come up here."

"Oh my God," thought the girl. "It's started!"

Gurlie laughed. "Where did she go? I don't want that woman snooping around the house. Send her away. Tell her to go back to Brooklyn."

"But I can't."

"*You* can help me as much as *she* could."

"Me?"

"All right. But I don't like to be told I'm sick. I'm not sick. I don't need a nurse in the house." And she got up from the bed with a violent gesture, but sank down again, blowing out her cheeks, realizing her heavy belly was too much for her. "Why do we women have to go around like this and the men get off for nothing? Go on, go on. Bring me a cup of coffee. It smells good. Where are the children?"

The night passed uneventfully. Another day to wait. Everyone was getting nervous, everyone but Gurlie.

"You should not lift your arms like that," the nurse told her.

"Why not?"

"Because the baby will be born with the cord around its neck."

"Cord around its neck?" Lottie had heard the nurse from the next room. "What does that mean?"

"Nonsense," said Gurlie. Nevertheless she did not throw her hands up again. "I'm sick of staying in this house. I want to go out and get some air."

"I would be careful," said the nurse.

Joe, who had still been sleeping with his wife, had spoken of taking a room in a hotel in the city until the event was over.

"Not on your life," said Gurlie. "You stay here where you belong. You are responsible for this. I want you to know what a woman goes through."

For a moment his temper flared, but he downed it at once.

"Put your hand here."

"Na, na, na, na!" He hated that sort of thing. She grabbed his hand in her rough way and laid it upon her bare belly.

"What is this for?"

"I want you to feel what I have felt for the last three months. There, feel that!" The infant in her big belly had given a powerful kick.

Somehow it made him laugh; perhaps it was the power of the kick or a feeling of manly competence that he had been able to get her that way, that she had come to term. "That's a funny thing," he said. "To feel a baby kick before it's born."

"So you think it's funny, eh? I wish it was out and he could kick you."

He laughed again. "Suppose it's another girl?"

"You can have it if it's a girl."

"All right. We'll give it to Hilda. She always wanted to get married and have a baby. Give it to her. She can take it up to the farm in Vermont and feed it from a cow."

So once again Joe left for his early train in the usual way. The girls went to school. Magna had listened half through the night but the nurse, Mrs. Jacobsen, slept soundly.

After Gurlie had had her breakfast and Mrs. Jacobsen had questioned her without any satisfaction, she told her patient that she had run out of clean uniforms and would like to go back to Brooklyn for a couple of hours to replenish her wardrobe.

"Go ahead," said Gurlie. "Stay all day. I'm not going to have this baby until January."

So Mrs. Jacobsen had taken the eleven o'clock train and gone and that was that. "She'll be back tonight," said Gurlie. "Good riddance. Now I feel free. Nobody is watching me as if I was a sick hen. Whoopee!"

But Magna was shocked and thought her mistress, although she had wonderful courage, a little crazy at times.

"Don't look so scared," said Gurlie. "You're not going to have the baby."

"God forbid!" said the young woman.

"I bet you'd like to," laughed her mistress.

"Not yet," said Magna, seriously.

"Have you taken any chances?" said Gurlie.

"Oh, no, no, no! The man I'm going to marry is in Seattle," said she.

"Oh there are plenty of good-looking fellows who would make love to a pretty girl like you."

Magna blushed crimson and walked from the room. What a woman! she thought to herself, to talk like that at such a time.

When Joe returned from business that evening the house was strangely quiet. He listened, but though he could smell supper cooking, he didn't hear anything. "Yoo hoo!" he called. Little Flossie came running from upstairs.

"Hello, Daddy."

"What's happened? Where is everybody?"

"Magna's in the kitchen cooking supper."

"And where's the nurse?"

"She's gone to New York."

Then Gurlie called to him. "Is that you, Papa?"

He was furious when he heard what had happened. "The *Gottverdammte Dummkopf.*"

"Don't yell at me. I don't like to be yelled at," said his wife. "Nothing has happened and I feel fine. Let her take her time. And don't say anything to her when she does come in. I tell you I never felt better in my life."

"Magna said . . ." began Lottie.

"Magna has too much mouth," her mother cut her short. "Supper is ready."

Mrs. Jacobsen came in about eight o'clock, said she got lost, missed the train and had to wait for an hour. Joe turned his back and walked out of the room—relieved.

At three o'clock in the morning his wife wakened Joe by punching him violently on the arm. He didn't know what had hit him. "Wake up," she said to him. "Rub my back."

"I'll get the nurse."

"No," she said, "don't wake her. I don't want her fooling around me yet. It's just my back."

"Has it started?"

"Yes," she said. "Now I feel it!" And she was silent a moment with both hands on her belly, as she sat on the edge of the bed. "Put your hand on my back. No, lower down. That's the place. Now it's going away." And she stretched out again on the bed and closed her eyes.

"How long has this been going on?"

"I just woke up. Leave me alone, I'm all right now."

Joe got up, lit the light and confirmed the time by consulting his watch that was lying on the dresser. He began to dress.

"Where are you going?" she asked him. "Nonsense, come back to bed. It's not coming yet. I'll tell you when to go for the doctor." So Joe put down his underwear and got under the covers again.

"It's cold in here. Better let me go down and open up the furnace."

74

"I'm sweating," said his wife. "Don't make it any hotter. Go back to sleep."

But there was no more sleep in the house that morning. In another fifteen minutes Gurlie had another pain, low down. Joe began to dress—anything to get out of the room.

"Don't wake the children."

"I know," he said, as he went to the library where the nurse was sleeping heavily. She didn't answer his knock, so he had to go in, which he detested, and tap her on the shoulder. "Get up," he said, when she opened her eyes, and left the room. He didn't want to talk to her and didn't like to see her woman's clothes lying on the chair. Returning to his wife's bed, he told her he was going to get the doctor.

"No," she said, "I don't need any doctor now. I'm all right. Just tell that woman to get me a cup of tea."

"Tell her yourself," said Joe. "I'll turn on the heat."

She put him out of her mind.

The nurse now in her professional capacity began to take hold. She was master of the situation, or thought she was, and knew what to do.

During the days she had been there the woman had made big pads of newspapers covered with old sheeting basted loosely together to cover the bed. "Get up," she told Gurlie. "I want to put this under you."

"What's that for?"

"To protect the bed. Here are your slippers. Now you must walk."

"I'll sit here," said Gurlie. "Get me a cup of tea. Why must I walk?"

"That's what makes the baby come. Now, up and down, up and down."

"Get me a cup of tea," Gurlie repeated. "Go on, do what I tell you."

By four o'clock the nurse came creaking downstairs to

tell Joe, who was sitting in the front room reading, that she thought he had better go for the doctor. Joe didn't answer by more than a grunt but walked into the front hall, put on his heavy coat, and went out. It was a good half-mile across the hill. The night was still and cold, no stars to be seen. It might snow.

Dr. Armitage was a tall, thin man who wore a short, pointed beard. He knew Joe and told him to come in a moment while he dressed, standing there rubbing his eyes, his sandy hair rumpled about his ears, in a blue bathrobe which kept opening in front.

"Sit down a moment. You think it's coming soon?"

"I don't think there's much time to lose," said Joe.

"Oh well, in that case . . ."

"Can I smoke in here?"

"Yes, go ahead." And after what seemed an age he came downstairs fully dressed, a necktie on, his hair neatly brushed, quite spick and span. Joe looked at him and wondered at his deliberateness. Time was passing.

"We'll go out and hitch up now."

The little mare took her time as, side by side, the two men, Joe holding his cigar—the doctor didn't smoke—went up one street and down the other until they arrived at the scene of the confinement. He blanketed the horse, patted her nose, picked up his bag and walked up the front steps where Joe was already holding the door for him.

It was nearly five o'clock by this time, and Gurlie was in full labor. "How are you, Doctor?" she said in one of her cramp-free intervals. "Everybody is worrying but me."

"You seem pretty comfortable," he said. "Are you having strong pains?" He looked questioningly at the nurse.

"No," said Gurlie. "This is nothing." But just then she was seized with a good one, got to her feet and, holding onto the back of a chair, her feet apart, head bowed, grew red in the face with her effort.

Everybody waited. Joe had come upstairs and was standing in the door. He thought it would come on the spot but the doctor, who remained sitting on the edge of the bed, didn't stir.

"How long have they been keeping up that way?"

"This is Mrs. Jacobsen, from Brooklyn, my nurse," said Gurlie puffing as she came out of her contraction. "Ask her. She must be good for something. This is my doctor," she said to the nurse. "What do you think of him? Ha!" She laughed her raucous laugh. "Why don't you examine me and tell me if it's coming all right? I tried to feel if the head . . ."

"I can't do anything with her," said the nurse.

"You'll have to stop that," said the doctor. "You can do yourself harm that way." And, as she had flopped herself down on the bed: "Stay there," he told her, "until I can find out what's going on." With that he started for the bathroom to wash his hands, the nurse following him.

"Come back here," Gurlie called to her.

"I have to speak to the doctor."

"Don't be telling him any lies about me."

Joe came in then to talk to his wife. "How do you feel?" he said.

"Oh, you make me sick," she told him.

The anger surged up into the back of his neck. "Well, if you don't want anything," he replied, "I'll go downstairs."

"Come here," she said. "Rub my back. Never mind. No, I don't want anything. Go away—and if the children wake up, keep them out of here."

"She's a terrible person," said the nurse to the doctor in the bathroom while he was scrubbing his hands. "I can't do anything to make her listen. But I think everything is ready." She helped him tie on his gown as he held his hands out in front of him to drain the solution from them and followed him into the room.

"Lie down now," she said to Gurlie. "The doctor wants to examine you."

"No. I want to go to the toilet."

"You can't go now, I tell you."

"I'm going," said Gurlie. "Get out of my way." So she pushed the nurse aside while the latter looked at the doctor in despair. "You'll have the baby in the bowl!" she told her angrily.

"I know what I'm doing."

"At least put on your slippers."

"Leave me alone."

"Go with her," said the doctor, patiently. He merely looked down at the floor and waited. Pretty soon Gurlie came back.

"I didn't do anything."

"I didn't think you would," said he.

"Don't you ever smile?" said Gurlie to him. "I never saw you laugh. I should think in your practice seeing us women when we are having babies would make you laugh."

"No, I never feel that way," said the man, father of eleven babies of his own. Boy, girl, boy, girl, all the way down the line, till people spread the rumor that he had discovered the trick of the sexes. Maybe he had.

"Oh, that's what it is," said he, examining her.

"What is it?" said Gurlie.

"The head is right here. And you, Mrs. Stecher, you'll have to stay in bed from now on. That's right—" as Gurlie seized the sheet that had been rolled into a rope and tied to the bed post for her to pull on— "Wonderful! I can just begin to see it."

"What color is its hair?" said Gurlie between grunts.

"I can't tell," said the doctor.

"What can't you tell?" said Gurlie. Just at that moment there was a big gush of fluid and the woman's legs were drenched.

"There it goes," said the doctor.

"Good," said the nurse, "now it will come." She put next to the doctor the chair covered with a towel on which was standing the basin of antiseptic fluid. "Keep the sheet over you!"

"No," said Gurlie, "I don't want it."

"But you must keep yourself covered."

"Agh," said Gurlie. "He's seen more than that."

"But you must cover your skin."

"No, I don't want to be covered." And she pulled up her knees and put her whole strength into the effort this time so that the head of the baby could be plainly seen. "Let me get up. I want to move my bowels."

"What can we do with her, Doctor?"

"No, you can't get up," said the latter quietly. "Let it go if you have to."

"But in . . . Oh, here it comes again. Oh, do something for me. What good are you? Take it away. Pull it out. It's right there, I can feel it."

"Give her a few whiffs of chloroform."

"Here it comes again!" And with that Mrs. Jacobsen began to drop the chloroform into the handkerchief. At first Gurlie didn't notice it, but then with the next deep breath, she got a lungful, and knocked the woman's hand away, coughing herself blue in the face. By that time the pain was gone. "What is that?" she asked him drunkenly. "I don't want any more of it. No, take it away. I'm all right. Just leave me alone."

Joe heard the commotion downstairs and listened for the children, but not a sound. Magna, though, was up and dressed. She went down to the kitchen, lit the lamp and closed the door.

"Here it comes again." Gurlie let go of the sheet and grabbed the doctor's shirt sleeve. Letting go of that, she took a pillow in her hands and pushed it against her mouth. Throwing that away she gave one brief scream.

"Here it is. Good girl," he said. "Well done. It's slippery as an eel. Put your hand on her belly," he said to the nurse, "and push down."

"Take your hand away," yelled Gurlie threateningly.

"No, stop that," he spoke sharply. "Do you want to hurt yourself? Leave the nurse alone."

"Is it here?" She raised her head from the pillow.

"Keep your head down," said the nurse. Gurlie brushed her aside. "Is it all right?" The doctor was having his troubles holding the thing. Just then its first wild cry sounded through to Joe's ear. He leaped to his feet. Spasmodic yells followed one after the other. He looked at his watch. Five-fifteen. Magna came to the kitchen door.

"Is it born?"

"I guess so," said Joe, and he started upstairs.

Just as he reached the top step he heard the doctor say in his steady voice, "It's a boy."

Joe stopped dead.

"A boy!" said Gurlie. "I knew it! Hooray."

"Keep yourself quiet," said the nurse angrily. "You have still to deliver the afterbirth. Keep quiet."

"Let me see it," said Gurlie to the doctor. "Hold it up." He did so with the cord uncut, holding the baby's bottom to the mother so she could distinguish its sex.

"That's good. Now let me sleep," and she rolled her head to one side. "Take your hand away from my belly. I don't want you to push on me like that."

"All right, Doctor, I think it's ready to come now," said the nurse and she squeezed out the afterbirth, Gurlie hanging frantically onto her wrists.

"What's that?" said Gurlie.

"Keep your legs apart," he said to her. "Now lift up till we take this pad out from under you. That's right. Now we can tend to the baby. Go to sleep. Hagh!" said he wearily. "These low beds, down in the middle, are not the best thing for my back. Now, young gentleman," he said to the baby, "we'll look at you. Pretty nearly eight pounds is my guess." He tied the cord, put the drops in the eyes, rolled the infant over to see if his back showed any defect, counted his toes and fingers. The baby blinked his eyes, let out another lusty yell or two, and quieted down, until the nurse could finish making over the mother's bed and bathe him.

Such excitement! And now it was all over.

Joe came in and kissed his wife. "You were fine," he said. "It's a boy."

"I knew it would be a boy," she told him. "How much does it weigh?"

"About eight pounds."

"That's a big baby. Is he all right?"

"Yes," said Joe.

"I'm glad that's over."

The doctor was washing up. It was just beginning to turn light. Joe looked at that little puckered face, the eyes opening and closing from time to time, the infant grunting and twisting from side to side. "He looks cold in that sheet. Don't you think a few drops of whiskey would do him good?" he said to the doctor, who at the moment came into the room drying his hands. He sat down on the edge of the bed and grasped Gurlie's belly in his grip.

"Don't do that," she cried, grabbing his wrists. "That hurts."

"We have to do it," said he, persisting. "There, you're doing fine."

"Don't you think we should give the baby a little whiskey and water to suck on? He looks cold," said Joe.

"Let nature take its course," said the doctor. "If the good Lord had intended him to have whiskey when he was born He would have sent a flask of it along with him."

So after all was quiet and the doctor had left and Gurlie was asleep, the nurse took the baby down to the kitchen to bathe it. Magna was entranced. "A little boy. Let me hold it. Isn't it heavy? So big! How can it be?"

Flossie could hardly believe her eyes.

But Lottie merely gazed at the little thing in a bored way. "Disgusting," was all she said, and turned away.

8

The leading women of the town, and at that time they were mostly the Presbyterians, adopted Gurlie as their own. She was bold, she had unbounded energy for public affairs, she was gay, loved a party and knew how to get others to work for her. That didn't all come out at once, but from the first they liked her and that was enough. There were those, of course, who thought her indelicate, to say the least, but even they had to acknowledge that she got things done once she undertook them.

"We need people like that in this town. They're all asleep here. If we don't wake up soon there won't be anything left of what we once were. We haven't a park, we haven't proper paving on our main streets, our street lighting is a disgrace, and she has a wonderfully talented daughter."

"Doesn't look a bit like her."

"Her husband's a very pleasant man to talk to and a shrewd businessman, they say. He's a printer. Prints the United States money orders."

"I thought they were printed by the Government."

"My husband says it was a shady deal, though, the way he got the contract."

"I heard that, too. Bob says it wasn't at all shady. He bid for it like anybody else. Here she comes. Is everybody here?"

"What were you talking about by yourselves here in the corner? I bet you're saying something that isn't true. Tell me about it," and she laughed her raucous laugh. She didn't care what they were saying.

"We were saying what a wonderful musician your daughter is, and so beautiful . . ."

"Beautiful? That stick?"

"She has such lovely eyes."

The Presbyterian church occupied a dominant position in the town near what might be called the civic center, a triangular piece of land a block long where two of the main streets joined. It was contemporaneous with the castle and had been built at the same time, largely from the same fortune. The old church, now the library, stood across the street with its wooden bell tower, from which the bell had been removed, staring silently at this crossroads of the town's interests, the firehouse and old school.

"Has the ice cream come?" asked Gurlie, who had organized the musicale.

"It's too early," said one of the women. There were three of them in the kitchen laying out the plates, teacups, forks and spoons. Gurlie was gone again as the people were beginning to arrive.

"Wait till my husband gets home and finds me gone. He's going to raise hob."

"Didn't you tell him?"

"No. What he doesn't know will never hurt him. Did you have your supper? I didn't eat a thing. These cakes look wonderful."

"You're going to get awful hungry before we get to them. The music comes first. How *is* Ned these days? I heard he's been sick."

"This weather! He's all right, though, but last month he was terrible. He's better than he was last year. How many cakes are there? Only six? Do you think we'll have enough? And this one's awful small. Who brought this one?"

"Never mind."

"Oh, I know. It isn't really very good, is it? Tell the truth. I don't see why people send cakes like that. Either give something good, or if you don't want to give anything or you can't afford it, just don't give. But to send a . . ."

"It's not a bad cake," said Mrs. Coburn.

"It all depends on how you look at it. But don't mind me," continued Mrs. A. "I've got to say what's on my mind. You never talk, do you Mrs. C.? You're deep. But that's not me. I've got to come out with it. She was lucky to pick such a good evening."

"She seems to be always lucky," said Mrs. D.

"You're right at that, some people are always lucky. It pays. I love her daughter. Those big eyes. But she's timid, isn't she?"

"I don't think she's pretty. I know those moony kind of girls."

"That comes from being so tall. They have such long legs they have to lean over so as not to be so conspicuous. I'd rather be small the way I am. Wouldn't you?" she said, addressing Mrs. C. "Oh, but you wouldn't express an opinion. Her mother isn't so tall. Neither is her father, in fact he's short or at least medium height. He's a lovely man. I wonder where she gets her long legs. She doesn't look like either of them."

An elderly lady came in at that moment bearing another cake covered with waxed paper. "I thought I'd never get here," she said. "I had to wait until the last minute."

"Oh, look at this, isn't this wonderful!" said Mrs. A. "You always make such delicious cakes. You're a darling. Look at *this* one, girls. This is what I call a cake. I'm going to have a piece of it before we take them around."

"Shh!" said someone at the door. "They can hear you out in the room."

"Oh, I'm sorry. I always forget. How many are there going to be?" she continued in a lower tone of voice. Gurlie, who had been talking to some of the more prominent guests, thought that there would be almost a hundred present.

"Oh, my God! We won't have enough cake."

"Yes, we will. We have ten now, and if we cut each into twelve we'll have more than enough."

"Oh, you're always so practical! There's nothing more to do here," said Mrs. B., taking off her apron. "I'm going out front. You'll be glad to get rid of me won't you, darlings? But I'll be back." And she was gone.

"I'm glad to get rid of that whirlwind. But she's got a good heart," said Mrs. D. "Are you going to sit out front for the music, Mrs. A.?"

"No, dear," said the heavy, quiet woman. "We can open the door a crack and hear everything from where we are. We'll just put out the light. Oh, here's the ice cream at last. I'm glad you didn't arrive in the middle of the music."

The Sunday school room was going to be crowded to its capacity. Everyone was there—at twenty-five cents a ticket.

They were stepping over each other to get into their places. "Why do people always take the first two seats on the aisle? They'll do it every time, and leave the others empty. Must be they're afraid of a fire," said the big-bellied Mrs. Janus.

"How're you, Hank? You coming to hear the music too? How's tricks?"

"The wife drags me to these things. Can you smoke?"

"No."

"How're things in the lumber business?"

"Sawing away. How's it by yourself? People giving you any trouble collecting?"

The man addressed was the town's assessor. He never answered direct questions.

"What have they got on the program for us tonight?" and he took his glasses out of his vest pocket and in his ponderous way he began to look over the program. "Printed," he added. "Ain't that something? We're getting stylish these days."

"Yes, her husband got them out for her."

"Hum, they do things right in this church, I see. So. Singing and—what's this? Who's this fellow Back?"

"Bach," said his wife, correcting him.

"Bock. I thought that meant beer."

Lottie and the two singers, Miss F. and the baritone, were in the minister's study nervously looking over their music. In the middle of the program her name was down for a Bach suite, which she had insisted on playing; her mother had wanted her to do something more popular, but she wouldn't give in.

Gurlie, fidgeting, had been standing near the door until the last minute. Now she left instructions with a young man who had been taking tickets to make the latecomers enter quietly.

"Leave it to me," he said.

Then she went into the study to tell the players to begin and sat in one of the last row of seats, hoping for the best. Just at that moment, Mrs. A., from the kitchen, came up and plucked her by the sleeve. Beckoning her to follow, she went through the kitchen door, closing it behind her. The accompanist was just beginning the opening passages of the first song. Miss F. was on the platform.

Seeing her smaller daughter Flossie standing there, "What's happened?" Gurlie said to her.

"Papa sent me," said the child boldly, knowing she had done nothing wrong.

"What did he send you for?"

"The baby's crying."

"Tell him to give it a bottle of water to drink. That's no reason to send you here to me at this time."

"He gave it some water, but it wouldn't take it."

"Tell him to put the baby on its stomach. Burp it."

"He did that, but it began to cry more."

"Let it cry then, it isn't going to hurt it to cry."

"It's been crying for over an hour, he says, and he wants you to come home."

"I can't come now. I have too many things to take care of. Tell him to do the best he can. Go on, tell him what I say."

It was a good quarter-mile back to the house, and though the spring evenings were growing longer, darkness had begun to fall.

"He says you've got to come home." The child would not budge.

"You better go," said the quiet Mrs. A. "We can manage everything all right. If necessary, you can come back. We'll be here for two hours what with one thing and another."

Gurlie was furious when she arrived. He had the baby in his arms downstairs and was walking up and down with it. It was asleep for the moment.

"You!" she said coming in at the door. Flossie didn't wait to hear, but went immediately to her room.

"That's what comes from your society foolishness," he began.

Seeing that he was really angry and nervous, she was smart enough to laugh. It struck her as ludicrous. "What good are men? You can't even take care of a baby."

"No. We aren't born to feed them like a woman. This is your job. But you want the vote, you want to go into politics while you let your homes go to hell. Here, take it."

"Here, give him to me," she said, taking off her hat and coat. Sitting in a comfortable chair, she unbuttoned her dress and put the baby to her bulging breast.

"Now get out of here, and don't start any more arguments. Where are you going?"

"I'm going out," said Joe.

"No you're not. You're staying right here so I can go back as soon as I have nursed him."

He didn't answer, but started out the front door.

"Hey, you," she said. But he was gone. She didn't make any further effort to call him, knowing he was just bluffing. After ten minutes the baby, satisfied, released the nipple from his sleepy mouth. She took him upstairs, placed him in his crib. He was drunk with his full belly and didn't stir. "Darling," she said, and left him. She could smell Joe's cigar. So she put on her wraps and her hat, walked out and told him, where he was sitting on the front steps, that she was going back to the church, kissed him on the mouth and left.

"Agh," he said, "you're a fool."

"Ta ta!" she said, waving her hand at him and walked with her waddling duck's walk off into the darkness, which was now complete.

"What happened?" she asked the ladies who met her at the door of the church. "Is it over?"

"No, no. Only the first half. That daughter of yours is wonderful. She's really a musician."

"I know that," said Gurlie. It was the intermission and everyone was looking for her.

"What happened to *you?*"

She whispered to one of the ladies on the committee, Mrs. D., who sniggered and looked down. "What happened?" asked her neighbors. "She had to go home to . . ."

"Oh, no!"

"Yes, really."

"I didn't know she was nursing a baby," said Mrs. C., coming back into the kitchen.

When Lottie heard it in mid-flight of her dream she was terribly embarrassed.

"Well, when the house falls down, you blame the architect, not the bricklayer," said Mr. T.

"What was that?"

"So when it stands up you give *him* the credit. It's a

damn good concert, I say. But all this classical stuff is too much for me. Did you hear what happened to Max Weber this week? A month ago he lost his false teeth one night down the toilet. Yes, he did, and wouldn't do a thing about it. Wouldn't listen to anyone, but had the dentist make him a new set. Cost him two hundred dollars. Two days ago he had the plumber to clean out the drain. What do you think he found? Sure. Not a nick or crack. Just as good as new. The man came up with them just the way they were when he lost them. Two hundred dollars down the drain."

Lottie and the old accompanist were in the vestry. The door was shut. The singers were out receiving the congratulations of their friends. But Lottie didn't think she had played well and didn't want to see anyone.

"Don't be foolish," said the old man. "That is a difficult piece and you played it well. How old are you?"

"Past thirteen," said Lottie looking her questioner straight in the eye.

"Do you like Bach?"

"He's the only one."

"That's a little drastic," replied her friend, "a little advanced for the town you live in, at any rate. You do live in Riverdale?"

"Yes, but I'm not going to stay here always. I'm going abroad." There wasn't the slightest prospect of her going abroad at the moment, but she wanted to sound big and that was what came into her mind.

"Abroad?"

"Yes, to study. To study music."

"Lucky girl. So music is your whole life. Don't you like to dance and go out to parties?"

What does he think I am, thought Lottie to herself. But she said, "No."

At that moment Gurlie came flying in at the door. "What are you two doing in here? Everybody is looking for you. Come out and show yourself." She gave the man, whom she did not know, a quick look.

"This is Mr. Bellows, the accompanist. He's from out of town. We've been talking."

"Very nice," Gurlie said. "Now get along with you. Hold your shoulders up. Don't be so sloppy. Look at your hair."

In the kitchen there was a great deal of coming and going among the waitresses carrying ice cream and cake. The fixed rows of chairs had been broken up to make informal groups. The women were gathered together. Some of the men were smoking, sitting or standing apart. "Those damned wooden-bottom chairs weren't made for Christians. Glad to get up and stretch. How was the school-board meeting last night?"

"They're talking about putting up a new building for the high school."

"I guess we've got to have it sooner or later, but maybe this ain't the time for it. There's lots of things we need before that."

"You ought to have heard that little guy, Page, he is a great talker. Had them all tied in knots on parliamentary law, wouldn't give up the floor and they couldn't make him. It was good fun."

"My dear, I *love* to hear your daughter play. But couldn't you ask her to choose something a little lighter? There are some things by Schumann, for instance, or some of Chopin's études. But Bach! Our people really aren't up to that, are they? Tell the truth. I know you are a musical family and some of us . . ."

"What a picture she makes! I love to see a young girl at the piano. She honestly makes it speak. Don't you like to see young people perform? They are so innocent-looking and that beautiful music . . . It seems to come from their eyes—you can almost say that, can't you? It seems ridiculous to say the music comes out of their eyes. But music is the language of the soul they say, and the eyes are its windows. So it's natural . . ."

"Oh, come off, she's just a kid. She does all right."

Lottie, who had to listen to all this, was very grateful for that touch of common sense.

"Are you going to play for us again after some of the others leave? Come on. Something simple that we understand."

Here it comes, thought Lottie, who hated them all, but had to keep on smiling with one eye on her mother—going about among the various groups seeing that everyone had a good time.

"How much did we take in?"

"Twenty-six dollars and twenty-five cents."

"Why, that isn't bad at all. You'll clear at least fifteen, or even more."

Lottie had to play again after more than half the guests had gone. Some were still standing in the entry; the women in the kitchen with the door closed, washing the dishes, could still be heard and had to be shushed. Lottie did a Chopin prelude. After the applause the racket began again.

At last it was all over. The dishes were washed and all put away, the cake plates returned to their owners and Gurlie could leave. As the janitor said good night to her, it was getting toward eleven. "Papa will give me the devil," she said.

But Lottie was looking up at the stars. It was a lovely spring night, everything so still, the air so warm. "Oh," she said, "I wish I could stay up all night."

Gurlie yawned. "I'm glad it's over."

"Look at those stars. I don't feel a bit sleepy. People are such fools to go to bed."

Joe was in bed asleep. He wakened when Gurlie entered.

"Has the baby been good?"

"Yes."

Lottie did not turn on the light, not to waken her sister, but undressed in her room quietly and, going to the window, stood there in her long nightgown looking at the stars. She stood there a long time, perfectly still, not knowing what she thought except that, in her still excited mind, after the music, it felt good to be so still, as if with her clothes she shed the vulgarity of the whole town, as if she were bathed in music—and the night.

Night is the best time, night, to be naked, if she only dared, alone. It was the sadness of early youth. She'd like to go bare onto the lawn and stand completely away from the house. She had no wish to dance, just feel her skin touched by the night air. For a moment she half thought she'd do it. She had the nerve. Nobody need know.

But my God, if they saw me! Just to go out and stand naked under the stars. They'd think I was crazy. No one understands. They all have dirty minds. All of them.

She raised her hands to her hips, then turned reluctantly and crawled into bed, stretching her long, skinny legs out, her big feet, laying her hands at her sides, evenly, looking up, seeing in her mind the pure starry sky, hearing the music as if truly of the spheres and so fell into a dreamless sleep.

9

"I hate boys," said Martha. Flossie agreed.

It was a bad time for males at the beginning of the century. The mortality threatened to be high. It's funny to be a girl instead of a boy. Or a boy and not a girl. Which comes first? Why? Of course it had to be, everybody knows that. But it's that they won't let you decide: I want to be a girl. So you're a girl. And vice-versa.

The fury of the sexes, for one thing, doesn't mean much to little girls. Boys get the itch much earlier. It makes them hateful.

"The only one I like," said Flossie, "is Tom."

"Who?"

"Tom Barry, he's nice. I go down with him when he gets bread. He eats it on the way home. Hot."

"Do you eat it?"

"No. We don't eat hot bread."

"What does he do?"

"He pulls out pieces of the crust and just eats it. His mother is furious when he gets home. Other boys are too fresh, but he's nice."

It began when the Van Riper boy was brought home in a cab from the station. The commuter train he expected to take to work had run over his left leg just above the ankle.

His mother happened to be on the front porch when the cab he was in pulled up in front of the house. She shrieked. You could have heard her a block. It was awful. They didn't dare take him into the house. He lay on the porch. She wanted Dr. Armitage. The other doctors were for cutting off his leg, but she wouldn't let them. He told her she was right. He's a good doctor. He knows.

"Boys are awful. They smoke. Even when Papa says they mustn't. I see them smoking all the time and they do other things. I see them. Peanuts Howley—Beansie. Do you know him? He lives near you. He's awful. I hate him."

"I never want to get married. Some girls, though, are just as bad. They encourage them. If they wouldn't encourage them, they wouldn't be so fresh. They don't care what they say."

"They talk dirty."

"What do they say?"

"Everything. I won't even repeat it."

"I haven't any grown brothers."

"You're lucky. I wish I had all sisters."

"Buckalew, did you hear about him? He was trying to knock some chestnuts out of a tree last fall. He fell and landed on the telegraph wires. Right across them and then he turned over and fell the rest of the way. And broke both legs. What they won't do!"

"And I heard of a boy that went into the old copper mines."

"Where are they?"

"In Lyndhurst. Down by the meadows. He was quite old, about seventeen. The boy in front of him had a rifle over his shoulder, a Winchester, I heard. And it went off and shot the other boy in the face. Tod Nelson, his name was."

"Did it kill him?"

"Yes, of course."

Flossie had never heard of such things.

"They go swimming in the meadows at a place called Little Bend, bare naked."

"In the mud and everything?"

"Yes, in the mud."

It was a rainy day, and the two little girls were bored. "What is there to do? Look, it's stopped now."

"It's stopped raining," Flossie said to her mother. "Can't we go out and skip rope?"

"No, it's too wet. You can't go out."

"I don't see why everyone can't be like my papa," Flossie confided after awhile. "I love him."

"Does he ever spank you?"

"Sometimes, a little. It never hurts. But when Mama spanks it hurts. She hits hard. I got spanked yesterday. I forgot to come home on time. I met Lucy Young, and I didn't get home until almost six o'clock. I couldn't help it. I didn't know what time it was."

"My mama never spanks me. She always has my papa do it. He doesn't really spank me. But he whips the boys, and I'm glad of it, only he doesn't do it half the time when he should. I could tell him lots of times when he ought to spank them."

"Does your father go to New York every day?"

"No, he has an office in Riverdale. He's a lawyer."

"Does he come home to lunch every day?"

"Yes, almost."

"That's funny. Sometimes I go to meet my father when he comes home on the train at night. He often brings me presents. Does your papa bring you presents?"

"No. Do you play with dolls?"

"Not any more, but I used to."

"Haven't you got any?"

"Yes, I have a big one my uncle gave me."

"What's her name?"

"Susie. She has a china face and blue eyes that open and close. But I can't play with her because I might break her face. I don't like her, anyhow. She's too big. I liked rag dolls. I made them myself."

"How?"

"Like this." Flossie looked around and couldn't find anything to make a rag doll out of until, on her sister's side of the clothes closet, she came up with a piece of an old petticoat. She stuffed some paper, for want of better, into the middle of it to make a head, tied a narrow ribbon round it to make a neck—and: "There you are!"

"I used to have dozens of them. Oh, it's still raining." The little girls looked disconsolately out of the window awhile, watching the rain splash on the sidewalk and collect into a shallow pool at the lowest point, which happened to be just where their front walk started from the street.

"How are you going to get home?"

Lottie was at the piano playing over and over again a passage from some piece she was learning by heart. She always got stuck at the same place, a passage where the left hand came in with runs up and down the scale while the right hand was emphasizing the melody in chords. The time was what seemed to bother her. She played it over and over while the little girls watched the rain. The muffled sound of the piano below them seemed to express something of the rainy mood.

"What are you going to be when you grow up, do you think?"

"I'm going to work for my father," said Martha. "He has a woman in his office. I'm going to take her place. I can help a lot. What are you going to do?"

"I'm going to be a singer."

"You can't sing," said her friend. "Anyhow you have to have lessons to be a singer."

"No you don't. If you have a natural voice you just sing like a bird. Didn't you ever hear a robin redbreast singing?

That's the way I'd like to sing. Next to that I'd like to dance. Oh, I wish I could be a dancer. I'd dance all around."

"Yes, but you can't earn a living being a dancer—unless you teach."

"I don't mean that," said Flossie. "I'd just like to dance and dance and dance. I wish we could go out and skip rope. Let's skip rope here in the room."

"You might shake down the ceiling," cautioned her friend. So they decided not to try it. "Do you always wear your hair in braids?"

"Yes," confessed Flossie sadly.

"So do I. Let me fix your hair for you. Let's make believe we're grown up. I watched my sister. I can fix it the way she does." So Flossie sat on the floor while Martha unbraided her blond hair, untying the ends where her mother or perhaps Magna had finished it that morning. "Don't you love your hair loose?"

"Yes, but now let me unbraid yours." Martha submitted to the operation. Then they both admired themselves in the glass.

"I think our hair is beautiful, don't you? Oooo!" she spread her arms out and postured. Flossie did the same, throwing her head back and running around the room crazily. Martha followed her. "Aren't we silly?" she said.

"Aren't we?" Flossie agreed, and they both laughed. "Hair is funny. What good is it? I wish I could cut it off."

"You'd look like a boy."

"I tell you what we'll do. Shall we dress up?" But they couldn't find anything but some of Gurlie's shoes which they put on, loosely, having removed their own to do so. "You can't dance in these." Then Martha began to rebraid Flossie's yellow hair in a single rope which she coiled up into a bun on the back of her friend's small head. She combed out her front hair to make a bang, then stood back and opened her mouth in surprise.

"Look at yourself!"

The effect was startling, as every mother knows. Flossie looked at her small features in the glass with the adult coiffure. It frightened her a little. She didn't like it.

"No, I don't like it, either. It makes you look old." They decided they'd put their hair back the way it was before, each helping the other. They were bored.

"It's really stopped raining now. I think I'd better go home."

"Oh, don't go. I have no one to play with."

"No. I've got to go. I'll see you tomorrow. If I don't go now, I'll get all wet."

After her friend left and waved good-bye to her as she ran off down the street, Flossie stood at the window for a long time. As she looked, the rain began again to come down hard. It was like being at the bottom of the sea. One looked up through the water and—there was a green light. You could see the other fishes swimming around. Terrible ones, sometimes, with big eyes and long tails. Did you ever see a fish like a girl, with hair in twin braids? And one with blue eyes. Papa had read her the story of the princess who was a mermaid—in a book of fairy tales. The good fairy had promised her that she could walk.

The rain was coming down in buckets. Martha would be caught in it. But anyhow she had an umbrella. And rubbers. So she wouldn't get very wet and catch a cold.

The mermaid had been promised, so the story said, that she could have feet and walk, part of the time, or something like that. But it would be like knives when she stood up, as if she were walking on knives, gingerly, that's what she had to suffer for it. Flossie walked about the room as if she were walking on knives, gingerly. That was cruel. I wonder why that was? But it was worth it to be a human being. Otherwise she lived in the sea. Of course there are mermaids. There must be. But the good fairy had promised her she could have feet, and dance and someone would come for her and . . . But if she stayed too long it would be like she had to walk on knives.

Her papa often read stories to her in the evening. He had always read her stories. Once she put a whole row of rag dolls on the window ledge in the kitchen and told them the stories again. But she was too big for that now.

If you're a mermaid and live in the sea, she thought, looking out of the window into the rain, it would be like this—except that I am not wet but dry and I can walk on my feet and it doesn't hurt me at all. She heaved a sigh and was happy.

Suppose it never stopped raining but kept on and on until "the waters rose," as it said in the story they had read to the children one day in Sunday school and "the floods came," and you could see naked women with horrible looks on their faces, five or six of them, with cats and dogs lying on the rough stones, just with the tips of them sticking out of the water. You could see other tops of mountains, just the last tip sticking out of the water. Naked men and women with little babies in their arms whom they were holding up to save —only they couldn't—because the rain still was coming down in buckets and soon they all would be drowned.

It would be wonderful to be a mermaid then.

It might rain again like that. The water would come higher and higher. First the meadows would become a lake, then the waves would come to the shore. Martha's house would be flooded first because it was nearer the meadows. But she'd have time to come up the hill. It wouldn't come that fast and . . .

Flossie was frightened. She turned around in a hurry and went to be near Magna, who was boiling cabbage for supper in the kitchen. She had the door closed, to keep the smell of cabbage from going through the house, she said. "Is it still raining?" Magna asked her.

"Yes," said Flossie. "Hard." But Magna didn't seem to mind, which was what Flossie had waited to see. She hadn't minded at all. Yesterday it had been a beautiful day, she remembered it because she had gone with Lottie to play with her friend Nala. But a big boy was sitting on the front porch talking to Nala's older sister, Mary, and neither Lottie nor Flossie—not even Lottie—had dared to walk up the steps while he was there.

So they stood there undecided.

"What do you want, my dears?" Mary had said.

The big boy was there, so that they didn't even answer her. Lottie, at least, didn't answer and Flossie was too little to speak when her sister was unable to do so. So they just stood there, dumb.

"Are you looking for Nala?" Mary said.

Still they stood there without answering.

At that the big boy—he was almost a man—had said, "Come on up, little girls. I won't hurt you." At which Lottie and Flossie had turned abruptly and, without looking back, had hurried home. That was Flossie's first meeting with her future husband.

10

"Riverdale is such a *nice* town—it's really a privilege to bring our children up here," Mrs. W. began. "We have such *good* schools and our teachers are such ladies." The flattered young schoolteacher wondered what was coming next. She grimaced and blushed. "You're from one of our best families yourself. Wasn't your father a minister of the gospel at one time?"

"Yes," said the young teacher briefly, knowing that her father, while truly a preacher of the gospel, as the shrewd woman well knew, was of a small, poor and particular sect not at all popular in the town.

"But the town is growing and there are many undesirable elements getting a foothold in it now." She let out a deep sigh. "Isn't it hot today? I must have hurried."

"Let me take your wrap?" The young teacher, after all, did have to clean up her desk and get out. All but one or two of her fifth-grade pupils, who had been kept in, had been dismissed. "Excuse me a moment," she said to Mrs. W., the mother of one of her nicest girls, and she turned from her, sitting there fanning herself with a book.

"You may leave now, William," she said to one of the boys. She waited a moment until the boy scrambled up at the unexpected reprieve. "And you may leave also, Joseph. I will speak to you tomorrow." Joe followed his friend.

"Who are those two little boys?" said the woman.

"They're very troublesome," the young teacher said. "I had to keep them in."

"As I was saying," said Mrs. W., who had shrewd eyes, an arrogant air, "we can't afford to be complacent. If the older families, those who may be said truly to represent the better element in the town, do not stick together, it won't be long before we're all lost. I'm a Southerner. It's only by sticking together that the South has maintained some vestige of its old aristocracy. What would you suppose would have happened if we had let every Tom, Dick and Harry into our schools and our houses? How are any decency and manners to be maintained unless . . . ? And it's the mothers who must see to it. The little girls who are to grow up and marry here must be protected."

The young teacher was in thorough agreement. How, in fact, are the precepts of the Lord to be maintained other than by that small minority in which her family took such pride, a pitifully few staunch believers in the true church, that indomitable, small, indestructible, faithful . . .

"Next year, when the new park school is opened . . ." It was to be the first modern building in the system, the first attempt on the part of the Board of Education to meet the growing demands of the town. "I understand," the alert Mrs. W. continued, "that we're going to have two fifth grades, one from the west side of the town and one from the east. Now I live on the east side, not very far from the center, but I have been thinking—my little daughter has most of her friends on the west side, where the better families come from, I think it is fair to say. Oh, I don't mean the West *End*, but . . ."

The young teacher, who was shrewd enough herself, in a modest way, began to get the drift of things, and found herself fully in agreement with what was being intimated. What a relief it would be to get rid of a few of those downtown boys and girls too, who so persisted—she couldn't for the life of her explain or excuse it—in breaking the rules both of the school and of God, also.

"Now, what I was thinking," went on Mrs. W., "was, if you think it a good idea, I wouldn't presume to suggest anything that would interfere in any way with the proper running of the school, but if you think the idea a good one maybe you'd speak to the superintendent of schools, Mr. Mewhinny, and get him to select a nice little group of girls and boys who could have you for their teacher."

At last it was out, and Mrs. W. watched the young teacher's somewhat expressionless face, which in this case blushed crimson without altering its expressionlessness.

"Well," said the young teacher, "it would make a very interesting group." Secretly her heart leaped at it.

"It would be such a wonderful thing! And it's so fair. All the little boys and girls who play together and go to their innocent little parties would otherwise be broken up. They form a homogeneous group, they go to the same churches, their mothers and fathers know each other, they belong to the same sets, to the Masonic Order, the same clubs. It is their right to remain together and continue their solidarity; it was a good world. It would be wrong, positively destructive of everything we hope to preserve in Riverdale, if they are driven apart now. I think it would be a very bad thing, don't you?"

This brought it right up to the young teacher to make a decision, as Mrs. W. had intended. "Speak freely," said her tormentor. "I want to know your candid opinion. Because if you think I am saying anything improper, I hope you will have confidence in me enough to tell me so, as a teacher and as a townsfellow. Can you see it from my point of view? The point of view of an interested, a deeply interested parent, who wishes to preserve the best interests of the town she lives in, one of the mothers of the town? I want to be corrected if I am wrong, I don't wish to force anything on you that you do not approve of. But if you think I am right . . . Don't you think it would be a pity to separate all the children who have

grown up together in school and admit another element . . . ?
Well, let's be frank, an element that is not, sweet children
that they all are, that is not quite so desirable."

The young teacher was a little frightened at the thought
of approaching the principal and wondered how she'd go about
it.

"Well," said Mrs. W., preparing to go, "you don't have
to commit yourself now. I didn't come here to trouble you
at this time of year when you are so busy preparing your final
examinations. But I had to come now before the vacations.
We have to get ready before the new school term begins
or it will be too late. Oh, by the way, what are you doing this
Friday afternoon? I have a few of my friends who are coming
to tea. If you care to drop in sometime between four and five,
I'd be so happy to see you."

Mrs. W.'s teas were well known in the town. She was a
wonderful pastry cook and a charming hostess. "Will you
come?"

"I'll try," said the young teacher, who before that had
never in fact been invited to any teas in the town, certainly by
the better people. "I'd be very happy to."

"Well then, good-bye, my dear, and if you think well of
my little proposition, which is, after all, nothing but an idea,
which occurred to me the other evening, that I thought would
be of benefit to us all . . ."

"I think it's right," said the young teacher unexpectedly,
much to the older woman's surprise and satisfaction. "We are
going to have two fifth grades in this building next fall and it
is only proper that friends should remain together."

So the following September, when the classes assembled
in the new building, little Flossie (after all, *somebody* had to
be sacrificed) found herself cut off from those she had become
accustomed to be with for the past few years and grouped
with the less desirable elements of the town.

She went home in tears. Even her best friend, Martha,

was in the other, more select, group. She was heartbroken and Gurlie was up in arms and personally affronted.

"Who do they think they are, in this town?" she said to her husband that evening. "No, they can't do that. I'll take her out of school. I won't have it."

"It's a good thing," said Joe. "She'll get to make some new friends."

That infuriated Gurlie the more. She began forthwith to attack her husband. "What kind of father are you? Haven't you got any pride? To let a lot of stupid people order you around?"

"Go see the superintendent. Isn't her new teacher as good as the other? Find out about it. Don't go off half-cocked. Maybe he had to do it that way, maybe it was a mistake. If you speak to him about it, it can be arranged."

So Gurlie went, for the first time, to the superintendent of schools with her complaint. She had to wait while he disposed of some other business, boys and girls coming and going, new assignments, and then she was admitted. A secretary was at work on some papers nearby.

"Well, what can I do for you, madam? May I have the name?"

"Mrs. Joseph Stecher." He instantly noticed the slight accent, sensed that trouble was ahead and, Irishman that he was, decided to be tough. A tall, thin man, with angular features and the nervous manner of one always anxious to get away, he seemed to imply: Hurry up, get it over with, I have many more important things to do than listen to you.

Gurlie had a habit of closing her eyes when she talked. Perhaps she was watching her opponent through half-closed lids but, her face raised, facing Mewhinny, her eyes partly closed, opening them wide for a quick glance once in a while, she told him her story. He had heard it before.

"Well, Mrs. Stecher, I'm sorry. But we can't do anything about it now."

"You can't, eh?"

"No, we can't. The classes had to be divided into two groups, and this is the way we've done it."

"Is that so?" said Gurlie. "Well, I'll tell you one thing, that's nothing but favoritism. You've kept my little girl from being with her friends and put her in . . ."

"Somebody had to suffer. We can't please everybody."

"Well then, why have you been so careful to please somebody else?"

"Do you accuse me of being partial?"

"Yes," said Gurlie, "I do. You have gone out of your way to do this. You are not the superintendent of one group of pupils. Your salary is paid by the taxpayers to represent all of us. You have to treat us all equally. It is not fair if you choose one set . . ."

"Do you accuse me of being unfair?"

"If you do something that is unfair, you accuse yourself of it."

"My dear Mrs. Stecher, I was hired to run the Riverdale schools. I wasn't told how to do it. They left that to me. I am sorry if your little daughter has been divided from her friends, though you exaggerate the situation. She sees them every day on her way to and from school and on Saturdays and Sundays. She has a good teacher, one of our best. But we cannot change our rule for any individual."

"Yes, you can if it's unfair . . ."

"Mrs. Stecher, that's your opinion, which I do not share. Your opinion is not my opinion. I run the schools as I please." And he got up and went to the door.

Gurlie wanted to slap his face but, white with anger, her eyes wide open now, she got up also and, without looking further at him, walked out of his office, down the corridor and into the street, crossed the little park and went home.

"That's not the last I'll hear of that," said Mewhinny to his secretary.

That evening Joe got it full blast. "Oh, forget it," said he. "The child is well rid of them," meaning the children of the better families. "What's the matter with the ones she's with? Aren't they as smart as the others?"

"No," Gurlie put in, "they're all stupid children, the worst in the whole town. All the bright ones are in the other section."

"Well then she won't have as much trouble being the smartest. I think you're making a mountain of a molehill. Forget it."

But Gurlie was not going to let up. It stuck deep in her crop. She had to beat them down, she had to win. She had to put that stupid Irishman in his place. "What kind of a name is that Mewhinny? He's impolite. Insulting. Are you such a ninny that you're going to see your wife insulted in the schools? We've got to move away from this part of the town. I want to live on the hill where the best families are."

"Here it comes," said Joe. "You're as bad as they are. If it'll make you any happier . . ."

"Do you know anyone on the Board of Education? Go to him. Raise hell. But I won't let that cheap Irishman beat me. Will you play second fiddle? If he had any brains he wouldn't be just a schoolteacher. You . . ."

So Joe went to a fellow German, a cocky little man on the Board of Education, who took the matter up for him. "We can't change it now. But your wife is quite right. It was a bad business. Next year we'll divide the classes alphabetically."

"Next year!" Gurlie was furious. "I'll take her out of such a school."

11

A cornet, its tones clear and deliberate that quiet May morning, shattered the distance. Seized by it, the whole neighborhood listened: *Oh promise me* . . .

Oh promise me that some day you and I . . .

It came suddenly, half the first verse, unexpectedly into the sunshine as if a very heart would break. Then as suddenly ceased, cut off short.

"Let the boy play."

"Not on Sunday morning. People want to be quiet."

Dinner was cooking. The odors of it filled the whole house.

Without telephones, innuendo and direct attack were the only weapons a good woman had with which to defend herself from her neighbors in those days.

Small and peppery, Mrs. Mason was all the more infuriated to see her great, placid husband, a genial giant of a man who was never angry, take things so easily.

"Why do you get so excited, Ella? They don't mean to hurt you."

"They don't, eh? You're blind. Did you hear that those Stechers down the street are sending their daughter to Germany to study the piano? *That* costs money."

"Joe's a good fellow. Darn nice man. I like him."

"What about his wife? She's stuck up. She's so stuck up

she can't talk to her neighbors. She wants to join the Women's Club. Her! She had Mrs. Smith, 'the rich Mrs. Smith,' come for her in a carriage the other day. Who comes for *me* in a carriage? I have to hear complaints of my boy from the neighbors, from his teachers, from the police, yes, from the police. And I have to bear it. Not you. Me. I'm the one. But I tell you they'll never get anything out of me. If I saw him breaking their windows with my own eyes, I'd never admit it. They couldn't tear it out of me with a team of oxen. Let 'em try. I'll defy them to the last breath out of my body— and that Stecher woman's at their head." She went out to the kitchen a moment to glance at the roast. Frank sighed a sigh of relief. But she came back madder than ever.

"—with her *grand* piano. Boasting to me that it was a Steinway. I don't know yet how I'm going to do it, but before I get through, I'm going to show them up. It may take me a year, but I'm going to make them sorry."

The fourteenth of February, St. Valentine's Day, was a great one in the Stecher household, awaited each year with ever mounting interest as Lottie, especially, grew older. But Flossie wasn't far behind. They always received the frilly little paper messages of love from Auntie Olga, Auntie Hilda and always a very beautiful one from Joe's brother Oswald in Chicago.

Mrs. Mason was at the paper store the cold day before St. Valentine's when the idea struck her. She had really gone in there for a moment to warm herself after starting home with her purchases from the bakery. There wasn't really anything she wanted at the paper store. It was just an excuse.

But the place was full of valentines, pretty ones with frilly paper lace about them, flowers and billing doves. "Ridiculous. Who ever sends me a valentine?" Her husband used to buy them for the children, but they were too big now. But she kept reading the silly verses, just the same, as the feeling returned to her frozen fingers. She took her woollen gloves off and clenched and unclenched her fists to make the blood flow in them. "They're pretty, all right," she said to herself, and kept walking along the rack. Once in a while she picked up one and opened it, reading what was inside.

"Awful! I wonder who writes such stuff. And sells it? I could do better than that."

She was just about to leave, had, in fact, put on her gloves again when she came to a shallow box of gaudily colored sheets, a penny each, comics, which attracted her. "A penny each. That's more like it. That's what they ought to be, not ten cents and even a quarter. A quarter each! What do they think people are?" She began to thumb through the sheets, taking off her gloves once more the better to handle them. Now her interest suddenly awakened, she didn't at first know why.

She picked the first one up and read:

TWO OF A KIND

Here you're pictured with a creature
Your likeness both in mind and feature
Which ranks the highest, you or it,
Is hard to tell, you must admit.

Looking at the picture on the flimsy sheet she saw a crudely drawn splayfooted man in checkered spats facing a pig in a pen, its forefeet up on the boards. He had on a green hat much too small for him, a shirt with the collar of broad striped green and white turned up about his neck, while the pig on its hind legs was staring up into his face. There were twenty or more such cards to choose from. She was fascinated and began to go through them.

This was a heavy-set woman in a big plumed hat, her big feet solidly planted. In her hands she held the reins, a bag hanging at her waist labeled "cash" in bold letters. A little man, drooping with fatigue, the bit in his mouth, hat in hand, was being driven before her. The verse read:

To bridle and bit you meekly submit
 Like a horse that's been trained to obey.
A horse? No, an ass would be more in your class,
 Such a lack of all spunk you display.

She was fascinated. "I've got to have some of those," she giggled. "It'll be fun." She didn't know exactly what she was going to do with them, but now, thoroughly warmed, she went through the entire stock. Looking about guiltily to see that she was not observed she read greedily all the vicious legends she came to. "Hit Me Hards," it said on the ticket above the tray where the comics, so called, were exhibited. " 'Hit Me Hards.' I know a lot of people that I would like to."

Even then it didn't completely come into her head what she was going to do. She bought a nickel's worth of them. Then, after Mrs. Smiley had rolled them up in a piece of paper, she paid her nickel and, replacing her gloves, bowed her head as she walked out into the cold. The wind forced her back for a moment against the building but, clutching her various bundles, she staggered off home, laughing to herself.

It wasn't until next morning, lying in bed, warm and comfortable, that the light dawned. She began to giggle to herself. Her big husband lying beside her looked around suddenly thinking something had gone wrong. But she got up before he could say anything. He was glad to find her in such a merry mood.

"What's hit you?" he said, when she came back from the bathroom.

"It's St. Valentine's Day," she chirped. "Isn't that wonderful?"

"What's wonderful about it? It's about as sloppy-looking, thawing sort of a day as I've ever seen. I might as well stay home."

"It's a beautiful day! I feel like a young girl." And she started to sing, her beautiful voice carrying the strains of "Annie Laurie" till her daughter, on her way to the bathroom in her turn, poked her head in at the bedroom door in amazement.

"Mother!" she said. "So early in the morning?"

"Well, you can't expect a woman to be a drudge *all* the time. Are your brothers up?" But the girl only shrugged and went on her way.

Mrs. Mason had the five valentines hidden in her bureau drawer. All day long she pored over them making her selection: one was to go to Mrs. Beckman, next door, and one to that other woman whom she especially wanted to humiliate, that upstart whose husband had so recently made a pile of money, perhaps honestly, you never can tell. Pig, that's all she could say, but she couldn't find the proper verse to express her contempt. She had a pig valentine, but it was for a man, not a woman, and she wanted one for a woman.

Finally she made her selection—going back to it twenty times during the day and laughing outright at the face she would make, the contemptible thing, when she saw herself for what she was—a servant girl, pimply-faced, ignorant, dirty. . . . Ha ha ha ha! Her heart was singing within her as she searched in her desk and found, happily, two plain envelopes of different sizes, slightly soiled; one had been accidentally folded at one corner.

What she planned was to wait. Her big boy was too timid. No. The ten-year-old was the one! He had his mother's blood, everybody blamed him for everything that went wrong in the neighborhood. Well, this time they'd be right.

"Who do you want me to take them to?"

"As soon as it gets dark, before supper, I want you to go next door—and to the Stechers', on the corner. Put these two envelopes inside the entryways, ring the bell and run! Don't let them catch you."

"Let me see them." She showed them to him. He was delighted.

"And you musn't get them mixed."

"No, I won't get them mixed."

"*This* is for Mrs. B. and *this*, in your right hand, is for the other woman. Now, as soon as it gets dark, before your father comes from work, come back here and I'll give you a nickel apiece if you're a good boy and do what I want you to."

"Make it a dime apiece," said the boy.

"All right, a dime each *if* you don't get caught. You'll have to be pretty fast to deliver the *two* of them. Do you think you can do it?"

"You mean *me?* Huh," he said, "watch me."

So that evening she took him outside, her heart beating excitedly, and surreptitiously handed him the two envelopes. "This in your right hand and this in your left."

"I know," he said. She opened the front door and pushed the boy out and, with flushed cheeks, went back to the kitchen to do her cooking.

Gurlie heard the bell and sent the maid to see who was there on that winter's night, so late in the evening.

"No one!"

The maid, a little frightened, was about to go back into the house, when she saw the envelope and read on it, "Mrs. Stecker," in a childish hand.

"It's a letter," she called to Gurlie, after she had closed the door.

"A letter?" said Gurlie, coming down the stairs. She looked at it. "That's a child's writing. Oh, it must be a valentine," and she looked at the girls who had come to see what was going on. "Oh, that was sweet of you," she said, putting her finger in to open the envelope and withdrawing the contents. Magna was also looking on.

She unfolded the missive and her face went serious. She

looked at the girls, whose faces were blank and began to read, but not aloud.

WHY THOSE AIRS?

You carry your nose high, to be sure
For a recent recruit from the ranks of the poor.
Such haughty and arrogant airs, 'pon my word,
Make you look pompous, snob, altogether absurd
To those who recall how humble and low
Your station in life was a short time ago.

"Now I wonder who could have sent me *that*."

"Let me see," pleaded Lottie.

"Please let us see it," said Flossie. "Is it a funny valentine?"

Gurlie was mad. She handed the envelope to Joe when, a half-hour later he came puffing in at the door. "It's getting cold," he said.

He hadn't taken off his coat. "Looks like . . . Let's see the envelope. What would a child want to send you that for? Probably one of your neighbors."

But when the next day Gurlie saw Mrs. Beckman, they looked at each other, not wanting to be the first to say what they were thinking. But when they found that *both* had received valentines, they agreed that that boy next door had done it.

Later they caught him. Gurlie took hold of him by the collar. "I didn't start it," he said. "It was my mother."

"Vulgar," said Gurlie to her neighbor. "I wouldn't believe it." They were disgusted.

12

The day would be perfect. What luck! Stecher, knowing his wife's love of lilacs, had that morning cut an armful from the bush in the yard, gathered them early before the sun could reach and drain them of their fragrance.

The day had come for which they had all waited, all except the baby who was still too young to know. But for Gurlie, it meant the home country, which she remembered in the aura which childhood endows, a disappointed childhood, but a glorious one for all that. The old people were still alive, old Peter, her cousins. All the might-have-beens before her father signed that fateful note, before everything had been lost, were awake in her mind. Gurlie wanted to see if it really was so marvelous, what she had lost, as she imagined it to be. Now or never. She would be proud to show them that she did not have to come back a beggar.

The girls had said their good-byes to their school companions, Flossie eleven, a big girl now, and Lottie, a young lady, all in a dream. The ostensible reason for the trip was for her, Lottie, to enter the conservatory at Leipzig to continue her career. She would stay an indefinite length of time, perhaps three years or more. And when she returned—they would not know her! Meanwhile Norway, romantic Norway, the land of Ibsen and of Grieg, of Peer Gynt and the *saeter* girls, and of trolls who lived in the mountains—and music! Music, that was the goal of all living, the garland of a peaceful world.

"You take good care of my man," Gurlie said to Mrs. Emory, when, almost at dawn it seemed, the woman who was to take the house over had arrived. "Feed him well."

"Oh, I'll take good care of him. All Southern women know how to cook. Does he like biscuits? I'll give him biscuits for breakfast every day. Oh, we'll get along fine."

"My wife's a good cook," said her mild-looking husband. "She'll take good care of him."

"And hurry up and find a job for yourself," said Gurlie, "now that you have a place to live." Gurlie was not subtle. The fellow looked at her with no expression to his face while the two little girls who were to take the places of Flossie and Lottie hid wanly behind their mother's skirts and refused to say a word.

"Say good-bye to the kind lady," their mother admonished them, when the cab was finally at the door. "Come on, be smart." But they would say nothing. Flossie looked at them with a feeling of resentment as the ones who were to live in her house and sleep in her bed. Lottie didn't even notice them.

Her friend, from Maryland, had providentially come to Gurlie when the trip abroad was first mentioned. They were looking for a housekeeper for Joe. "Oh," she said, "I've got just the person for you. A lovely lady, a real lady, a friend of mine. They're of the old South. They've been unfortunate; her husband lost his job."

Joe laughed when he heard it: "A bum!" but made no stiff objections otherwise; after all, he could stand it for six months if he had to. As a matter of fact, Gurlie had known of the woman for some time. She was giving painting lessons, painting on china, in a small apartment over one of the stores on Main Street. Lottie and Flossie had both been her pupils— just until the time—it was lucky she could do it—her husband could find employment suitable to his talents. "He's really not used to the menial . . ."

"Well," said Joe, cutting the conversation short, "have you forgotten anything?"

"You have the tickets?"

"I've got the tickets in my pocket."

"Well, good-bye, remember what I told you," she said to Mrs. Emory. "There's plenty of jam and jelly and dozens of jars of tomatoes and beans in the cellar."

"Oh, we'll take care of everything."

And so the door was closed and the trip begun.

"Don't expect me for supper," Joe had said. The arrangement was for Mrs. Emory to give him an early breakfast. The rest of his meals he would find for himself.

Now the ship was their world. Pangs of uncertainty and loss were completely forgotten. The *Oscar II* was enormous to the eyes of the children, like a big hotel. In among its intricate decks was a door, like hundreds of others, which revealed a little room with bunks, one above the other—people running everywhere, weeping, laughing, old people hobbling along, children, in the semidark of the narrow passages. A smell, not unpleasant, of some strange environment. And now, from somewhere above them, was a long, deep blast that shook the very air and a fine rain began to fall which made the girls apprehensively look up at the sky.

"Well, good-bye," Joe was saying.

"Nonsense, you don't have to go yet." And Gurlie grabbed her husband in the bear's grip which always embarrassed him. "Stay with us a little longer."

"Papa!" said Flossie, in alarm.

"Let go of me."

"Come with us."

"Stop all this nonsense," he replied. "All ashore that's going ashore!" sang out a voice beside them. Joe took up the girls one at a time. Flossie flung her arms around his neck and wept. Lottie merely said good-bye, excitedly. He kissed the baby, who tried to get away, and finally he kissed his wife, who took him by the hair and refused to let go. "You mustn't leave us," she said, knowing he had no choice.

And there he was waving from the dock as the ship, its horn letting out short blasts, water spouting from the openings in its huge sides, began slowly to move.

There was the shouting of the farewells—down there! with faces looking up—some were already beginning to run toward the end of the pier. They lost sight of Joe in the rush. And the next thing they knew, they were out in the river. The Statue of Liberty was behind them and the sea began.

From that moment the ship's company sprang suddenly to life. There was the captain. They owed their lives to him.

Deep inside their world was an engine, which at various vantages on their walks they could smell, or feel the beating or hear the throb as they passed along a corridor. Most of all, wherever they went, they were surrounded by the sea, it held them and their little world, which rose and fell underfoot with its life—from which they were protected only by a narrow rail which a young sailor was intently rubbing down. For ten blissful days this would go on, after which they would have left America behind, and crossed the ocean, sailing—though you couldn't call it sailing any more—from the New World to the Old.

By nightfall the Nantucket lightship had been passed. Their first meal had been eaten, they had walked the slowly swaying decks and had gone to their cabin, undressed—Lottie pre-empted the desirable upper berth—and now, in the absolute silence of the night, broken only by the sound of the ship's creaking, had fallen into a deep sleep.

One thing Joe had not told his wife—he had kept it from her the whole last week not to disturb her anticipation of a happy and comfortable vacation—was that somehow, by someone not yet found, two sheets of government money-order blanks had disappeared from the serially numbered order. It was a serious matter, for upon discovering the thief and the return of the stolen goods might easily depend the contract itself.

But there were nearer, though less important matters, claiming his attention at once.

The next day after the departure of the tourists, Mrs. Emory was at him to start a garden.

"You always have a garden, I gather."

"Let your husband do it," Joe had told her.

"Oh, but he's not strong enough. It's his back. It wears him out to have to dig."

That's too damn bad about his back, thought Joe.

"Maybe you could get somebody to just spade it up a little for him, and plant it. Then he could take care of it."

"No, a garden would be too much trouble," said Joe. "I wouldn't want him to strain himself, and I'm too busy. But if you want to get someone to come in and do the heavy work, go right ahead."

"Now that's too bad," said Mrs. Emory. "I thought we could have a right smart patch of greens."

"In fact," said Joe to his wife later, "the sucker never did find a job."

"Don't talk that way. They're friends of Mrs. Moore," Gurlie admonished him.

"I don't think he ever looked for one. He was always taking his ease, smoking my cigars, when I offered him one after supper."

"I thought the arrangement was that you were going to take your own supper in the city."

"Well," said Joe, "it was cheaper to eat at home."

"You mean you paid them for it?"

"You didn't think they were going to give it to me for nothing."

"How much did you pay?"

"A dollar a day."

"What? But the arrangement was that they were to have the house furnished in exchange for taking care of you and giving you a breakfast."

"They had to have something to live on. How were they going to pay their bills? I paid them. He didn't even cut the grass. I paid for that, too. They had luck, though. Oswald sent me a barrel of Armour products, like he usually does before Christmas." Oswald, Joe's brother, was employed by Armour and Company in Chicago, and every year, about Thanksgiving time, expressed them a barrel of choice meats, hams, a side or two of bacon, a tongue and various potted delicacies.

"Did you give that away, too?"

"No. I took out a ham and a side of bacon and told her to use them. They swiped the rest of it before they left."

"What!" said Gurlie. "Why that's stealing."

"But when you're so genteel it can't be that. That's just taking what is due you. It's a new method discovered in this country by Christopher Columbus."

"When did they leave?"

"The day before you came back. They went back to Maryland. I paid them off and told them to go."

"Did you give them money, besides?"

"Glad to get rid of them."

"What happened to all the preserves I left in the cellar? And the jellies and jams?"

"The poor children, they were nice little girls. They had to be fed up, it's going to be a hard winter. I told her to feed it to them. I don't care for it. She did a nice job on the cellar, left your shelves absolutely clean."

"What? Everything? And didn't she preserve any grape jelly from all those grapes?"

At sea one day little Flossie, alone on an upper deck, wandering, came to a place where you could look far below down a hatchway to what seemed the very bottom of the ship. Hot, sweet air was coming up from the place and there, from above, she saw a man in a white hat with trays of little cakes onto which he was squeezing, from a gun, white figures decorating them. She saw him fill the gun, then very quickly he would make the white snake come out and lie in loops and curliques ending, finally, with a little dab in the middle to give each cake a finish. He was very quick and clever at it, doing one cake after the other until the whole tray, which had just held plain cakes before, was full of lovely pieces ready to serve.

She watched him a long time as he made what seemed to be hundreds of little cakes. Until finally with the heat and the bakery smell coming up in her face, she felt suddenly ill and had to turn away. The sea air soon revived her, but when she saw those cakes at the supper table that night she didn't want any.

Every night before they were sent to bed—for Flossie had successfully pleaded to be allowed to remain up till nine o'clock like her sister—they had seen the flares of phosphorescence over the side, small globes that came agitated to the surface as the ship plowed among them, then faded away. Steadily eastward, into the rising sun, a sun which had come up from the mists over Russia and still farther away, from the hardly ever seen or even thought of land of China. Eastward. But Gurlie was returning "home" again, not to stay, of course.

It was a fine ship. The Norsemen were the great sailors, though the Swedes were pretty good too. Like the Danes. They were all pretty good at sailing the seas, those Scandinavians. Ha! Ha!

It had been different on the small ship she had gone out on, alone, a young girl—after all, only twenty years before. She had said then, with deep resentment, that she would show them one of these days, she'd show them that a Hansen wasn't so easily beaten. The trip, on a cheap ticket, following

the sun—as Leif Ericson, who discovered the country, had
made it, was to the West. Always to the West.

The slow roll of the *Oscar II*, as Gurlie sat in her deck
chair, the children off somewhere with others their ages about
the deck, the baby asleep in charge of a stewardess below, had
made her think comfortably of that experience—of the deter-
mination, the intense hopes of those days.

There had been an American actor, a young man, a singer,
who had noticed her among the third-class passengers, her
snub nose alert, evasive blue eyes and blond hair tightly
gathered in a bun at the back of her bullet head. She was
erect, amused at the others, and laughed derisively at their
antics. She was not shy. He was a singer, had sung parts in
musical comedies on Broadway. Yes, she had heard of Broad-
way. It was interesting.

He had livened the solitary voyage for her. She had
studied him shrewdly. They had had lots of fun together. But,
as the voyage progressed and they came closer and closer to
America, if his intentions had been serious, he never spoke of
them. He, too, had probably been studying her and had dis-
covered, no doubt, that though she laughed with him at the
peasants, sang to their accordion playing and played with
their children, gay and full of animal spirits, she had a habit
of making him ridiculous at the slightest approach to romance.
He didn't get anywhere with her. That small, round chin was
made of iron. He had found those eyes a wall—built for de-
fense from which to sally on raids. She ended finally by
frightening him; she made him feel small. But on her part she
had never quite forgotten him. She had a purpose: to hold
her head up, to justify her family name, and to be rich. She
felt a restrained power in her own compact body. She was no
beauty, she knew that, but she was healthy and she was
smart, in a way.

This was the *Oscar II's* first trip. The Norwegian consul
to New York and his family were aboard. The ship did not go

up to Christiania, but stopped at Christiansand, outside the harbor, where a tender came out to get them, and they were taken ashore. A small ship, the *Motala*, was to take them up the fjord to the capital city.

The *Oscar II* was well out to sea again when that evening the little transport started. Almost at once, Gurlie noticed that the consul had disappeared from among the ship's passengers. Hers was a first-class ticket, but she found herself surrounded by the strangest people. And almost at the same time, night having come down, the little ship, hardly more than a tugboat, began to pitch and roll as it headed around a point into the North Sea. Then all hell broke loose.

Slap! It began as the first heavy wave struck them and the little vessel shuddered. *"Gud! Gud spaare us!"* a woman shrieked nearby. *"Oh Gud!"* sounded all about them. The girls were delighted. Slap! and the little ship rose on its beam end and rolled with a twisting motion as the screw came out of the water and the hull shuddered. It was too late then to do anything about it. No meal could be served. And there was no relief as, from the force of the storm, the vessel groaned.

Gurlie made her way to the galley and demanded that they be fed. The cook merely shook his head. Impossible.

"How long is this going to go on?"

"We'll be in Christiania by tomorrow noon."

"But is the ship safe?"

"Oh yes." A wave smashed full on the ship's beam so that Gurlie had to cling to the side of the hatch. "Do you mean to say that this will keep up all night?"

"We should be in the fjord by morning."

All the passengers but Gurlie and her family were seasick. No meals were served. The night through they stayed in their cabins and clung to the edges of their berths. Then in the morning it had passed as a bad dream and they were running up the fjord. At places you could practically touch the rock walls as the little ship seemed to squeeze through. Then they would come to places where the water opened out into a wide bay with mountains going straight up from the water. It was worth it to stop at all sorts of little towns—of only a few houses, at times—in that beautiful springtime country. It did not, however, stop Gurlie from going to the shipping office on her arrival and demanding satisfaction for having been put on such a boat.

"That is not first-class passage!"

"No," the agent acknowledged.

"What happened to the consul?"

"He waited for a larger boat that came later."

"Then why . . . ?" she was furious.

"It was the first passage of the *Oscar II*. They were not ready." It ended by Gurlie getting her passage money returned. Meanwhile the children had got such a view of the Christiania Fjord as they could not have dreamed of having otherwise.

They went first to the city itself to live in the apartment of Gurlie's old cousins, who were to die so miserably in the Second World War, the whole building burned to the ground, the doors locked against them, two helpless women, because the Germans thought that a member of the underground was hidden there.

There they stayed a month, then at the end of June went south to Frederickstad, to the old farm which had been Gurlie's paradise as a child. There it was still, just as it had been in the past, unchanged, even old Peter, who never had been anything else than old, still there unchanged, almost a hundred now, but still as hearty as ever.

America seemed a dream as she stood remembering the ships anchored in the river where the wheat fields came right to the water's edge. Just as then, the masts of the sailing vessels were still there, though fewer now, standing above the wheat at the bottom of the field. She had climbed to the very tips of those masts when she was no more than nine years old. Not a horse in the pasture that she had not mounted and galloped over the ditches and through the brush.

Here Tante Karen still presided. The little girls were made much of and the baby, a boy! The only boy—well, not quite, but such a blossoming boy, with tightly curled yellow hair! Before Gurlie had been there a week it was decided that this boy, no one else having come back to claim it, should be the one to inherit the farm when the old aunts should die. It was agreed, and Gurlie saw to it that it was part of the will before she quit the country.

But Lottie and Flossie were in fairyland. They had been impressed in Christiania by the tall white lilacs growing profusely in the streets of that small capital city. They were almost trees, reaching to the second floors of the houses. Their perfume filled the streets on fine days and all days were fine, so it seemed.

But here on the old farm, hundreds of years old—where they themselves might have been born but for the fatal weakness of the man who had lost it all and precipitated them to the ends of the earth—this was pure delight to the little girls.

Lottie especially felt as if she were living in the age of the trolls.

They lived at the farm for a month while Gurlie visited about the country. The whole great room of the second floor was theirs. In each of the four corners was a high four-poster bed. Gurlie and the baby had one, that's the way it began, and Lottie and Flossie another. There they slept, under the roof.

After the hands had gone to the fields, breakfast was brought to them in bed, by Tante Karen: cakes! of all sorts, which the girls ate with surprise, and big goblets of milk.

"Now rest and take your time. There is no hurry and you have come a long way." Instantly thereafter they were up, staring from the windows. But the thatched house was so quiet that by force of the hushed voice of the old lady and the stillness about them, they soon crept back into bed and were at least quiet for another hour.

Then downstairs for the real breakfast: an enormous

meal. Two kinds of fish, bread and cheese, eggs and a huge jug of the richest milk or deep plates of clabber, called filibunke, thick with cream over which they spread sugar and ate with large spoons. What a meal! and the day hardly begun. That was in the front room downstairs—not the big communal dining room at the back of the house, where the other meals were served, and which the girls especially loved.

But for a month every morning Karen would come to wake them bringing the little cakes which were Flossie's favorites, diamond-shaped, made of puff paste—how did she cook them at that big open hearth, which was all the fire there was—pastry an inch and a half high, flaky, delicious? Lottie preferred the sweet breads. And they would drink the coffee and milk, while Gurlie in the far bed would be having her coffee black and strong, with little Paul sitting in the middle of her bed with her.

Karen and her sister, who managed the old farm, had never married. They adored the baby as if he had been the Christ child Himself. It should be *his* estate, *he* would perpetuate it. That suited Gurlie fine.

They went from there to an island near Sarpsborg, a wooded island, where at midnight once, the sun low in the sky, they picked lily of the valley growing wild among the leaves.

Then these ecstatic days were over. Summer was waning toward the fall and the business of the trip had to be resumed. Lottie must be entered at the conservatory in Leipzig. Some place, some trustworthy and conservative family had to be found with whom she could stay and, after she had been found to be satisfied, when she should signify her ease of mind, and was working well at her piano, they would leave her and return home.

"But she is not yet fifteen!" said the Norwegian aunties. "How have you the heart to leave a young girl like that and go so far away?"

"Nonsense!" said Gurlie. "You are here."

"But she is so young! She doesn't know anything."

"I do so!" said Lottie. "I want to stay. I don't want to go home. I want to stay in Germany. It must be very romantic."

"Romantic!" said the aunties. "Can't you stay here with us or near us? We have good teachers in Christiania. Grieg did not need to go to Germany. He became a great musician right here."

"They do not have great piano teachers in Norway," said Lottie.

"But who are you to need great teachers? You are just a young girl. For the next four or five years the teachers here will be plenty good enough."

"No. Don't listen to them," she said to her mother in English, afraid that she would have her dear old aunties on her neck; as bad as being at home. "No, my father said I must go to Germany. The best teachers are there."

"Well, if your father said that, then you must go."

"We are going to Germany," said Gurlie. "It is all arranged." She, too, wanted to see Germany and the continent. She was growing restless in Norway; it was too rural, too confining, she found. Why come all this way and not see Berlin, some of the sights of the great world? "She will be all right."

Lottie, for once, was grateful to her mother. Imagine being in Norway, so close, and then to miss the life of a really great conservatory in Bach's city. She had already begun to plan it all in ecstatic dreams.

"Why do you go to Leipzig? So far! Saxony is so far."

"The Grand Conservatory in New York recommended it. For instruments, for instruction in playing the piano, it is still the best," said Lottie.

"There are other places nearer."

"Arthur Nikisch is still there and Kubelik. Berlin and Dresden for the voice, but for the pianoforte they recommended Leipzig."

"They have the reputation," said Gurlie.

"Well, if you must have the reputation . . ."

"And there is the Gewandhaus, which is very famous. And it was Bach's city."

"Oh, but he is long since dead."

"To play Bach well you should go to Leipzig to study him, where you can hear his great motets and masses. They perform them every week just as he did when he lived there," Lottie volunteered. "His house is still standing." That particular was not true, but Lottie was convinced that the great Johann Sebastian's presence was something that lingered in the air of the old Saxon city. She had wanted to go and live near him the moment Leipzig had first been mentioned as a place to study abroad, and she had fixed on it. Her mind had never for a moment wavered. Leipzig it must be.

And now at last the great day had arrived, the day when they should leave Norway and begin the final adventure.

"This is not going to be like the trip we had when we arrived," said Gurlie.

"No, no, madam. This is a much better boat."

"I should hope so," said Gurlie.

The *Kong Ring* on which they steamed into the North Sea this time was indeed a better ship. Bound for Hamburg, it was crowded with first-class passengers who made much of the young and vivacious young mother making the trip with three children. There was, especially, a gallant gentleman who took Gurlie entirely under his wing. Lottie was the heroine, the talented young pianist from America who was to be a student at the conservatory in Leipzig. A concert on the ship was quickly organized, for that very evening, at which, sizing up her audience, good middle-class people without musical distinction, Lottie played a piece, from memory, "Moonlight on the Hudson." Her teacher in New York would have murdered her had he known. It was a tremendous success.

The second night, the night before their arrival in Hamburg, Lottie and Flossie were told to go to bed early. When

Flossie peeked, as she did, she saw a group about a table drinking beer, laughing and talking gaily.

In Hamburg, their friend put them and their baggage into a hack which he, too, mounted, taking them straight to the sleeper for Leipzig, and at last he bade them good-bye.

In Leipzig, after the first night in a hotel, Gurlie bought a paper, looked up "Rooms to Rent," found one out near the Rosenwald at a Frau Franke's. This estimable lady was heavy with child. She showed them three rooms with kitchen privileges, which they could have at a reasonable price. The next-door neighbors were a young married couple. The wife proposed that if Gurlie bought three new beds, she would repurchase them later at half what she had paid for them. It was agreed and Gurlie moved in.

Within a matter of weeks the infant with which Frau Franke had been so obviously pregnant when they arrived was born. The next day she was down on her knees scrubbing the front steps of her house as usual.

"*Aber* Frau Franke!" cried Gurlie when she saw her that morning, "you shouldn't."

"Why not?" said the woman, sitting back on her haunches and looking up at them standing about her.

"It is not good for you."

"And who is going to do it if I don't?" said the woman.

As the weeks went by and Lottie and her mother would be at the conservatory making arrangements for the details of her classes, Flossie and the baby would be left at Frau Franke's to amuse themselves as they could. Meanwhile a place nearer the center of the city was discovered, in the home of a couple with a small boy who was an invalid, little Fritzl; they had a small business as caterers, *aufsteurer*, a very reliable pair, who were glad to have the added income from renting a room to a girl pianist, who could practice as much as she liked in the house, they wouldn't care.

There, before they left, Lottie had been installed. She

was thrilled at her new associates and teachers at the school; it was so engrossing to her that even though her mother and sister were still in the city, she had almost forgotten them, wished them away before they had gone, and by the first of December hardly knew that they had departed. Before they had been a week at sea she forgot them entirely—except at moments when she looked about her a little surprised and found that they were not there.

At last she had her love, music, in her arms! The food at Frau Janecke's was a little plain, but what is food when the blood has already been warmed by such great names as Bach, Schumann, Beethoven, Brahms, Chopin and Scarlatti? For three years she would continue—attending the concerts at the Gewandhaus, on Thursdays at the *Motetten*, learning to know that world. Through her ears she drank the heady liquors of an ancient mastery. Those above her in school she envied and, being young, strove to rival and beat them.

Her other love was the ancient city itself with its memories of Goethe and his dreams: she was too young to take part in the life of the university, but she knew of Auerbachs Keller, where Faust had seen the devil. She knew the romantic background of Barfuss Allee, the narrow, twisting streets and old houses. She lived in a dream, studying at her liberating instrument, in which she found a companion and a confessor, her link with the glorious past—her pianoforte, to which she could go and, touching it, actually placing her hands upon it, she could feel herself lifted from the earth to enter a nearer world than her mere family could ever supply.

Alone with her piano for those three years, her rupture from the family ties would be complete.

13

The Town Improvement Association, which Gurlie had enthusiastically joined, merely took up the women's time and gave them something to talk about, according to Joe.

But Gurlie gave his head one of her affectionate shoves, which always infuriated him, and said, "Mrs. Smith, the rich Mrs. Smith, is coming to take me to the meeting tomorrow in her carriage."

"Tell her to turn her horses around and drive you out into the country. It'll do you more good."

But Gurlie persisted. "The women are all right. They can show the men a thing or two. And by gorry," adopting her favorite Irish brogue, "we'll do it. You'll see."

"All you'll do is boost the tax rate."

"At least we'll get something for it. We built the new school by talking and fighting. Now we're going to get a park for the town."

As a matter of fact, there was a triangular block-long patch of woodland similar to the one occupied by the Presbyterian church and adjacent to it, a block to the south, which was ideal for the purpose. It was owned jointly by the local druggist and an old lady who needed the money and hoped to sell her section for building lots. The council wanted it, but didn't want to pay the price.

"If we can get it at a reasonable figure."

It was at that point that the ladies started to work.

"How much did we clear?"

"I'm sure it was over a thousand dollars. But wasn't it wonderful, really wonderful! My favorites were the little tots in the rose dance. Weren't they just darling? I tell you, in this town we do have the most beautiful children you ever saw. Don't you think so, Mrs. Holbrook?"

"They were really very cute. And, for the short time they were at it, they were well trained."

"They're intelligent, ha ha ha ha! Don't you think it shows? It's the home training they have."

"I think that gives us enough to buy . . ."

"And did you hear? We have been deeded the rest of the property, we really have. All of it."

"No!"

"Yes, it's true. We're going to have a park. We're going to have the honor of presenting the council with the deeds. I tell you, it takes women to do things. A big feather in our caps. And it's been less than a year we've been working for it. But this really put it over."

There was the sound of a gavel being pounded on the wooden table and the thirty-odd women came rapidly to order.

"Huh," said Mrs. Jessup, in a loud whisper, as the room quieted, "they come out of their hiding places all right when there's any roses to be handed out. But they didn't . . ."

"Ladies, will you please come to order?"

". . . when there's work to be done. Half of them . . ."

"Order, please.

"We're going to dispense with the usual order of business today in order to hear the report of the Kirmess Committee, which I know will please you all. As some of the members have to leave early, we shall have that first."

A round of applause drowned out the rest of what the chairman had to say. "Oh, I'm so glad we don't have to go through all that preliminary rigamarole. Get right to the heart of the matter."

"With your permission, the chairman of the committee, Mrs. Holbrook, will now take the floor. And I think it would be very nice, the whole affair having been so eminently successful, if we all showed our appreciation by standing. Mrs. Holbrook, we offer you our congratulations."

There was a polite clatter as the ladies, getting up from their chairs, talking, laughing, applauded.

"She's a smart woman in spite of herself."

"Look at her hair. Why is it that the brainy ones are always so sloppy."

"Shh!"

"Do you want me to read it all? It's pretty long."

"Read it! Read it!" Some of the ladies, it must be admitted, hadn't been to see the children dance, the tickets, at a dollar and a half for the series, had discouraged them, and, well, they wanted to hear all about it.

"Wouldn't they?" snorted peppy little Mrs. Jessup. "They wouldn't give you that much! They're the kind that would put their old mother in a home when she's too weak and deaf to be any use to them any more and forget her. Oh, I know the kind. There's a woman on our block I could choke whenever I see her. What I know about the way she treats *her* mother . . ."

"Shh!"

"Of course, you have heard that the whole entertainment was a tremendous success. Many things contributed. We had a good instructor."

"We know that."

"Shh! She'll hear you." The committee chairman half-turned, but smiled benignly and continued. "I don't know how to begin," she said. "Shall I start with a list of the dances?"

"Yes, do," said the Chair. "I'm sure we'll be glad to

hear about that, especially as some of you were unable to be present."

"They're the ones that always appear at the church meetings and put a nickel in the collection basket."

"Order, please."

"The littlest ones shall come first."

"Oh, they were so cute! The darlings . . ."

"Well, to begin at the beginning: The plan was to run the dances for a whole week. Every evening and two matinées, Wednesday and Saturday. And we were blessed with perfect weather—so that we played to capacity houses. It was wonderful, so encouraging! The whole week! The committee on decorations had put in great masses of dogwood blossoms, which were renewed every night, or morning rather, at the sides of the stage. Very beautiful. And there were colored paper streamers across the ceiling to cover the bare beams. Very well done. How did they get up there to do it?"

Everyone laughed.

"Well, let's begin with the flower dance, I think it was the flower dance. They were the little tots. Some of you younger ladies had children in that dance. Of course, there was not much they could do. But they had on their little flaring dresses of pink chiffon, they curtsied, and bowed, each holding up a flower at the end. It's remarkable to think what a really skillful coach can bring out of even such little ones. Little girls. Yes, there were no boys in that dance."

"They were so funny. When one of them would stop dead in her tracks the others piled up over her. They had to push her to get her started again."

"Order, please!"

"The next age group was the twelve-year-olds: the rose dance. It was very popular. All girls. They wore flower hats and rose-petal skirts. There were from twelve to sixteen individuals in each dance and each dance took about ten or fifteen to twenty minutes to perform. We had two pianos, yes. We're very grateful to our pianists, Mrs. Wade and Mrs. Hasbrook, for their parts. What would we have done without them?"

Another round of applause.

"Then there was the tarantelle—I haven't been giving you the names of the children who took part in the dances. Should I have done so? It would take a lot of time."

The ladies thought it would be nice.

"Well, for the fairies there were Lucy Wheaton . . ." and she went on giving the names.

"Oh, she's a darling."

"Ethel Moorhead, Jessie Wheeler . . ."

"Do you know her mother? No one does. A strange woman. She doesn't belong to any of our clubs."

"Paddy Price, Joyce Haggerty . . ."

"A Catholic?"

"Yes, I think so."

"Frances Devereau and Katherine Campbell . . ."

"Her father is the lawyer, you know. They say he has tuberculosis. I hope his child hasn't got it. You never can tell, when you get a crowd like that, rehearsing in a dusty old hall, day after day, what they may be spreading."

"And Florence Stecher . . ."

"That's her mother sitting over there. Look at her smile. They've just been abroad. What do you think of her? She sure has come up in the world. But I like her. She's got the old ginger. We need people like her."

The Chair intervened at this point. "I wonder if it's wise to go on reading the names. I'm afraid it'll take too much of our time as we have other important business to consider."

"Shall I drop it?"

"No, no!"

"Very well, but be as brief as you can."

"Well, in the rose dance there were Katherine Hanson, Mabel Dalton, Jean Armitage . . ."

At this point two of the members took advantage of the attention being directed at the speaker to whisper to their immediate neighbors and tiptoe to the exits. Several turned and looked at them.

"She has to be home by four o'clock to take care of her supper. He's a typesetter on the New York *World*, the night shift. Who's the other one?"

"She doesn't come very often. Her daughter was one of the fairies."

"I suppose that's all that interested her."

"The butterfly dance, with lights, was performed by four of the older girls in flowing skirts of pastel shades. Very skillfully done."

"Oh well, of course. But the true spirit of the kirmess is the little ones. You can't get that effect in any other way. It's crude, of course, but weren't some of those . . ."

"She hasn't said a thing about the boys. Some of those are handsome, and can they dance! That Charlie Bishop, who danced the duet with that girl, what was her name? The gypsy dance? Do you know his mother? She's Spanish or something. She usually comes out to our meeting. I don't see her today."

"All in all, a wonderful success."

"You've heard the report of your committee. Have you any questions?"

"What was the total attendance?"

"Twelve hundred and forty-eight."

"Wonderful for Riverdale."

"It's getting late ladies, but, before we close, I have to ask you if there is any old business, any unfinished business that we ought to bring up? Any new business?"

"Madam Chairman, I hate to inject a sour note into these proceedings . . ."

There was complete silence in the room. Everyone looked at the speaker; it was Mrs. Nagel, one of the older and more respected women of the town.

"Yes, Mrs. Nagel, you have the floor. You needn't stand. I'm sure it will not be necessary."

"Oh no, I'm a little stiff from sitting here so long listening to such a flattering report of our young people's activities, but I can stand." She got slowly to her feet. "I wanted to ask what is being done, if anything, about that family that seemed to be having so much difficulty feeding and clothing its children. The . . . What was the name?"

"O'Halloran," said Gurlie in a loud voice.

"Thank you, Mrs. Stecher. The O'Hallorans. What has become of them?"

There was a hurried consultation on the low platform between madam president and her secretary. The president turned to the meeting at large and said, "Can anyone enlighten us on what has—what the present status of this case may be?" She waited a moment. "I'm sorry, Mrs. Nagel, but I myself cannot give you any details."

"Oh that's all right," said the elderly lady. "But someone, there must be some committee member who can report on the case."

"I am chairman of the committee," said Mrs. Lowell. "I was hoping this would not come up. We are having some trouble over that case."

"What kind of trouble?" asked Mrs. Nagel.

"Well, it's hard for me to explain . . ."

There was an awkward pause. "Surely," said the elderly lady, "it can't be as bad as that."

"I'll tell you what it is," said Gurlie, standing, as the chairman of the committee gladly took the opportunity to sink into her chair. "The priest of the local Catholic church has interfered. He won't let us do anything about it."

"But," said Mrs. Nagel, "am I right in believing that the woman is in dire straits and that her children cannot go to school for lack of proper clothing?"

"That's right," said Gurlie.

"Well, what are we going to do about it?" said Mrs. Nagel.

"What can we do?" said the president. "We can't interfere with the church."

"And let the woman starve? Someone should at least go and investigate. We can't let the thing drop. It's inhuman." And the old lady sat down. As she did so she was still speaking. "I wish I were younger." The room was deathly still.

"I'll do it," said Gurlie.

Everyone turned in her direction.

"Good for you," said Mrs. Nagel.

"Very well, Mrs. Stecher. And may I say you are appointed with power to act if need be. And report at the next meeting. Thank you. And now, ladies, will someone make the motion to adjourn? It's been a wonderful meeting and I'm sure we're more than proud of the committee in charge of the most successful kirmess, the most profitable enterprise for a good cause, the purchasing of a park for the town of Riverdale, that we have ever enjoyed."

"I make a motion that we adjourn."

"All those in favor . . ." And then the meeting broke up, the ladies made for the door as Mrs. Nagel and Gurlie stood talking together at the back of the room.

14

Women can stand on the street and outtalk a man any day in the week no matter how sturdy his legs may be. It was like that when Gurlie met Father Kelly outside the house where, as the administrator for the Poor Fund in Riverdale, she had just been to see the O'Halloran woman and her children. Father Kelly was mad. Gurlie was ready for him.

The other women, sensing the delicacy of the situation, and being not a little scared, had gladly let her take on the job. It was her meat and gave her a chance to show up the others, besides which she was a really courageous woman. She had nothing against Catholics, though some of the others were in favor of barring all aid to them. That made Gurlie genuinely angry.

"The children are starving," she protested.

"The priest should take care of them."

"But if he doesn't do anything . . ." said Gurlie.

"That's his business, the church's business. We only get ourselves into trouble if we interfere."

"And let the children go needy? Not on your life. We're not interfering with their religion. We're only trying to help a lot of poor children. I don't care what the priest says, the children need help, and we should give it to them and see that they get it. Leave it to me."

They gladly left it to her.

"To hell with the priest," Mrs. O'Halloran had said, when Gurlie went there to see what could be done. The place was clean, as far as she could see, though the kitchen blinds were torn and the bit of linoleum on the floor had all the pattern worn off it in front of the tubs and on the track between the door and the cook stove. "What has he ever done for me?"

"We don't want to do anything to hurt your feelings," said Gurlie.

"I've got no feelings any more from living with that bastard, begging your pardon. He's not been home for a week. The drunken bum is in the jail in Jersey City."

"Is that where he is?"

"I don't know where he is. It's what Father Kelly told me. And what good to me is that bit of information? And what does he say on top of that, but that I'm to take him back like a good Christian woman—with six kids—when he gets out? You can see the youngest of them there, not a year old. And that's what I got for taking him back the last time. And where is 'his good Christian woman' going to get the food and the poor clothes to do for the rest of them?"

The two women looked at each other like fighters after the bell rings, waiting for the other to lead.

At that, Gurlie left the woman saying she'd hear from her later in the day. But no more had she reached the street than she ran into Father Kelly himself.

"How do you do, Father Kelly?" said Gurlie. "Isn't that who you are? I've heard a lot about you."

"You have, have you? What have you heard?"

"I'm Mrs. Joseph Stecher," said Gurlie. "I'm glad to meet you."

"So you're Mrs. Joseph Stecher. It's a pleasure."

"It's a fine day, isn't it?" said Gurlie.

"Yes, it's a fine day, and what are you doing here, Mrs. Stecher?"

"What are you doing here yourself, Father?" said she.

That stopped him for a minute. In the interval Gurlie went on, "There's a poor woman in there with a lot of children. The town's been helping while their father is in jail. Have you any objections?" She had made up her mind to take nothing from the priest and the sooner they had it out the better. "The poor soul seems very deserving," Gurlie went on. "I hope you're coming to bring her some help from her own people."

"I can take care of her; she doesn't need anything from the town."

"That's not what she says."

"What does she say?"

"She's in great need."

"Did she say anything else? Did she?"

"Now Father Kelly, I'm not a Catholic. If she has anything to say to you, that's her business. I'm not here to tell you what she said or didn't say. I'm here to provide her children with the barest necessities. I'd be glad if you can take over the responsibilities. Until you do, I'm going to come in and see that she gets what she needs."

"Oh you are, are you?"

"Yes, I am."

"Well, suppose I order you off the premises?"

Gurlie laughed her open and maddening laugh. "I'd pay no attention to you," she said. "Look, Father, the woman's in need, we have a fund got up by the women of the town to help in such cases. It's interdenominational, we have nothing to do with religion. Mrs. O'Halloran is helpless. I came in here and found the children cold and hungry . . ."

"Why didn't she come to me?"

"She did come to you. She told me herself. Maybe it's your intention to help her. Meanwhile—and I think her husband has tuberculosis besides—she should have . . ."

"She should have waited until I could . . ."

"It's over a week now."

"Well, keep off here. I can look after my own."

"When she tells me, I'll keep off, as you say. But until then the devil himself couldn't stop me. And I'll give you a piece of my mind, besides. This is a good town, we're interested in our poor. When we find them in need we'll help them, and you can't do anything about it. I don't care who you are."

"That's big talking, Mrs. Stecher."

"And you'll find it's big doing. And you'd be a fool to fight us."

"The Catholic church . . ." the priest began.

"You think more of your church than you do of the poor."

"We think of the souls before we do of the body," said the priest. "Of the souls of everyone in the world. We can't always help the downtrodden and the outcast as we'd like to. But their immortal souls are precious to us. That's our business."

"Then you shouldn't try to interfere with those who want to help their poor bodies. We're not interfering with your business. All we're doing, and you say yourself that it's not your first concern, is to give these poor people and their innocent children something to fill their stomachs and provide them with some warm clothing. Is that harming you?"

"No, I can't say that it is," said the priest. "But I'll not have you interfering with the woman's duty to her church."

"We're not," said Gurlie. "We're only following Christ's own words when he said to feed the poor. In Norway," Gurlie couldn't help but adding, "everyone is taxed for the poor fund."

"That's where the responsibility should lie, with the Government. When the church has more power in this rich land, it may be that there will be greater justice for the starving."

"We can't wait for that. So we'll keep sending our regular weekly allotment of groceries and what we have for the children."

"You needn't bother," said the priest stubbornly. "And good day to you."

He turned and walked toward the worn wooden steps that led to the front door of the tenement. Gurlie turned and followed him. He stopped. "Where do you think you're going?" he said.

"I'm going to see if this woman wants us to send her any more supplies."

"I forbid you to follow me," he said.

"You can forbid all you please," said Gurlie, "but I'm going to see for myself what's what."

"Oh you are, are you?"

"Yes, I am."

"Well I'll say one thing, you've got a gall fit to . . ." He stopped. "I just wish I had the power over you," the priest went on. "And it won't be long before I have it. We're building a school now, and we'll soon show you who runs this town."

"You'd think you'd use some of that money you're using for your school for this woman and her children."

"We've got money enough and to spare."

"Sure, and you got it out of people like her, from all I've seen."

"Woman, you're talking to a priest. You're talking blasphemy . . ."

"I'm talking nothing but common sense," said Gurlie.

They stood there under the old elm, while a heavy woman with some affection of her knees came haltingly near. They had been aware of her for the last few minutes as she came nearer and nearer.

She was watching the priest and the sturdy, well-dressed woman standing facing each other at the foot of the steps. As she got close by, puffing as she progressed, she said to the priest, "How are you today, Father Kelly?"

"I'm fine, Mrs. Lomax, and how are you?"

"I'm doing all right, Father," said the woman cheerfully. "It's a fine day."

"Yes, it is a fine day." And she passed.

"Let's go in together," said Gurlie. "I want to hear what Mrs. O'Halloran wishes me to do. She's in need, but if she doesn't want any more help, she can say so. I'll tell the committee and that will be the end of it. But I'm not going to take it from you."

"You're a hard-headed woman," said the priest.

"My ancestors were Vikings," said Gurlie. "They weren't afraid of anyone or anything . . ."

"Not the devil himself," said the priest, admiringly. "Well I'll promise you one thing. I won't do anything to discourage her."

"Will you give me your word?" asked Gurlie.

"I'll give you my word," said the priest. "Don't you trust me?"

Gurlie looked at him and laughed. "I don't like to," said she, "but I guess I'll have to."

"Do you realize whom you're talking to?" said he.

"Sure," said Gurlie, putting on an Irish brogue, "and I think I do now. It's a good-hearted Irishman I'm talking to. Isn't it right I am?"

"I wish to God I had you in my parish," said the priest. "I'd put you to work till we'd have the school built in a year. What was the name you told me?"

"Mrs. Joseph Stecher, representing the committee of the Town Improvement Association."

"Yes, I've heard of that. I understand they're getting a park for the town. Now, that's a good thing, and I'll see what I can do to help you along."

"The town needs a park. We've raised over a thousand dollars toward it recently when we gave a kirmess. Did you see it?"

"Yes, I did stop in one day. Just to see what was going on. Some of my people were in it. So good-bye, Mrs. Stecher, I'm glad I met you. Will you let me go in now by myself? Or will you still want to follow me to see that I don't browbeat the poor woman? I think we'll get her husband out of jail by the week-end. And I'll tell you one thing, I'll dress him down till he'll think twice before repeating this breach of decency and order."

"So I'll report it's all right to keep sending supplies until the woman tells us to stop."

"Yes, and I'll back you in it," said the priest.

15

At twelve Flossie went often on errands to the city alone. The occasion would be, perhaps, that Auntie Hilda had come out to make dresses for the entire family, staying as long as two weeks sometimes at a stretch. All day long the work would go on.

First Gurlie selected the materials, Flossie naturally telling her what she wanted. Then the styles would be chosen, the stuffs purchased, to be either accepted or rejected when they they arrived in the house. It was a time of considerable importance to everyone. Hilda was a good dressmaker.

Then the work began, the designing, the cutting. There would be not quite enough material. The lining would be lacking by half a yard. Flossie, armed with her samples, would take the train of a Saturday morning, make a quick trip to McCreery's on Twenty-third Street, and be back by noon with what was wanted.

McCreery's, on the southeast corner of Twenty-third, was *the* place for silks. It was a wonderful place also for all dress goods. And down Sixth Avenue only a few blocks, was O'Neil's, Adams Brothers, Simpson and Crawford's and Gimbel's and that first marvel of the multidepartment stores, Siegel-Cooper, where at the bar Gurlie would always stop for a dozen raw oysters, while the girls waited and watched the attendant scoop up the small hard crackers from a barrel back of the counter where the oysters, by the bushel, stood before them, to fill the bowls on the counter.

"Meet me at the fountain," was the popular word of the day.

But her favorite trip, also on Saturdays, when Lottie was still in Europe, was to Grandma's on Russell Street, Brooklyn. The Norwegian colony was centered at Greenpoint, still beautiful with its little park where the children would be playing, and the Norwegian church around the corner on Lorimer Street, her Uncle Einar's grocery shop not far off.

About mid-morning she'd take the train at the Erie station in Riverdale, often finding a friend to sit with. Arriving in Jersey City, there was the walk through the old waiting room, smelling of the rotting piers beneath it, the wooden benches, occupied by sleepy stragglers, or perhaps a tight knot of odd-looking immigrants, of unknown origin, Magyars or Latvians, the men smoking odd-shaped pipes, wearing what looked like Alpine hats, the women, in silk, embroidered kerchiefs, wearing heavy and voluminous skirts, the children wide-eyed, often sick, clustered about their leaders while an interpreter, harassed-looking, in a shabby overcoat ran back and forth explaining what was wanted of them. In their coat lapels they wore tickets of identification, or perhaps they were their railway passes. Flossie glanced at these people, wondering to what particular place they could be headed, like cattle bound "west." She was not too young to realize that within a year or two many of them would be on their way to financial success in the new country.

Trucks loaded with heavy bales would be coming in to the ferries, so that you had to wait for them to pass, the powerful horses, their hind legs straining, their heavily shod hoofs slipping on the boards of the ferry entrance, or up the incline, if the tide was in. The cries of the drivers echoing under the roof of the ferry house made her pause. But then, following the other passengers, she'd step aboard the blunt boat, the gates would be closed, the hooks loosened as the chains rattled and clanked in the iron chutes and they'd be off, the whistle blowing, into the river!

She would sit near a window as the greased planking of the slip passed close by, till she could see the gulls flying or sitting at a safe distance on the water among the river débris about them.

New York harbor was always beautiful to her. Over there somewhere in the downtown section was her father's printing house. She loved the leisurely Twenty-third Street ferry run. Not long before, one of the ferry boats had been rammed in midstream and, springing a leak, slowly sunk, after all the passengers had been safely removed. Its single narrow stack could be seen still sticking up ten or fifteen feet above the opaque greenish river water.

But what she loved best was the Jersey shore, with Stevens Castle on its high ridge above the docks, above where the North German Lloyd and the Hamburg-American boats were tied. They occupied the whole shoreline, some of the finest ships and the fastest, too, of all ocean liners. Beautiful ships! The *Kaiser Wilhelm*, perhaps the very one on which the immigrants she had just seen in the Erie waiting room had crossed, its orange stacks standing out prominently beside the sign over the docks: "*Nord Deutscher Lloyd.*" She loved those boats.

At Twenty-third Street she took a crosstown surface car for the long ride to the East River ferry on the opposite side of town. Then again a ferry—a short ride this time—and another car, a green band about it, the Greenpoint car. You got a transfer here to another car, on Lorimer Street, getting off finally at the corner of Russell Street, near the little park, from which it was only half a block to Grandma's house. The Stoltzes lived next door, and Mathilda, the Widnesses, and many other friends. That was before the neighborhood changed and all the Scandinavians moved out to Bay Ridge and Uncle Einar sold his shop and moved to Vermont.

Arrived on Russell Street, in her flimsy flowered hat, her round, straight legs and the short skirts of a girl of twelve, her small face with the shrewd, proud blue eyes, her grandmother, never an exuberant person, would look her over, shake her head in assent, meaning, you'll do, tell her to make herself at home, and go back to the kitchen where, as often as not, she would be in the midst of her baking. She was forever at some sort of undertaking there.

Perhaps a crate of eggs would be broken in transit to her son's store. You can't waste such things—and you can't sell them. So Grandma would have to make cakes—not *a* cake, but cakes. Flossie had seen eight or ten delicious sponge cakes in the large crock in the pantry, carefully laid down. She'd keep them for a month or more, their lasting qualities enhanced not only by the tablespoon of *brauntwein* she'd always mix with her batter, but in addition by the cupful of the brandy she'd put at the bottom of the crock, covered with paper. When the tight-fitting lid of the crock was put in place this tended to fill the container with a preservative to keep the contents in perfect condition for later use. When you'd remove the lid to take out a cake, as Flossie had often done, the odor, the scent of the brandy mixing with the pastry odor of the cakes themselves, was something exciting, a sense of Norway, the old farm and all the excitements of Christmas, Easter and intimate gaieties about a table, the snow falling in the street and familiar faces close about one in a warm room.

Flossie would sigh, after traipsing the streets, ask her grandma if there was anything she could do. Perhaps it was to grind some cardamom in the old brass mortar. Otherwise she would play tiddlywinks with her small cousin, take up one of the many romantic books Hilda had about the apartment, or practice the piano—she was taking lessons then—otherwise she'd just sit and look out the window at the children playing in the park.

Olga had written that there was a package for her. Dear Auntie Olga, she would always make up a package, something rescued from the Learys, where she was the housekeeper, a dress, several yards of lace, two or three pairs of the most beautiful slippers—thrown out! Toys for little Paul. All sorts of things. Her wealthy patrons would say, "Here, Olga, here's something for you. Get it out of my sight, I'm sick of it!" And Olga would take it, beautiful things, sometimes—they'd be packing, getting ready to go to Saratoga Springs for the racing season.

At supper they'd have *fiskeballe*, potatoes, from Vermont! And—Flossie loved it—plum pudding served in a high glass dish, a bowl supported by a stem you could grasp to pass it around. Flossie loved her grandmother's plum pudding. The prunes were strained through a sieve, a little cornstarch added, sugar, whatever else, and then served with cream, plenty of it. The old lady insisted on that. The family might have lost its money, they were no longer rich, but that made small difference to the old lady. When it came to the table there could be no diminution of the former abundance; she lavished what she had upon family and friends.

Uncle Einar would be there, and Hilda, and, of course, Einar's small son, into everything. Flossie was always happy at such times and felt quite the young lady—her sister in Germany, her baby brother at home, Grandma fussing over her, undressing later in the spare room, climbing into the big old-fashioned bed and sleeping, sleeping like an angel.

Sunday morning, she'd help with the eggs at breakfast, help with the dishes, dress again and go to Sunday school around the corner with her small cousin, Sunday school carried on in the Norwegian language, which she could understand with a few lapses. The effect of it upon her was indescribable, the white stalls, the colored windows, very plain but giving a certain luxury to it all, the old-world appearance of the men and the women, and the new generation of American-born children still marked with their parents' ways. This girl from New Jersey felt quite different from the others. But she couldn't help liking it. It made her proud. She felt secure among them even though she was glad not to have to be bound by their life.

When Sunday school was out, sometimes her parents would already have arrived with little Paul all the way from Riverdale, and Gurlie would already have begun to assert herself. Flossie would hug her beloved father and glance with misgivings at her brother, hardly more than a baby. The Sunday papers, the *World*, with the Yellow Kid, would engross her while she listened to the men talk of the recent Croker scandals—to which she listened while pretending not to do so.

Veal for dinner! She knew it. This was the big meal, this was a continuous ritual for the old lady. "You cook too *much!*" Gurlie always told her. And always the same answer, that a body must be fed to keep well. There was no use arguing. And you had to eat! Flossie did her best, but her father, a slightly built man, would not take more than he wanted. He simply would not—much to the old lady's annoyance. But even she couldn't move him.

"I *know* when I've had enough," he would say. And as she could not speak English, she'd ask her son or Gurlie if he didn't like what she served him. She appeared hurt. She'd want to give him more. She'd even put a second helping on his plate in spite of his protests. He'd always leave it.

At three o'clock, the gang began to arrive. This was a year-round ceremony, as long as the family was not in Vermont on the farm. The whole neighborhood took part in it—until finally poor Einar, former sailor, gentle and unable to resist his mother, went broke. His grocery business couldn't keep up with her.

All the Norwegians knew, so long as Ma Hansen was there, that they were expected for *Kaffe* at the home on Russell Street; in fact if *everyone* was not there she would ask her son what had happened. This was her weekly social event in which she, mother of them all, keeper of the faith, carer for the tradition, guardian of morals, rememberer of the old days, prided herself. Elvira and Stoltz would be among the first to arrive. Joe would have to submit to it, though he was not of the same breed.

"Good!" would say old Captain Guldbrandson, as it happened, one of Joe's favorites. "I'm glad to see you!" and he said it in such a way that you felt it was so, he was indeed glad to see you. "How are you? You look fine." And he'd come beside Joe, take his cup of coffee and one of the delicate cookies in his enormous paw, smile so that his false teeth shone brilliantly, and ease his massive bulk down into the sofa. "Ah, there's Gurlie." And he'd struggle to get to his feet again, balancing his coffee cup. But Gurlie would push him back, as over his features spread a big boyish smile. "How are you?"

"Agh," Gurlie would say, "don't ask about me." And she'd turn her back on him and walk off.

"How's the business? You making a lot of money?"

"A million a week," Joe would say, seriously. "I'm up to my neck in it. She spends it as fast as I make it. I'm broke."

"That's too bad," said the old captain seriously, with a wink. "I bet . . ." But the beautiful Elvira entered, queen of the group, and a real queen in size and demeanor, full-breasted, with a look in her eye, which she turned full upon Joe.

"Let me sit beside you gentlemen." And she sat between the old captain and Stecher. Gurlie saw it from across the room, and came immediately toward them.

"She is always making love to my husband," said Gurlie to the old captain. "I have to watch them. He loves the ladies. You wouldn't believe it, would you?" Joe hardly knew what to say. "Come with me," his wife said to him, pulling at his arm. "I want you to meet one of my oldest friends. I used to go to school with her when we were little girls."

Elvira Stoltz, recently married to a struggling bank clerk, was only a few years older than Gurlie's oldest daughter. Why, Joe had even wanted, only recently, to buy her a mink wrap and in all seriousness had proposed it to Gurlie, who was scandalized. "What is the matter with you?" she had told her husband. "You can't do things like that."

More and more people from the neighborhood dropped in—and stayed. The old lady was in her element. Box after box of sardines and anchovies from the store were opened and served! Coffee was served and sometimes chocolate for the children, with milk and cream in abundance. Her pastry was famous. Port and sherry! Stoltz was a sturdy drinker; he stuck to the brandy, of which he had glass after glass. "This is something like it!" he would say. He was employed by a Norwegian bank, a thick-set man with a bottomless belly, later to die suddenly of a cerebral hemorrhage, poor chap, an event long predicted by his associates.

The room got hotter and hotter until someone opened a window.

"This is what I call a good time," said young Heilbrun, a man who they whispered had a good mixture of Jewish blood in his veins, husband of the woman Einar should have married, and would have, if Grandma had had her way. She never got over it. Childless now, Mathilda was one of the intimates of the group. "This is what the Norwegians are famous for!" Heilbrun said. "Eating and drinking and . . ." Being partly of another race, but still attached to the group, he was the one to say it and mean it. "They're a wonderful people."

What everyone was waiting for, having already had enough coffee, port wine and brandy to sink a ship—one of their own daring ships, like his tent to an Arab—was the buffet supper!

"This is really it, what the old lady is famous for!" said Heilbrun. She overheard what he said as she was passing, and said something to him rather sharply in reply. He jumped and bowed. "I beg your pardon. I should not have said that, Frau Hansen. But you cannot deny your smörgåsbord is the finest in the world." She was pacified, remarking, "You drink too much. You forget yourself. You should be ashamed."

"What happened?" said his wife, coming up.

"I called her an old lady. I should have my tongue cut out sometimes."

"Forget it. Here's good food. I'm hungry," said Stoltz.

"You hungry? Are you ever anything else?" his wife observed, and turned away.

"Now *my* wife's sore at me. Come on, let's have a drink." But the old captain and Joe both refused. "What a drinker he is," said the old man, who with his lame leg had not moved from his place on the sofa all afternoon. "I have known men like that in the old days, two or even three bottles of whiskey every day would not satisfy them—and they are never drunk, just normal, they seem to need it, they drink it like water— it makes them strong. Stoltz is like that, good healthy man. But he works in a bank. That I do not understand. The men I have known work with their bodies, out of doors. He must be a very powerful man."

Joe laughed and puffed his cigar. "That costs plenty," he said.

"Yes, now whiskey is expensive," replied the captain.

The herring salad was brought in, on a big open platter, an enormous dish which everybody hailed with exclamations of delight to please the old lady's heart. She was proud of her herring salad. A place was made for it on the table about which the guests gathered as if they were starved, although they were already bursting with their surfeit.

As they smacked their lips over its salty pinkness the old lady stood back and urged them on.

So the day passed, and Joe began to look at his watch and to say that they had better be thinking of home. Gurlie was approached, and after many protests from the others finally went in to the room where the baby was sleeping. Flossie began to put on her hat and her coat.

"Oh, Auntie Olga's bundle!"

"Agh," said Joe, who hated to carry bundles. But the bulky dress box containing the articles Olga had sent was brought out and retied.

"Have you heard from Lottie?" asked the sympathetic Mathilda. "How is she doing?"

"She's doing fine," said Gurlie.

"Ah, the poor child, all alone that way in a foreign city."

"Don't call her a poor child. She's lucky to get such a chance. And she's not alone. She has many companions of her own age, all doing the same thing."

"But if she is sick?"

"She isn't going to be sick. And if she is sick, she'll get well. She's happy."

"And how long is she going to be there?"

"As long as she wants to; three years, perhaps."

"You won't know her when she returns."

"She'll be the same lanky thing she was when she went away."

It was an evening early in May—the evenings were getting longer—as Joe and his family went to the corner to wait for the trolley, just at sunset. Mathilda waved from the window. Gurlie just nodded her head. And there they stood waiting, Gurlie holding little Paul in her arms. "Put him down," said her husband. "He can stand up." Joe had Flossie's overnight bag in his hand, his derby hat a little on the back of his head, while Flossie, holding her father's other hand, carried Olga's bundle.

The evening was beautiful, thank goodness, but Stecher was in his usual restless mood when out on these family jaunts. Flossie half-heard what her parents were discussing.

"Never again!"

"You seem to have a good time. Her reputation is no better than it should be. You might say she had to leave Norway because of the scandal; since she was sixteen years old she has had one man after the other."

"Agh, leave her alone," Flossie's father replied. "Whenever a woman is good-looking, the rest of you cats can't do enough to drag her down."

At that moment the car came clanging to a stop before

them and they all got in. There was only one other person there, a man well-dressed, but with his eyes shut, who almost fell off the seat as the car jerked to start up again, opened his eyes, looked at the newcomers, then at once, his head slumped forward, went to sleep again.

"Drunk," said Gurlie.

"He should have been with us," said Joe.

"No one was drunk," said Gurlie.

Joe chortled disgustedly, "They were all drunk."

"Nonsense, you're not a sport."

"That man Beha didn't know what he was doing."

"Einar's a fool to spend his money on such riff-raff. He'll go broke."

"He's broke now, only he doesn't know it. That simple little party this afternoon must have cost him fifty dollars."

"You're crazy," said his wife.

"All right, figure it out. Three bottles of the best brandy to begin with. Do you know what that costs? And he'll do the same next week. And all summer, at that farm in the mountains, he'll have them all on his hands, besides. The old lady must think he's a millionaire."

"Change here," the conductor called in to them. And out they piled to stand on the street again until the Greenpoint car came by. There were a few more passengers to listen here, so that Flossie heard no more talk. Little Paul, half-asleep, sat on his mother's lap while Flossie, her bundle on the empty seat beside her, stared idly about.

The ferry over the river to East Twenty-third Street was a short run. Another trolley, waiting outside the ferry house, made it easy for them. It was getting rapidly dark now. Then, at last, they were on the West Side ferry. This was what Flossie had been waiting for. Gurlie sat inside with little Paul while she and her father went out to stand at the prow of the blunt boat for the long run to the Erie slip, then a short train ride home, across the dark meadows.

She loved this night ride, the water, so near them, dark

and mysterious rushing by, the movement of it as it rattled under the prow throwing up spray, so that you had to stand back not to be soaked.

Then far ahead, on the right, she could see lights in the sky coming and going. "There's where we left from," she said to her father, "when we went to Europe last year. It was so beautiful at night."

"Ya," said her father, "that's the place. Those are fine ships. The Scandinavian-American, the Holland-American, the Hamburg-American and the North German Lloyd." You could see them below the dark outline of the Castle. It made Flossie think of her sister—alone there, to the east, over the dark interval of the ocean.

It was frightening, mysterious, the vague forms of passing boats with lights, one above the other on a short mast, dark bulks slugging along behind a straining tugboat, a hawser stretched between, hardly moving beyond them. Flossie looked at her father to see if everything was all right.

And then, at last, you could really make out ahead of them what the lights over the long piers were about, with their brightness and dullness, regularly alternating. It was a very exciting ride, this, down the river at night. The breeze, a warm, river-scented breeze, blew her skirts about and roared in her ears as she clung to the broad hat and stood close at her father's side. Now she could read the letters.

"Look!" she said.

The letters, which had been at an angle before, so that it was hard to make them out, finally became clear, going on and off regularly, spelling out their enthralling message:

"Trips to the Orient"

Then after you had had time to absorb that, the message was modified:

"Trips to the Mediterranean"

On and off, off and on vis-à-vis the river and the New York skyline for everyone to see. Flossie looked toward New

York then back again. It was a proud message. There was nothing like it from the other side. The Jersey side was best and of all the ships, of course, you had to omit the Scandinavian-American line for special reasons, the German ships were the finest, her father's ships. Suddenly she felt sleepy and wished she were home.

16

"Whaa!" said Gurlie, letting out one of her raucous shouts. "Do you remember her coming off the ship!"

"What was the matter with me?" said her elder daughter. She was hurt.

"What was the matter with you?" said Gurlie hilariously.

Lottie remembered the whole incident only too clearly: two and a half years at the conservatory, a kid of fourteen and then fifteen, now sixteen, living, breathing and eating music, music, music every day, every night; dreaming, waiting to begin her concert career and then—that! To meet her parents at the pier in New York and to hear Gurlie let out that roar of laughter at first greeting.

The poor kid had looked down at herself not knowing what to make of it.

"Where did you get that dress?" Not, "How are you, my sweet child? How have you been? Did you enjoy the trip, tell me?" Oh, no. Just, "My God! just a little Heinie! A little German hick, arrived from the old country. Who gave you that dress?"

"Nobody gave it to me," said the girl. "I bought it and Mrs. Janecke fixed the yoke up for me with that lace."

"I suppose she had to, you skinny thing. And that high collar you had on."

"I did not have on a high collar. I had a string of pearls wrapped around my neck. It was a long string."

"Well, what's the difference? That bertha, hanging down. I guess you needed it. Why don't you gain some weight?"

Oh, if she could have taken the next boat back to Leipzig that instant! She didn't like this country or anything in it. She wanted to go "home" again. To Germany. To music. To her future as a great artist.

And now a month later, the showdown.

"Let me go back to Leipzig, Father. Please!"

"No, you've had enough of that. You can't even talk English any more," said Joe. He wanted her to get a teacher in New York and return to high school. "One lesson a week from a good teacher should be all you need."

"But, Dad, what good will that do? I can't get to be a concert pianist that way. I can't. And I don't want to go back to high school. I've had enough education."

"Don't make a fool of yourself," said Joe. "You don't know anything."

"I know music! I know what it means. I know I've got to work, work, work, to give my entire time to it and even then, sometimes, it isn't enough. I can't go back to high school and be an artist. I'd rather quit the whole thing."

"That's up to you," said Joe picking up his paper.

Gurlie was listening.

"Then why did you send me to Europe in the first place— for three years to the conservatory—if it was not—if you didn't want me to go through with it?"

"It was your mother's idea."

"Stupid," said Gurlie. She got up from the table and took some plates into the kitchen; they had just finished their Sunday dinner. Joe lit a cigar as Lottie picked up the napkins, folded them and went to put them away in the sideboard drawer.

"Now, look here," said Gurlie coming into the room again, "let's have this thing out." Lottie turned about and held her breath waiting for what would happen next. After all, her entire future depended upon it.

Joe didn't move.

"She says all her teachers at the conservatory were disappointed when they found out that she was not coming back."

"They know what side their bread is buttered on."

"They said she had talent and urged her to return."

"And the fall term begins the first of October," put in Lottie, picking up hope. "If I take the steamer next week I'll be there just in time. Frau Janecke said I could have my same room again, isn't that true, Mother? That would be heaven! Heaven!"

"No," said Joe finally. "Listen to me—we have enough artists"—his lips curled up in a sneer as he spoke—"in this family."

"In your family, not mine," said Gurlie.

"That's right," said Joe. "In my family. In your family they are all bankrupts!"

The light flared in Gurlie's eyes. "Not me," said she. "I'm no bankrupt—lucky for you. And I wasn't when I married you. I had a job. I had a good job."

"Listen, Lottie. You'll never be a great artist."

Lottie couldn't see how he could tell that. "Why not?" she said.

"Great artists are born, not made. Look at you. In the first place, you're a woman. In the second place, you're already sixteen years old, it's too late, and you're not strong enough. To be an artist you have to live like a pig. You can't live a normal life; you have to have luck or be a gypsy. I don't want my daughter to be one of those people. I don't want any more artists in my family. I've seen enough of them."

"Agh," said Gurlie, "what kind of an artist was your sister? All she did was show her legs . . ."

"She earned money for it," said Joe, "so she was an artist. Music is fine, but I don't want a professional musician in this house. I want her to go to high school and learn something. That's enough."

"Go in and play him some music," said Gurlie to her daughter. "Maybe it will get some sense into his thick head."

"I don't feel like playing," said Lottie. "Not today."

"Go on," said Gurlie, "unless you've already forgotten how. Let him hear what you can do."

Lottie was in the front room playing Bach when Flossie came downstairs. She went up to her father, who was reading the *Sunday World*, still at the dinner table, and said to him, "Have you finished fighting?"

Joe looked up at her, not understanding.

"What?" said Gurlie from across the table.

"I heard you fighting."

"Oh," said Gurlie. "Where were you?"

"Upstairs."

"You were upstairs all that time. I thought you had gone out. You see what your children think of you," said Gurlie to her husband. "Fighting." She burst out into her raucous laugh. "That was your father," she said to Flossie. "He's Dutch."

"Agh," said Joe, "don't talk that way to the child."

"Who talks what way? You are the one that frightened her so she was afraid to come down."

"Can I keep this dress on? I want to go out and play," said the young girl.

"Go ahead, then," said Joe. "Or maybe you'd like to stay in and hear your sister play Bach for you?"

Lottie was putting everything she had into her playing, longing, remorse, bitterness and a last good-bye to her departing life.

"Agh." Joe got up and left the room. "I think I'll go for a walk."

"Take your daughter with you, then," said Gurlie. "She's more like you than the other one. Take her down the street, and don't come back until you're in a better mood. Do you hear how she plays? God, I'm sick of it."

"You too?" said Joe. "No wonder you want to get rid of her."

"That goes on all day long. I wish you would send her to Germany again. Give us some peace. You can afford it."

Never, never, never, never! thought Lottie to herself, hearing very well what they were saying in spite of the music. It will never be. Unless I can borrow the money from somebody else—she was no longer a child and she knew it. In fact, she was absolutely certain of it, much older than her parents. What do they know of the world? If I could borrow the money . . .

She had known of a girl who got money to stay in Europe and go on with her music. She was a little older, true, but not so much older than Lottie herself. Why not? And she knew what went on, in spite of Frau Janecke's denials. You can get money if you want it badly enough. And she needed money desperately, now.

Meanwhile, the family forgotten, her fingers were flying over the keys.

Then her mind began to wander. Coming over on the boat there had been three of them in the cabin, three girls from Leipzig returning to their parents in the States. One of them was crazy about men. She wasn't very good-looking and rather silly. Any man that looked at her she thought was trying to flirt with her. It was ridiculous. But some girls are that way. She was pretty hard up.

Men, men, men! That's all she talked about day and night until her companions got sick and tired of it.

So they put up a game on her. There was one man, especially, that she was daffy about—not the best-looking on the ship, but unmarried, or at least not traveling with his wife—who had fallen into stride with her one day and so continued for several turns around the deck. Later they had played shuffleboard together and she had jumped to the conclusion that he was in love with her. This gave Lottie and her companion their malicious opportunity.

While Dorothea was out mooning around one morning, near the bar entrance, waiting to attract her lover's attention, posting herself now at one point of the ship's rail, now another, her two cabin mates, who had secured several sheets of the ship's note paper for their purpose, were composing a note.

It was to be brief, but to the point, a love missive in discreet terms from the object of their friend's adoration to his beloved Dorothea, asking her to meet him that evening at a certain hour. He had, they wrote, something important to tell her. She would find him standing at a certain place on the afterdeck, a white handkerchief displayed prominently in his hand. It took the girls a good hour to write it, but it came out well. Her name was inscribed upon it, they tipped the steward, and had him deliver it to her at the cabin door that afternoon while they were out.

She was completely taken in and quite innocent in her reactions; told them everything. They felt a bit remorseful at that but had to go through with it once they had started. She was thrilled. Her excitement was astonishing to behold and they did everything to increase it. They congratulated her, praised the man's appearance and encouraged her to give herself to the experience without reserve now that she had the opportunity.

"This is what you waited for all these years. We envy you! And you must promise to tell us all about it afterward." She promised.

Poor girl. The only person she saw at the trysting place that evening was a man with a terrible cold in his head who had his handkerchief on display merely to blow his nose with it. She waited and waited, but had to come in at the end crestfallen.

"The dirty skunk!" sympathized her companions. She wept; she was broken-hearted. "He's just laughing at you.

Don't give him the satisfaction of seeing how you feel. Cut him dead when you see him in the morning." And that is what she did.

Broken-hearted. That was the key. How could she get to Germany unless her father gave her the money? And get the money? It wasn't as easy as all that—unless her mother would help her. Meanwhile she took it out on the pianoforte, played and played.

"*Um Gotteswillen!*" Gurlie broke in on her an hour later. "Give me a rest. Will you quit that piano and get out of here? You're driving me crazy. It's about time we did *something* with you. Either go to school or anything else that will satisfy you."

She got up and went into the street, bareheaded, the way she was. She had seen her father and sister, out of the corner of her eye, disappearing earlier up the elm-lined road, and with a bitter, aching heart, turned in the opposite direction.

Bach under the elms! Lanky, tall with one shoulder higher than the other— "From playing the violin, too, when she was growing. It isn't right"—Lottie walked off into her dream, stumbling at the first cross street and almost falling.

"Hey, Charlotte!" called a girl's voice. Lottie didn't so much as lift her head. Everything lost: Easter or before Easter, the conservatory students were allowed to come to the *Thomaskirche* when no one else was admitted, of a Thursday to hear the *Motetten*, in Bach's own church, his own organ loft—almost you might say, his own choir—and hear! hear it, all to themselves and be transported. What did anyone know in this Godforsaken place?

The Barfuss Allee! Auerbachs Keller, where the devil had appeared to Faust. It was true. The devil had actually appeared to Faust in Auerbachs Keller. You could see where the tunnel had been (it was said privately that it led to the crypt of a nunnery in the neighborhood).

And the *Messe!* That was the time, in spring, when they came even from Rumania, remnant of the old mediaeval fairs, every merchant setting up his booth where you could go and buy all sorts of things: if you had the money—which she never had. But you could *look*, anyway.

The Gewandhaus concerts! The opera—remember the opera? For what would be the equivalent of fifteen cents in this country, you could hear the finest, the best singers in the world. And really serious plays like Ibsen, *Ein Puppenheim*. *Die Wilde Ente* at the Altes Theater at the northern tip of the Ring! Oh Leipzig, Leipzig . . . Her thoughts trailed off into space.

"Daddy, look!"

"What?"

"Black-eyed Susans! Let's pick some."

"Not in that dress. The grass is all dirty there." But the girl seemed so disappointed that he hesitated. "I'll climb up and get some for you." It was atop a little embankment.

"No, let me help. I'll be careful."

So they climbed the low bank—it was rougher going than at first apparent—and started to pull the flowers. Flossie couldn't do it; the stems were strong as wire. So he took out his penknife, which he kept at the other end of his watch chain, opened it and cut the flowers, a handful of them, closed the knife, and gave them to his daughter. His hands were chafed, the skin even slightly torn under one knuckle.

"Oh thanks, Daddy!"

And he lifted her down, out of the grass—she in her new flowered dress—onto the wooden walk again.

"Thank you."

"Look," said Joe to her tentatively. "Look," as she glanced inquiringly up into his eyes. "You're the only sensible one in this family."

"Oh," she interrupted him suddenly, "there's a little bunny!" Sure enough, just at the edge of the tall grass, there sat a half-grown rabbit, his jaws working rapidly, and looked at them. His eyes wore that look of eternal surprise and intelligence common to all wild creatures. Then he got down on all fours and started foraging again.

Joe leaned down to pick up a stone, but, seeing the look that came into his daughter's eyes, didn't throw it. When they turned again to the rabbit it was gone.

"I can't trust your mother," Joe went on. "Your sister's crazy, she wants to go back to Germany, she doesn't know what she's asking for. Look at her. I think what she really needs is a mother to look after her. You can't buy those things. Agh! She needs to learn to speak English. She needs to learn that the world isn't made of people who know nothing else but to play the piano. After all. Don't you think so?"

"Yes," said Flossie. "I agree with you."

"Shall we walk to the next corner, just to those trees over there?"

"Sure." They started to walk. "What shall we do with her? Shall we send her back to Germany—to get rid of her?"

"Don't you like her?" asked Flossie.

Joe didn't answer at once, but went along looking into the distance. "That's it, isn't it? I guess that settles it. She stays home and goes to school here. What do *you* want to do? Do you want to play the piano, too?"

"No," said the girl.

"That's right, you've got sense." And they turned homeward. "Do you know what your mother's idea of a genius is?"

"No," said his young daughter.

"A genius, according to your mother, is a person who gets something for nothing. Everybody is a genius who doesn't want to work and thinks he is one. That's what your mother thinks. She is a genius. Crazy."

17

"Oh, she wants to run everybody," said Lottie.

Elvira, who, after all, was not her granddaughter, and married, nodded with a smile. "She even wants to order me around the way she does Hilda."

"Hilda ought to send her to the devil. Poor Hilda."

"Well, I don't pay any attention to her. But it makes it hard *always* to have to fool her. Where is she now?"

Grandma appeared from the kitchen. She spoke to them in Norwegian. "Have you said good morning to Miss Guldbrandson this morning? You should go and speak to her."

"But she is so deaf, Grandma. And it is such a nice day to be out. She makes me mad."

"You have no heart, you young people. You should be ashamed of yourself."

"But Grandma, she's happy. She only wants to sleep. She's happy on the porch in her nice chair. She doesn't want to talk to us. Look what a fine view she has across the fields. She can see the barn and the cows and the wagons coming down the hill on the road and . . ."

"Go and talk to her."

"All right. But we were just going to pick blackberries."

"Where were you going to pick blackberries?"

"We found a wonderful patch yesterday—along the road

near the lake. They were wonderful. Just ripe. We better get them today because it might rain."

The old lady, with a doubting look at the girls, the tall young Lottie with her black hair curling around her head, her big pleading eyes, and the older, magnificently blond Elvira, who spoke with a strong accent. The girls held their breaths, waiting to see how their ruse was working.

"Um," said the old lady, with never a smile. "Yes, it might rain. You are not lying to me?"

"Never, darling. I was coming to ask you for the pails. Milk pails are very good for berries. May we have two milk pails? They are the best."

"No. Milk pails are for milk. Go out and get your berry pails. You know the kind of pails to get." And she walked out of the room with the big fireplace, stopping at the door to say, "You young people. Be back here for dinner. Don't keep me waiting." And she went out to sit with poor Miss Guldbrandson—and to watch to see if the girls went down the road the way they said they would.

Miss Guldbrandson was asleep, so the old lady sat beside her on her own comfortable chair.

The girls came out of the house onto the little side lawn behind her, jumped down the three broad stone steps by the bed of phlox to the grass edge, still slippery with the heavy morning dew of the Vermont mountains, to reach the grit of the road where they could regain their footing again.

They swung their pails ostentatiously so the old lady would see them as they went by, past the bergamot patch and the bluebells.

"Good-bye!" sang out Lottie, covertly triumphant—the old lady got it perfectly.

"Oh, well, they are young," she said.

"We'll be back with the pails full."

"See that you are," said Grandma to herself, turning away and going back into the house.

Down the road strode the two girls.

"Oh, I wish I was married," said Lottie to her friend. She had said this on more than one occasion during the two weeks they had been together.

"Well, why don't you, then?" said Elvira. "Seventeen is old enough for it. Then you'll find out all you want to know."

That effectively shut her up.

It was hot on the road, and the ruts turned their city ankles, especially Lottie's long, slender ones, never too firm. "I wish I had legs like yours," she said to her friend. "You are wonderful. Look at me, skinny, flat-chested. Look at my arms. And look at you."

"You have wonderful dark eyes."

"But yours are blue as the sky."

"You are very attractive," said Elvira. And again the conversation stopped short. "And you can play the piano like an angel. I envy you that. Did you have any romances in Leipzig?"

"No," said Lottie. "I was too young. I didn't see anybody I liked but my violin teacher. I felt like a fool."

"Poor Lottie!" said her friend, mocking her. "What you need is a lover."

They got to the main road from Brattleboro. Not a soul, not a wagon in sight. "What a place!" said Lottie. "You could die here!" The side road ran, turning and broken by several well placed thank-you-ma'ams, to the left into the heavy maple woods uphill. A few of Mr. Aldrich's cows stood at the barbed-wire fence in the shade chewing their cud.

Mrs. Aldrich came out of her kitchen door, seeing them approach, and went to talk to them. "Phew, it's hot in that kitchen. How be you? Having a good summer up here, are you?"

"Yes, wonderful," said Lottie.

"Berrying?"

Lottie, for reply, held out the pail. Elvira did the same, half-heartedly.

"There's plenty." With that she turned and went back

into the house. "Not very polite," said Lottie. They went lackadaisically up the road, keeping as much as they could in the shade of the tall trees. "Phew, it is hot." But just short of the lake, where there had been two or three larger trees felled last year to broaden the right of way, they found the berries and set to work picking them. Their fingers soon became stained with the dark purple juice. They had to be careful in brushing back their hair as they worked not to smudge their faces and their clothes.

When the sun was hottest they turned home, their pails loaded with the fruit. Lottie was watching over a butterfly on a milkweed cluster when Elvira brought her to with a start.

"Someone is coming up the road."

"Where?"

Something in Elvira's voice caused Lottie to stand stock still.

The boys were striding along at a good hiker's pace talking together, relaxed, carrying some bundles as if they had just been to town. Lottie's heart gave a leap as she realized what had occurred. You could hear them, just beyond a slight screen of bushes at a bend in the road, even half make them out, getting nearer. But they had not yet seen the girls, who simply stood there apparently unable to move, so that when they did see them they were almost face to face.

"Hey! What have we here?"

Everything had come to a dead halt. The boys stared. Elvira stared back and Lottie, following the example of her friend, stared also—especially at the taller and more direct of the hikers, who came up to them at a slower pace. "Hello," he said. "Been berrying?"

"Yes," said Elvira, conscious of her foreign accent.

"Yes," said Lottie after her, hoping this new find would prove someone who would at least stop and talk.

And they did stop and talk. Lottie had fallen in love at the first glance with the taller and better-looking of the young men and hoped Elvira would take the other. For they were campers who said they were with two others at the lake and that they had come from North Adams. The girls told them they were from New York, that they were staying at a nearby farm. Names were exchanged.

"Come and see us," Lottie surprised herself by saying to them, and: "Do come and see us," she repeated, and felt happily like a fool.

"We'll come," said the one whom she had looked at hardest. "Don't worry." And she thought he gave her a secret and meaningful glance. She blushed crimson. Elvira saw it. The other boy, not quite as exciting as the first, but a serious, smiling boy, had already started up the road. "Aw, come on," he said to his companion. "So long," and they were gone.

"What luck!" said Lottie as soon as they were out of hearing. "Do you think he'll really—do you think they'll really come?"

"Why not?" said Elvira.

"Oh, you're so matter of fact."

"What does that mean—so matter of fact?"

"How can we tell Grandma? We'll say that Mrs. Aldrich introduced us. We'll just tell her they're campers. What can she say?" Lottie felt as if she were blown up like a rubber balloon, as at the circus, tugging at the string and about to fly off into the empyrean.

"Isn't he marvelous!" she said to her companion.

"They both seemed like very nice boys."

Good, thought Lottie. She likes the other one. Then I can have mine all to myself. I wonder if he's just a flirt. "Do you think they'll be able to find where we live?"

"Unless they're very stupid," said Elvira. "It's the only farm on this road unless they walk right past it and go up to Emma's."

Lottie laughed.

"I tell you what. Let's tell Hilda."

"Then she'll tell Grandma," said Elvira, completing Lottie's thought. Hilda was on the lawn in front of the woodshed with the baby. "How is my little darling?" said Elvira, going up to them and flopping down on the grass, kissing her little boy and at the same time feeling his pants. "Oh, he's wet. Let Mummy change you."

Hilda began to make excuses. Elvira only laughed. "For what?" she said. "All babies are wet. That's nothing."

"Oh Auntie," began Lottie. "We just met the most wonderful man . . ." She changed it to "men." "You would like them. I hope they come to see us."

"What is this?" Hilda began.

"We picked them up on the road to the lake."

"Picked them up?"

"I mean they're camping at the lake and one of them is wonderful. There's another one for Elvira."

"But Elvira is married."

"Oh Auntie, it's just for fun. You tell Grandma we met some nice boys in the village and they're going to call on you! Help us, won't you, darling? My boy, the one I chose, has such a nice voice, and he's so big and manly. He had broad shoulders and pretty teeth when he smiles. And Auntie," leaning close, "I love him!"

Grandma was just coming from the "opera," through the woodshed passageway. She saw Lottie and paused long enough to say, "Oh there you are. Did you pick berries?"

"Oh yes," said Lottie, running up to her with both pails full, "Look!" as the old lady sampled the berries from the top step. "Very good." And she took the two pails into the house.

"His name is John and his friend, the dark one, has another name," said Lottie to Hilda excitedly.

"How extraordinary!"

"Oh, you mustn't make fun of me. He is beautiful, you wait and see. You will tell Grandma at lunch, you'll promise to tell her two nice young men are coming."

That night, as the girls were finishing the supper dishes, having helped old Miss Guldbrandson up the narrow farm stairs to her room, poor soul, they thought they heard Hilda talking to someone out on the porch. For a moment they didn't move.

"What's the matter?" said Grandma.

"Who is Hilda talking to?" Lottie's heart was leaping in her chest. "I'll go see."

"No. Stay here and finish your work. It is probably old man Widness coming back from the village." And the old lady, who never smiled, tidied herself at the small mirror near the stove and started out to see. Hilda met her, all smiles. Lottie waited in suspense.

"It is a young man."

"One?"

"Who came to see Lottie."

"To see me?"

"Yes, he says he is a friend of yours. Shall I tell him to sit down?"

"Yes."

The old lady turned around. "What is this?"

"They are friends of Mrs. Aldrich, from North Adams. We met them today."

"Yes, it is true," said Elvira. Lottie was prepared to lie her head off, to say it was a friend of a friend, that he was a son of someone whom—but . . .

"He is a very nicely spoken young man," added Hilda, God bless her, and in reply to a question in Norwegian from the old lady, she replied that she would see to it. Grandma went upstairs and Hilda returned to her guest on the porch. "Finish your work," she said when she was halfway up the steep stairs, and was gone.

Now the girls began to giggle together. "Why is he alone?"

The practical Elvira said, "Plain enough, he came to see *you*. Go out and talk to him. I will stay here and read."

"Oh no! Come with me."

"No, I'm a married woman. Go and have your fun."

"I refuse. Unless you come with me, I won't go. How do

I know he wants to see me? We met him together. You are the beautiful one. I don't know what to say to him. Please come, darling. We don't even know which one it is."

Though she knew well enough, having no more than heard the pitch of that voice which in the moment of meeting had seemed to be engraved on her heart forever.

"Don't lie to me or I will not help you," said her friend.

"Why didn't he bring one for you?" said Lottie loyally. "I don't think that's fair."

On the porch, when they listened, as they did from time to time, they heard Hilda laugh. An intense pang of jealousy struck Lottie to the heart. She looked at herself in the little mirror, her serious face questioning her as she did so. God, she had to go! Not now. What is the matter with me? She couldn't go upstairs. Grandma was there.

"Go," said her friend. "I want to look at the baby. Go. I will come in a minute." So, the moment having come when she must see for herself what her fate would be: "Wish me luck," she said.

"I do," said her friend, and threw a kiss to her as she walked out, stiff and fearful, through the room with the big fireplace, the guns the books, Hilda's harmonium—over the uneven, half-sunken floor, out onto the side porch and the cool night air. It was still light enough to see the cows coming in across the far pasture and her uncle with the dog following them.

Lottie paused, then taking her courage in her hands, rounded the end of the porch and saw Hilda, the young man facing her, his broad back and fine head bent forward talking earnestly. Hilda was entranced with what he was saying. Lottie had not yet been noticed.

"Oh, there you are," said Hilda at last. "This is a young man who says . . ."

"Hello, Lottie," said John.

"Hello, John." Lottie wasn't going to be beaten. "Sit down. I'll sit here." The light was fading over the valley, but enough was left for the young girl to know that her instincts had not been deceived, this was a man such as she had dreamed of, that she had never seen at close range. Such a man as she could hope and dare to call her own. In him lay the answers.

"He likes Chopin's music!" said Hilda.

"Chopin!" said Lottie incredulously, and then, to herself, I didn't come here to talk about Chopin.

"I have been telling him all about your three years in Germany."

The nerve of her, thought Lottie.

"He is so romantic!" Hilda said, out into the night.

"What?"

"His music has all the feeling of the heart. It is so delicate, yet so bold. It reflects the soul!" You and your soul, thought Lottie. You don't even know what music is. Aloud, she said, "Where is your friend Tom?"

"I couldn't pry him loose. He wouldn't dress."

"We wouldn't have cared. Nobody dresses here. Elvira will be disappointed."

"So I came alone."

"I'm glad." He gave her a quick look, as Hilda began again.

"Music is the language of the heart. That is why in this country they have no composers. Everything here is money, money, money. That is strange, too, because there are so many beautiful places here which should inspire people."

"Well, we've got the songs of Stephen Foster."

"I don't know his songs." Lottie didn't, either, but she kept quiet. "Tell me some of the names."

"Well, there's 'Swanee River' and 'My Old Kentucky Home.' "

"Yes, I suppose so. But those are Negro songs."

"Not necessarily."

"But what have you got to equal Schubert? I used to sing them when I was young." God, thought Lottie, don't start now!

"And do you know Tchaikovsky's 'None but the Lonely Heart?' "

"Yes, I've heard it."

"Do you sing?" asked Lottie, with a thrill. "You have such a beautiful speaking voice."

"Yes, hasn't he? I noticed it right away. That's why we were speaking of music."

At that moment Elvira appeared. It was getting quite dark where the old farmhouse stood hard against the little hill which protected it in winter to the north and west. But across to the east the tops of the long ridge, enclosing the little valley where the pastures lay, were still in the sunlight. It was a tranquil sight, the intense silence of the scene making it all the more appealing with the nostalgic sense that inspires all that semimountainous country.

John rose and moved a chair into the semicircle.

"Hello, John," Elvira said. "Where are the others?"

"Yes, we would like to make their acquaintance," said Hilda. "Another time you must all come, and we can sing."

"Wasn't it nice of him to come alone?"

"Yes," said Elvira. "Do you like it here in the country?"

"He is a musician," said Hilda. Oh God, thought Lottie. Why hasn't she sense enough to go in the house? "We were talking of the great music which has been left to us by such men as Schumann. He was a true romantic. And Chopin. I do not like Wagner. He is too coarse. What is delicate and of the soul in such music? But Grieg—you know Grieg?" To hell with Grieg, thought Lottie furiously. Why don't you leave us alone?

It was quite dark now and the night wind had begun. "Let us go inside. I am chilly," said Hilda. Hooray! thought Lottie.

"Let me get you your shawl," Elvira put in.

"Oh, it's not cold," said Lottie.

But at that point John got up and said he'd better be moseying, he had just come for a short call, and that the others would be expecting him back at camp.

"Oh no! You've just arrived."

"Won't you come in? We can have a cup of coffee and a piece of cake." But Lottie had made up her mind. Something had to be done to get Hilda out of the way.

"I know," she said, "it'll be dark on the road to the lake. Let's walk down to the main road with you." She knew that would settle her dear auntie! And she would have him near her for those few precious minutes. "Come on!"

"It will be dark for you coming back alone," said Hilda.

"Oh that's nothing. Elvira and I have done it often before."

So Hilda was left wistfully alone on the high porch and the two girls and the tall young man dropped down over the lawn—Lottie would not let him help her down the steps— sliding down the grass to the gravelly road, and at once were lost to the view of the lady in the dark above them.

"Good-bye, come again," she called after them. "Good-bye," he called back from the darkness of the hollow road. They could see her, standing above them against the light, though she could no longer see them. She breathed deeply, looking across the valley, and then turned and went indoors.

The road was pitch-black as it started into the tunnel made by the century-old maples growing along the stone fence at the edge of the pasture. This was exciting.

"I can't see a thing," said Elvira.

"Your eyes will get used to it."

"Oh, I'm getting into the ditch."

"Come up here," said Lottie.

"Here, follow my voice."

"Oh, I'm all right now. Are there any snakes here?"

"No, not in Vermont," said John. "Men are the only snakes you'll find here." And he laughed.

"Do they bite?" said Lottie.

"Not often," said John.

"That's too bad." And she sniggered at her own daring They knocked together in the dark deliciously. "Are you all right, Elvira?"

"Yes, I am all right. I wish your friend," she said to John, "had been braver. Was he afraid of us? I think he was afraid. You were very brave to come alone."

"I think it was wonderful," said Lottie. And then, she could scarcely believe it at first and almost cried out, for she felt something that she had never felt in her life before. It gripped her firmly, without hesitation, live, giving, governing her uncertain steps. It was an arm, his arm about her waist. She did not hesitate; she welcomed it. It startled her, but something within her at that moment surrendered. She was afraid only that he would withdraw it. She walked carefully so as to keep near him as she wanted to do. If he had released her then, her disappointment would have been as if the whole world had collapsed and she would have been left alone upon the crumbling edge of an abyss. It was her whole passionate resolve to keep that arm in that place, touching her, steadying her through life.

They were coming out from under the heavier trees now. Oh, keep your arm there, she wanted to tell him.

"Are you cold?" she said.

"No. Why?" he said unsteadily. His teeth chattering.

"I thought you were cold." She had sense enough not to say more, that he was trembling. She had instinct enough to not give him away to Elvira. She knew. She was thrilled. "You are beautiful!" he managed to say to her under his breath.

When they came out into the light where the heavy trees ended he did not remove his arm. So it was confessed. Elvira saw it out of the corner of her eye and stood a little way off. "Oh, why didn't your friend come with you? We could have had so much fun. Do you do your own cooking at your camp? What do you have to eat?"

"Bacon and eggs and fish we catch in the lake. Yesterday

we had barbecued steaks. They were swell. And fried pota-
toes."

"I wish we could cook you something. Do you like home-
made pie?"

So it was agreed before they separated at the end of the
side road to the farm, that the girls would come to the camp
the following Tuesday with two pies. Grandma wouldn't allow
it for sure. But Mrs. Aldrich's pies were famous in the neigh-
borhood. Without telling anyone, the girls would order them
the day before. Somehow or other, under one excuse or an-
other, they'd sneak away. They talked of it excitedly on the
way back. "Something is breathing there!" Lottie gave a
stifled scream. "Why am I so nervous? It's only the old cow."

Somehow they managed it, put on their sheerest, most
fluffy organdy dresses, and in haste lest they be questioned
and detained, got away—after lunch in the early afternoon.
Out of breath, they had run down the dirt road to get beyond
the turn before Grandma should see them. Puffing, they
leaned against a tree for a moment, carefully so as not to soil
their dresses before proceeding. There were heavy clouds to
the west, but the sun was shining and the world was brilliantly
lighted.

They were a pretty sight on the road in their light frocks
hurrying to Mrs. Aldrich's door. That good lady had delayed.
"Oh, the pies are ready," she guessed. "But they're still in the
oven. Pretty hot."

"Oh, we can't wait for them to cool. Leave them in the
pans. Make one bundle of them. I'll carry them," said Lottie.

Mrs. Aldrich slid them into a big brown-paper bag she
had, put a good layer of paper between them, tied them, still
hot, in a clean cloth, and the girls started up the road.

They were about halfway to the camp when the storm
broke. The first they knew of it was when the sky quite sud-
denly darkened and there was a thunderclap ahead of them
just over the hill. They were fairly caught. The rain began

almost at once. The girls took to the woods, stepping gingerly along among the tall weeds. Another lightning flash followed by a loud thunderclap terrified Lottie, freezing her mind. She saw herself doomed, a just retribution for her sins. She was a coward before a thunderstorm. She clung to Elvira, holding the pies level as best she could.

The terror of death was upon her. She was not resigned. It was at her the lightning was aimed to destroy her just now when she had been happy for the first time in her life. No one cared. She had always been alone. That was what music was to her, something into which she could escape, something to comfort her in a lonely world. Against that world the lightning was aimed. It was a world of sin. All her desires were sinful. A blinding flash of lightning instantly followed by a terrifying thunderclap filled the world about her. She thought her time had come. "That was pretty close," said Elvira. "What shall we do? There is nothing to do."

Then it really rained. And from fear for their lives, it turned to fear for their clothes. There was no adequate shelter. Lottie still clung to the pies, but the two girls were soon soaked to their skins. Their hats drooped, their sheer dresses clung to their breasts and their thighs. Then the rain, as suddenly as it had come, subsided and quit, a typical summer flash storm in the mountains. They looked at each other and began to laugh. "What sights we are!"

"Oh my God! The pies!" said Lottie, having felt something sticky down her right leg. "Oh!" and she collapsed. The contents of both pies, softened by the rain, had run out and all down the side of her dress.

"Damn!" said Lottie, her white hat hanging about her ears, looking down at her own sturdy legs to which the dress was stuck. Out of sheer instinct she pulled it away from where it was stuck to her belly. Elvira let out a hearty, chuckling laugh. She leaned against the beech under which they had sheltered themselves, finally, and threw her arms around it laughing.

But Lottie was mad. "What do we do now?"

"The way we are? Let's go home. We can't let them see us this way. Look at us. And the pies!"

"We can't go home," said Lottie. "We'll get the devil."

"We could go to Mrs. Aldrich's kitchen."

But Lottie was inconsolable. "All my beautiful dreams!" seemed to be written on her features. As if in reply to disappointment, at that moment the sun came out in all its summer brilliance, the storm had passed, and the air, freshened by the downpour, was as sweet as young love. Elvira, who was anything but dull, saw how it was and decided, in her devil-may-care way, to give her friend the support she needed to go on to the end of the adventure.

"Look! The sun," said Elvira. "We said we would bring them something nice. Come on. They will understand."

Lottie could have kissed her. And so they went along like drowned rats still holding the paper bag containing the ruined pies as evidence.

As they approached the tent under the trees they hesitated. No one was in sight.

"Yuhoo!" they called.

A strange head stuck itself out from between the tent flaps, disappeared again. Then the four campers piled out. "We got caught in the shower," said Lottie. "What do we do now?"

First they laughed their heads off. Then, having looked the girls over: "We can't just stand here looking at you," said Tom. "You gotta get yourselves dried off. Look, go on in the tent, we've got a fire in there, and see what you can do for yourselves."

That was fair enough. And that's the way it went for the next half-hour. For of course the dresses didn't dry, though the girls had taken them off and done the best they could with them by the smoky fire. Finally they put them on again, stained with the pies, sooty from the fire as they were, untied the flaps of the tent and came out into the sunlight once more.

They had fixed their hair and carried their hats in their hands. They were tall, good-looking girls and the boys now fully realized it.

"We haven't seen you at all," said Tom.

"Too bad we didn't have our bathing suits with us."

"Too bad we couldn't even take a walk together. Or a ride in your boat or anything."

"And we're leaving Sunday."

"Oh!" Lottie's heart sank. "Aren't we going to see you ever any more?"

"There's a dance at the inn Saturday night. Will you be there?"

"Yes," said Lottie, though it was the first she had heard of it. "Won't we, Elvira?"

"Yes," said her friend. And that's the way it was left, as the girls, Lottie holding John's hand, walked down the road on their way home. What else under the circumstances could they do? They said good-bye at the crossroad, the girls going on alone.

"He might at least have kissed me."

Elvira looked at her.

"You poor girl. We didn't have a good time. We must see if at the dance you cannot at least go behind the inn with him. You should have at least one kiss."

But they were approaching the house and Grandma would be on the lookout. "And if she finds out what we have been doing, she will make a terrific fuss. I can hear father *Donnervetter*ing when she tells him." They crept up the far bank at the back of the house and went around to peep in the kitchen window. No one was there. They got in at the rear door under the hill where the slop pails stood, tiptoed upstairs without being seen, undressed in a hurry, jammed their half-wet dresses in a corner, dressed in other clothes and —got away with it.

The dance would be the climax. It had better be. Here was the man whom she had sworn in her secret heart to love forever. "Love is like that," she said to herself. "Someone appears, someone you never thought of, someone you know at once was made for you and . . . he is the one."

"What did he say to you that first night?"

"When?" said Lottie, knowing full well what was meant.

"Miss Innocence, you know what I mean; the night we walked down the road together. What did he say that got you so excited?"

"Nothing," said Lottie. "I asked him if he was cold and he said no. He was shaking." Elvira laughed, Lottie did not know why.

"So he was shaking. That's very funny. And were you shaking?"

"No, I felt fine."

"I can imagine."

I'm not going to tell her what he said to me. And that night she dreamed she saw her father with a big beard coming out of a cloud. There was a flash of lightning, rain chased her into the woods where she entered a cave.

The night of the dance, by luck a beautiful evening, the girls hitched up old Charlie, and drove the three miles into town. The air was perfumed, the brook noisy as they came out of the cut beyond the Hall farm, crossed the wooden bridge and clattered past the first old white buildings of the town itself.

There was a good crowd at the tavern, but they had no trouble finding a hitching place for the horse, being careful of their pretty summer dresses. Hilda had come with them as chaperone.

"Tables?" They had to take a table. They hadn't figured on that. A piano, a violin and a horn were the music. They had already heard the sounds of the two-step as they approached the brightly lighted inn. There were Japanese lanterns under the trees. The evening was windless. The clipped grass of the lawns was bright green where the candles shed their glow under the trees. Lottie's glance went about the room looking among the laughing couples for her man. He was definitely not there.

But a group was arriving as the girls at a table, quite at the back, watched the dancers get up and the men put their arms about their partners' waists and move off upon the polished floor. It was they! Entering as the music began "The Mosquito Parade," they didn't wait, but grabbed their partners and began at once to dance. For they had girls with them! For Lottie the evening was ruined.

"Why didn't they at least tell us?"

John had the decency a little later to come over to their table and make his excuses: the girls had surprised them, had appeared quite unexpectedly in the afternoon. What could they do?

"Is that your girl I saw you dancing with?"

"No, I haven't any girls."

"The way she had her arm around your shoulder and snuggling up to you made it look that way."

"Don't be so obvious," Elvira whispered in Lottie's ear.

"Do you want to meet them?"

"No, I hate them. I don't suppose we'll see you any more. So good-bye."

"I'm sorry you feel that way," said John. "We couldn't help it. Well, good-bye." He held out his hand, but Lottie pretended not to see it. Another dance was on. John turned and left.

"You shouldn't have done that," said Elvira.

"Let's go home," said Lottie.

"No. Can't we have a dance together? Don't let them see they have made you so unhappy." So the two girls danced together. There were several who were doing the same. Twice as she passed near John she refused to answer his glance. "Look at the cheap thing he's dancing with. Look at the dress she has on." And she began to laugh. "Look at them all! I think they are nothing but factory workers. Horrid. What a fool I was not to see it! Come on, let's get out of here."

"So early home? I think it is a very pretty dance."

But Sunday afternoon Lottie could not contain herself any longer. She had to have the last word and without difficulty persuaded Elvira to go with her on a casual walk out to the lake. What else was there to do in this place?

So again they were walking that road once so exciting to their spirits, now a dirge. They saw a wagon coming and in it the four campers and all their gear. John was in the front seat. He motioned to the driver to slow down. It looked as if they would stop, but just as Lottie was expecting to greet her lover in her best and most forgiving manner the driver, without looking up, gave the reins a slap and they moved slowly past. John was saying something to him, but he didn't stop.

Then in her rage and frustration Lottie did something for which she was eternally sorry. Lifting her voice after the departing wagon she called out, "Good riddance to bad rubbish."

If the cart had stopped and they had turned back to ask her what she meant she would not have known what to answer. But fortunately or unfortunately it kept on and that was the end of it.

Three days later she got a letter from John asking her, in fact, what she had meant by such a remark. But it was all over by that time. She didn't answer him. On Monday the girls dug down into the bottom of the clothes closet to get their dresses, so they could wash them apart from the rest of the laundry. They were amazed at what they saw. The lovely white organdy was stained all colors of the rainbow, greens, rusty reds, oranges and purples by the mold. It was so bad, what with the soot added, that they thought the best thing to do was to destroy them.

18

"So this is the night for which you've been waiting ever since we came to this neck of the woods."

"Put on your shirt so I can tie your necktie for you. It's almost half-past eight and we can't keep the cab waiting after it comes."

Joe buttoned his dress shirt at the throat. Gurlie was sitting with her hair newly waved, her gold-spangled lilac silk gown pulled up about her plump knees, her low shoes before her, shoulders slumped forward looking appraisingly at her man. "Ah, you make me tired," she said. "You've been half an hour getting into that shirt."

"God damn it!" said Joe in a suppressed fury. "It's enough to choke a man. I don't want to go where you're dragging me. Send the cab away. Tell them we've changed our minds."

"We've been invited by our good friends, and if you want to act like a fool you can do it. But I tell you I'm going even without you if you act this way. I'll tell them you're sick if you want me to, but you're not going to keep me home."

"All right," he said. "I give up. Tie my tie."

"When I get these shoes on you'll have to do up my dress in the back. Get a shake on you. You look fine. You look fine in a dress suit. It makes you look distinguished. I bet you'll be the best-looking man in the room."

When the door was opened to them by a maid, the first thing they saw in the front hall was a stuffed bear cub holding himself erect as part of an umbrella stand and hat rack.

Upstairs Gurlie found no one else in the ladies' room, so that she had a chance to look around. It was a prettily arranged bedchamber with dark mahogany furniture, rather old-fashioned in style but of an established appearance, a large rag rug on the floor and "*Fête Champêtre*," by Corot, a sepia print, next to the mirror on one wall near the high-backed double bed. She took off her wraps and was standing preparatory to going down when a large, gray-haired woman appeared, her head in a light shawl.

Gurlie did not know her, made some excuse looking down, as was her manner.

"I'm Mrs. Mills," the lady said.

"Mrs. Stecher is my name," said Gurlie.

"I beg pardon? I'm a little . . ."

"Mrs. Stecher," said Gurlie louder.

"Oh yes, Mrs. Stecher. I have heard of you."

"Excuse me," said Gurlie. "I am going downstairs." As she descended she saw Joe's back just as he disappeared into a group of men. Gurlie went to the wide double door leading into the parlor where the club members were assembled. There was a great talking and laughing and there she stood, a smile on her face, looking about for her hostess.

No one had noticed her. It gave her a good chance to see these people. She looked about. At the end of the room was a full-length painting of Mr. Arents in hunting costume, a Jaeger hat with a feather in it on his head and carrying a shotgun at ease over his arm.

Standing with her hands joined before her, Gurlie played with the ring on the third finger of her left hand, turning it round and round, first one way, then the other. It was a large opal, her birthstone, for everyone else unlucky, but for those born in October a magic token on which one could rely. She wore no wedding ring. In Scandinavia the bride and groom exchange rings. When Joe refused to accept and wear one she also had refused—so it was left at that. Her hands were plump, the fingers thick and powerful, her full neck, bare, was decorated by a simple string of amber beads; smiling at no one, for that brief moment, even bowing slightly, she stood there, until her hostess suddenly realized the situation and with a little cry rushed to her side.

"Oh I am so sorry!" she spoke with a very slight German accent. "I didn't see you!"

"That's nothing," said Gurlie. "Who is that sitting over there?"

Meanwhile Joe was being introduced to the men in the dining room. The ladies, as usual, having congregated in one place for their preliminary chatter, the men, a little awkward in their dress clothes, gathered in another, about the decorated dining-room table.

"This is my friend Joe Stecher," the host and mayor of the town was saying. He had a high, bulbous forehead and wore strong glasses. A little, reddish-haired, balding fellow bowed several times as he put out his ladylike hand and in a falsetto voice said, "How do you do?" Joe liked him at once.

"Oh, I am so sorry!" said Mrs. Arents to Gurlie. "Come, I will take you around and introduce you. You already know many of these people, I am sure." And with that she led Gurlie by the arm, solid, round and bare to the shoulder, to some of the ladies who were already seated. "First let us go to see our old friend Mrs. Nagel. She is our patriarch—no, that would be a man. Matriarch would be a better term."

The old lady did not attempt to get up.

"This is the wife of a very prominent man," said Mrs. Arents to her, "Mrs. Joseph Stecher. Mrs. Stecher, this is Mrs. Nagel, one of our dearest and most beloved women . . ."

"Yes, I have met her," said Gurlie.

"You have met her? Of course, at the Literary Club." Then to the older lady, "Mrs. and Mrs. Stecher are our guests for the evening."

"I'm very pleased to see you," said the old lady. "Is your husband with you? I should like to meet him."

"He is with the men," said the hostess. "They are impossible."

Gurlie was conscious of being carefully studied by a dumpy little woman on her left who, as soon as she was brought before her, began to clear her throat and look nervously down at the carpet. "This is Mrs. Fletcher," said the hostess. "Mrs. Joseph Stecher." Gurlie couldn't see the other's eyes, could hardly, in fact, hear her say anything more than a mumble, with a smirk. She nodded her own head and moved on around the roughly assembled circle of chairs.

"Who was that? I didn't hear," she managed to ask her introducer as they moved to the next chair.

"Mrs. Fletcher, one of our new members."

"I couldn't hear anything she said," Gurlie observed.

"Oh, she's very shy. But her husband is just the opposite. They are very different. But she is very sincere. They are good members. This is Mrs. Greer . . ."

"How do you do?" said Gurlie.

The lady put out her hand which Gurlie, not expecting it, took with a firm grip, then let go as fast. "Her husband is the Borough Assessor. Mrs. Greer has a wonderful garden."

"Oh," said Gurlie, "that's good."

"What is the name?" said the lady in question.

"Oh, I beg your pardon. Mrs. Stecher, Mrs. Joseph Stecher." Then, turning to Gurlie, "Mrs. Greer was a Stuart, one of our New Jersey aristocrats. They have lived in Riverdale—her family, I mean—since colonial times."

"Good," said Gurlie. And looked hard at the erect posture, the courteous, self-possessed manner. Gurlie admired her.

"And this is Mrs. Lincoln, Mrs. Stecher."

This was a rather heavy-set woman, with a bold but sad smile, her mode of speaking modest and slow. She smiled at Gurlie and said, "I have heard of you. It is a pleasure to see you here this evening. We need women like you in the town."

"What has happened to those men?" said the hostess. "They are impossible. They always do the same thing; till the last minute, they keep to themselves. Sit here a minute, with Mrs. Lincoln, here is an empty chair. We will introduce you to the others later."

"Yes, please sit down. It's so tiresome to be dragged around and the names . . ."

"I can't remember any names so far," said Gurlie.

"Yes, I was going to say that. It's always the same. We will introduce ourselves again later. Is your husband here? Everyone is interested to know what he looks like."

Gurlie laughed for the first time, her raucous laugh. "My little Dutchman's all right," she said.

Mrs. Lincoln had to smile also. "Does he like you to call him that?" she questioned. But Gurlie had turned to her neighbor on the opposite side, who had patted her arm. It was one of her church associates.

"Glad to see you here," she half-whispered, and batted her eyes knowingly at Gurlie. "This is a nice group of people. Glad to see you. Oh, here come the men. It's about time. Is that your husband? With the moustache?"

"Yes," said Gurlie.

"He's handsome!" said the little woman. "Look how straight he holds himself. So that's your husband. Hm! He looks smart."

"Yes, he's a smartie," said Gurlie.

"How you talk!" said Mrs. Lincoln. "But don't you think we have a fine-looking lot of men in our club? I think so. I think we should be proud of them. I am. Um, yes, he looks the part!"

The tall host, in his thick-lensed glasses, was taking Joe around introducing him to the ladies, one by one. "And this," he said coming to Gurlie, "is the wife of a little German-born son-of-a-gun that's . . ."

"Wha!" said Gurlie. "Shame on you! That's no way to introduce my husband."

"I beg your pardon, *gnädige frau*," apologized the mayor.

"Go on!" said Gurlie. "Let him meet the others." Then, as the various men were brought before her by the hostess and introduced, she bowed, half-closing her eyes, and mumbled the semblance of names she could not rightly hear. She noticed, nevertheless, the heavy, the slow, the smiling, the blue eyes, those with abundant wavy hair . . .

At that moment, a lithe man of medium height came impulsively up to her and introducing himself said, "You are Mrs. Stecher. My name is Fletcher."

"What?" said Gurlie. "I can't hear with all this noise."

"Fletcher," he said. "I've been having a great time talking to your husband in the other room. He's a wonderful fellow. We need men like that in this . . ." He leaned down and half-whispered to her, "They're a lot of old fogies. He's got brains."

"Who are you?" said Gurlie, still not having heard the name right.

"Fletcher, Fletcher. That's my wife over there"—pointing to the shy, mumbling woman Gurlie had just met.

"Where?" said Gurlie.

"There."

"So you have met my husband," she concluded. "That's good."

At this point, just as a stiff, graying man in an old-fashioned full-dress suit was about to approach her, the tall host, standing below his portrait, banged the table near him with a gavel and brought the meeting to order.

All corners of the room were filled; old Greer had found a big, comfortable chair and was settling down for the evening. Fletcher was not so comfortable on a rather fragile Louis XIV gilt replica. Some were high and some were low. Three of the ladies were together on a sofa; Gurlie was in about the center of the room, comfortably placed, and Joe several chairs to the rear, inconspicuously backed into a corner.

The business meeting was brief; after the reading of the

minutes, comically phrased, at which a few of the ladies tittered, there were the usual committee reports, the treasurer's report. "Any unfinished business?"

Plenty, thought Joe.

"Any new business?" There was not a sound. Someone cleared his throat, but nothing came of it. "Well," said the president, "isn't anybody going to say anything to give your presiding officer a reason for existing? If not, ladies and gentlemen, before turning the meeting over to the entertainment committee . . ."

"Oh Otto, sit down. He's always up to something, and he has such bad taste."

"I'd like, if I may,"—addressing his wife—"to say a word or two upon an important matter. Ladies and gentlemen, I must remind you that among our club members are many distinguished names, some of the oldest in the annals of our illustrious country—not that many of you have done anything to deserve it." He paused. "On the other hand, there are those, like me perhaps, just off the boat, you might say, who represent—an increment . . ." He paused again.

What the devil's he driving at? thought Gurlie. Several of the ladies shot quick glances at her distinctly Scandinavian features, the turned-up nose, the blond hair, the heavy legs . . .

"Ladies and gentlemen . . ."

"Oh, come off it, Otto," Charlie Greer, the assessor with the gold tooth, prodded him. "Say what you have to say and give us a rest."

"I wish he wouldn't talk like that," fiercely whispered his upright wife to her neighbor.

"Ladies and loafers, let me introduce to you a man who is making a name for himself in the business world and his charming wife, our guests of the evening, Mr. and Mrs. Joseph Stecher." Gurlie grimaced and nodded several times. Joe's expression didn't change.

"And now with your permission, I'll turn the meeting

over to the entertainment committee. Mrs. Arents. It's all yours, my dear."

His wife rose. She stood at the end of the room near the piano and, holding her chin high, facing resolutely forward, her thin figure erect, spoke in a low but distinct voice, diffidently announcing her program.

"We will have first," she said, "a song by a very lovely lady whom many of you know." Then almost as an after-thought, she added, "Mrs. Clopp."

There was a little stir among the ladies, as if they were about to applaud. Gurlie looked and saw the singer, a pretty brunette in a white dress, who had appeared from an adjacent room—and she recognized the soprano from the church choir quartet. She had never before heard her name. "She is one of our high-school teachers," went on Mrs. Arents, "and will sing as her first selection, 'In a Persian Garden.'" Putting on her pince-nez glasses, which she carried on a black ribbon about her neck, she went to the upright piano against the wall to her left, and began to arrange the music. She would accompany the singer.

As Mrs. Clopp arose to take her place before the piano the men sat up to have a better look at her, and the women, who were hardly of the type, on the average at least ten years older and far more plainly dressed, stared at her stonily.

"Isn't she pretty!"

"White satin! On a teacher's salary! I don't know how she does it."

"It's probably her wedding dress made over. She's a widow, you know."

"She's very popular, I hear, with some people."

The piano began the accompaniment. After a few bars the voice came in. It was not an operatic voice, but a credit-able performance by an attractive singer. The applause was instant and sincere, especially from the men. Mr. Fletcher continued to clap for a good twenty seconds after the others had ceased. "Bravo!" he said, and smiled. His wife looked at him sharply.

There was a little consultation at the piano, a glancing at the new sheet of music that had been placed before the accompanist, then Mrs. Clopp graciously announced that her next song would be the well-known lyric, "Because."

"Um," said Gurlie, and nodded. There was great applause which the singer acknowledged with a smile.

"*Because . . .*" she sang lustily. "*Because God made the world . . .*" Joe was embarrassed. He didn't like any show of emotion in public places, even in a performer. It made him sweat even to hear it; he was glad not to be sitting toward the front. But he applauded along with the rest and that was that. He wished he were at home reading the evening paper. Mrs. Clopp sat down in her white dress beside Mrs. Mills, who told her she sang beautifully, and what a gift it was to be able to express yourself like that. Wonderful! The general conversation broke out again and the singer was forgotten.

"And now!" said the host and president, coming to his feet once more, "after that delightful interlude, to return to the business of the evening. It was really beautiful! Without further talk (Charlie) I give you Professor Grimes, who will introduce himself. Where has he gone to?"

A tall, bald-headed man, grinning from ear to ear, stuck his head comically in at a hall door from which, at once, he emerged dragging an easel on which he proceeded to place a large book made up like that for wallpaper samples, which he displayed before his audience.

"Thank you, Mr. President. Ladies and gentlemen, let's get on an informal basis before we go any further with the evening's proceedings. In one word what I am going to do this evening is draw caricatures, of you, here, to show you how it's done, to amuse you during the next half-hour."

A burst of subdued talking, back and forth, greeted this announcement.

"Don't laugh yet! Maybe it'll be you. Caricature is an ancient art, it is social criticism of the most acute sort—Hogarth, Daumier, there are many great names. Well, who will volunteer to sit for our first portrait? Maybe we'd better start with one of you gentlemen. What do you say? You, sir," pointing out Mr. Greer. The ladies obviously were relieved.

By the time the professor had done the first two or three, with broad rapid strokes, the tension among the members and their guests was completely broken. They were having the time of their lives, especially as the professor knew his audience and was genial enough, witty enough, courteous enough to the ladies and had a good eye. He brought out many characteristics among his sitters that had never been noticed by any of them before.

"We should have more meetings like this—what was it? the *brachycephalic* head of Herr Arents and the long head, the *dolichocephalic*—was that right, Professor?"

"Yes, that's quite right. You're a good student."

"—the *dolichocephalic* head of Fletcher, here. No wonder you like Frenchies, Fletcher. You must be one yourself."

Refreshments were, as usual in this house, dominated by the delicate pastry which Mrs. Arents was so expert in preparing. The two servants, in tasteful gray uniforms and white caps, went about noiselessly. The men, gathered together again in the dining room, were smoking.

"Why no. Is your husband here? I haven't met him. I'd be charmed, I've heard so much from my husband about him."

"Wait a minute," said Gurlie. "I'll go get him." So in she burst upon the men, who immediately got to their feet.

"Why don't you come in with the ladies?" said Gurlie to them all.

"Why don't they come in here with us?" said Charlie Greer.

Gurlie laughed. "I want you," she said to her husband. "Why, you haven't met anybody. Come in," she took him by the arm. But he shook her loose. "Come with me."

"Na, na, na, leave me alone."

"Leave him alone!" said little Mr. Hammond, in his high treble voice.

"I want him to meet the singer," she lied.

"Bring her in here," said Charlie Greer. "I bet she'd like a cigarette. Sit down." And he made a place for Gurlie.

"I'll come in a minute," said Joe. But Gurlie just stood there, so he carefully stubbed out his butt, taking his time, while she stood in the doorway. "Come back when you're through," said Mr. Fletcher, "and tell us the rest of it."

"All right," said Joe.

"What's the matter with you?" said Gurlie to him on their way across the room. "The ladies want to make your acquaintance."

So he had to talk to Mrs. Lincoln, to Mrs. Coates, to Mrs. This and That. It developed that most of the couples in the room were childless. Gurlie was an exception with her three children.

Later some of the men came in and sat among the groups of women. Mr. Fletcher went to sit with the singer whom the other women had left quite alone to eat her ice cream and sip her coffee. "You have a lovely, sympathetic voice," which was precisely what she did not have. He was a gentleman.

"I sing because I like it," she said. "But I have no voice. I am new in Riverdale. This seems a very pleasant group. Have they been meeting for many years?"

"I'm new here myself. But I understand that they've been meeting for the past twenty years, at least."

She cast an appraising eye around. "Are these the best people in town?"

"Well, you couldn't exactly call them the sporting set."
She laughed.

When Gurlie and Joe arrived home, after midnight, they went immediately upstairs. She took off her dress, kicked off her shoes, undid her corset and threw herself flat on the bed. "Whoof! Am I glad to get out of that!"

"Well," said Joe as he began to loosen his tie and high collar, "I hope you're satisfied."

"What do you mean by that?" said Gurlie, sitting up at once on the side of the bed.

"You wanted it, now you've had it. I hope you're satisfied."

"Didn't you like them?" But Joe had gone into the bathroom. Gurlie finished undressing, put on her nightgown and stood, when her husband came back into the room braiding her hair in its two short pigtails for the night. She was laughing to herself. "What a lot of old fogies," she said. "So that's the cream of the town. But I like them. I bet you can have fun with them when you get to know them."

"I hope I never see them again," said Joe.

"You will," said his wife. "I bet you they'll elect us members."

"God forbid," said Joe.

"Agh," said his wife, "you haven't got anything to say about it. I had a good time. They seem like simple good people—but I don't think more than two or three of them have any money: two artists, the penniless brother of a wealthy publisher. The Millses, of course, have money, or she has. The Carvers . . ."

"Yes, he was a nice fellow," said Joe. "I like him."

19

"And now," said Gurlie, the day after their introduction at the Literary Club, "we've got to move to the other side of town."

"You mean if we don't they won't take us in?"

"How could we entertain such people here?"

"Then we don't move!" said Joe.

"Ha, ha!" said Gurlie. "I saw a house, a beautiful little house, the other day. It was copied after the California bungalow style. It has windows on all sides to let in the sun. It is . . ."

"To let in the ice and snow, you mean. Na, na, none of that. What do we want with a California bungalow in our cold weather? Where is it?"

"Right in the center of town, back of the woods."

"What woods?" But that appealed to Joe.

"And it's cheap," said Gurlie.

"What you call cheap."

"It has a hot-water heating system," said Gurlie.

"I'll bet the roof leaks. Is there a garden?" There Gurlie was stumped.

"No there's no garden. And no chickens. A well-to-do Catholic family owned it. They are anxious to sell. There's no other house in Riverdale like it. It's very distinguished.

Very chic. I think I will begin to take French lessons as soon as we move in there—very few people here speak German."

"Do they speak French?"

"No, but a French class would be good for us. You can speak a little French. We can't have a full-size piano—the front room is too small—but we can have a good three-quarter size one. Charlotte must have a place to entertain her musician friends."

"What do they need? Any dirty studio is all right for that gang."

"Crazy musicians!" As little Paul called them. He was almost five now, blond wavy hair, a sturdy young ruffian.

So at last, to Gurlie's immense satisfaction, they moved to the better part of town to a house, a little smaller than she wanted, but a charming house on a small lot, near the surviving patch of chestnuts and oaks and beeches almost in the exact center of town.

The whole interior was redone, wrought-iron chandeliers, quite an item, were installed, the walls were covered with grass cloth, the latest in kitchen fixtures and new bathroom equipment put in, and along the entire front beyond the broad porch were planted white rhododendrons, small bushes, as Joe desired. "They'll grow." The rest was Gurlie's.

And there they began to live in the years just before the First World War.

These were Gurlie's best years, the years of her most pronounced success, from 1907 to 1917, while little Paul was growing up. The house was the center of all the main musical excitement of the town. Lottie was the princess, a tall, gangling girl with big, dreamy eyes. She was passionately loved, from a distance, not without awe at her accomplishment, by a dozen young men of the environs.

Those were the years when young women wore their hair high in the front on a framework known as a "rat," voluminous skirts and frilled petticoats. The years when Flossie, definitely not musical, no rival for her glamorous sister, nevertheless had her own admirers. Her straight legs, narrow hips, and high forehead were not unobserved. Having graduated from the nearby private academy, she was commuting daily to a school on Fifth Avenue across from the Goelet mansion and the Russell Sages', and next door to Anna Gould.

Those were the years when you could have a maid for fifteen or sixteen dollars a month—a maid like Ellen Anderson, who couldn't speak a word of English when she came. Gurlie would pick them out at an agency in New York. Some starry-eyed little Eva of some unpronounceable Finnish name, whose clear complexion matched her unruffled and serenely happy disposition.

Not a syllable of English could Eva speak. Right from the boat. She had a brother in Jersey City and another sister, like herself in looks, out west on a sheep ranch. Two years after little Eva was with the Stechers, loved and instructed, the brother died, of pneumonia as far as the family could understand. She showed the family his photograph and they all cried—for days, until the sunlight of her eyes prevailed again.

Once, after a big party at the house, served by little Eva, to the amazed astonishment of the men who were baffled by her peasant beauty and sunny smiles—a party that did not end till three in the morning, dishes piled mountain high at all vantages—Gurlie sank exhausted into a chair. There was a noise in the kitchen.

"What's that?" she said.

"Eva washing the dishes."

"Not on your life! Not that. Go to bed," she told the little maid. "Go, I tell you." But Eva started to cry and would not leave until Joe himself, whom she respected and feared, had to come out and order her weeping from the room.

The house was small, and Joe liked small girls, not big, lumbering field hands. They made him uneasy waiting on the table. One, good as gold, and a wonderful worker, a Finn named Gerda, had acne. That especially annoyed Joe. "Get rid of her," he told his wife. But Gurlie liked her and kept her.

One Fourth of July, in the morning, the women of the house downstairs, dressing, or in the kitchen, Joe went up on the third floor to hang out the flag. A staff projected above the entrance to the front steps of the house from one of the windows of the maid's room.

Joe got the flag out of the closet in the hall, downstairs. It was a big one. Holding it in his arms, he couldn't see exactly where he was walking as he went up the stairs into the completely unfamiliar room where the maid slept to open the window. Gerda's bed had been drawn in front of it because of the hot nights. Holding the loosely folded flag, he pushed the iron bed aside with his knee to make room between it and the window for his maneuvers and squeezed into the space with the flag in his arms.

As he did so, he stepped right into a chamber pot full of urine which soaked his foot and the floor.

Joe was wild. A fastidious man, orderly, precise, disliking all slovenliness, he dropped the flag on the bed, turned and fairly bounced to the room below, looking for Gurlie. There he began in a furious voice, speaking in German, roaring at her to take that damned maid by the neck and throw her out the back door . . .

Gurlie, who didn't know what had hit her, began to laugh, still not knowing what had happened. Everyone was gathered about to listen. Then he told them—he had stepped into a pot full of piss. "Let me at that girl. Let me tell her." But Gurlie would have none of it.

"You're not going out there in that state to talk to anybody. There's nothing the matter with the girl. She probably didn't have time to empty it. You're making a fool of yourself," she said, as he raved on. "It's your own fool fault. You had no business in her room at this time of the morning . . ."

"The flag . . ." was all Joe could say.

"You could have waited with the flag. What's your hurry? No, I will not let you talk to her. Go upstairs and change your shoes and socks. I'll tend to the girl."

"I tell you if you don't fire her, I'll move out," Joe warned her. "The slut."

"Stop it!" said Gurlie. "Don't let your German temper go like that. You're supposed to be an intelligent man. The poor girl, she'll run out the back door if you go in there now. And what will the neighbors think of you then? They'll think you're killing her. Do you want her to sue you?"

That cooled him down a little. "Agh!" he said, looking down at his wet shoe.

"Come here. Put your foot up," said his wife to him. "Let me loosen the laces, since you're so dainty that you can't even touch them yourself." And Joe gladly put his small, graceful foot up on a piece of old newspaper Gurlie found for him, and his wife untied the laces. "Now go and change."

"These are my best."

"We'll have her clean them and put them in the sun. Go on. Off with you."

The girls crept into the dining room where Gurlie had been finishing her breakfast when the storm burst on her. "What happened to Papa?"

Gurlie was chuckling to herself by that time. "Shh! Don't let him hear you. He stepped into a chamber pot in Gerda's room when he went up to put out the flag."

"Well, that's not so bad," said Flossie.

"No, but it was full."

"No! Oh, my God! And it went all over him?"

"All over his foot and the floor. I haven't been up yet to look at it."

"I think I can smell it," said Flossie.

"Of course," said her sister. They all sat down on the chairs talking in whispers.

"Does she know it?"

"Not yet," said Gurlie. "She must be more careful. It'll wait . . . No, she better go up right away."

"The dirty pig," said Lottie.

"Never mind that," said Gurlie. "You girls stay here in case your father comes back. I'll go out and talk to her. Don't say anything to make him angry."

But by this time Joe had come downstairs, taken his hat, and, slamming the front door after him, had gone out. "Good riddance," said Gurlie. "He's ridiculous. The poor girl. Gerda," she said, "come here. I want to talk to you."

The poor girl, having heard the rumpus without understanding what was the trouble, came through the swinging door, her eyes wide, her acne-covered cheeks confronting them, stood there. "Yes, ma'am. What is it?"

Then Gurlie, the girls half-suppressing their amusement, told her what had occurred.

"Oh my God!" said the maid, and without waiting to be told, rushed into the kitchen, grabbed a mop and, mounting the stairs at a run, disappeared above. Her face had gone white.

"Come back here at once when you have cleaned up," said Gurlie.

"Aren't you going to fire her?" said Lottie.

It seems that in Finland, the disfigurement of acne, as here also, had been a great barrier to the girl's social success. She had heard in the old country that if, when going to bed, you washed your face in urine every night, you could get rid of it.

"Is it true?" she had asked Gurlie and her daughters. At any rate, she had decided to try it.

"No," said Lottie, disgusted. Flossie immediately thought of those among her friends whom it might help.

"I am very sorry," said the poor maid, red in the face now from her weeping. "I know Mr. Stecher never liked me. It is because of my face. I am not pretty. Everyone says the same. So I thought I would try . . . Shall I pack my things?"

"No," said Gurlie who didn't feel like looking for a new maid at that time. "You're staying right here."

"But what will Mr. Stecher say?"

"Do what I tell you. It was not your fault, but his, for being so clumsy."

The girl took Gurlie's hand and kissed it.

"But," said Gurlie, "remember, no more of that kind of treatment. You understand?"

"Yes, ma'am. Thank you, ma'am." And she looked at the two young ladies to see what they might think of her. "I am so sorry," she said to them. "I am not dirty. I did it to try to cure myself. You must pardon me."

"It doesn't seem to have done you much good," said Lottie.

"That's cruel," said her sister.

"Well, do you want somebody smelling of urine waiting on you at table? I don't."

"Shame on you," said her mother. "She's as clean as you are."

20

Ursula Hendricks was not Flossie's friend. She was sixteen, a year older than Floss, and united to the still older Lottie by their mutual interest in music. Lottie played, Ursula sang and sang, in a deep contralto voice for which she was receiving expensive lessons in New York, a voice that made everyone, especially Lottie, sit up startled when they heard her. But taste she had not. As you heard her you wondered at the songs she sang. It was all out of proportion.

But sometimes in the winter when the weather was bad, and Lottie not available, Ursula, an only daughter in the twelve-room house, would say to Floss, "Stay with me tonight. Please stay. Call up your parents and say you're staying."

And that's what Flossie would do. They'd study their homework together—Ursula wasn't very bright at her school work. Supper was always a special treat; simple-minded Mrs. Hendricks would see to that. Then they'd go to Ursula's room, a beautifully appointed chamber, twin beds of bird's-eye maple, closets with dozens of dresses, hats, boots by the score and . . .

The telephone would ring and Ursula would be gone, leaving Flossie wondering while she waited, for an hour sometimes, after which the sallow-faced, dark-haired girl would come back exhausted and fling herself on the bed. Only to leap up as another boy would call and she'd rush off again. Flossie would be doing her reading or her algebra or writing a theme, but how could this other girl do anything? After a while she'd get Flossie to help her. Furiously she skimmed the pages of her assigned work, never finishing, wearying of it before she started.

Flossie, who admired her—she was a crackerjack on the school basketball team—could easily see why she never got anywhere. Oh, but—it was such fun to spend the night there, Mr. Hendricks with his goatee and quiet ways, poor Mrs. Hendricks, who threw her hands up in despair and could never deny her daughter anything, looked at Flossie over the supper table and shook her head despairingly.

"Are you allowed to jump up from the table and talk to your mother that way?"

"No," said Flossie simply.

"I'm so glad to have Ursula have good companions. So many of the girls that come here are good for nothing. And my foolish daughter follows them all. You must come often. Why don't you stay here all during the week, you and your sister? And Lottie is so musical! I try my best . . ."

"Oh, Mother, the girl is young," her husband would say. "Don't be so pessimistic."

Ursula would be out in the corridor, laughing and whispering over the phone. "Oh, I suppose it's one of those useless friends of hers." Flossie, who didn't understand what was going on, would be embarrassed, look down at her plate and eat very quietly. Neither she nor her older sister were used to such carryings on. The big house, the obvious wealth, the good food and—what crazy things went on there that they would never dare to do at home—made them conscious of a whole world of which they had never been aware up to that time. And they liked it.

Mr. Hendricks had some special skill or knowledge of the silk business in Passaic from which he made his money, but

Floss never could understand how such a man could have married such a woman; why even a child could see she was— well, ignorant. She couldn't go out into society. She couldn't talk. All she could do was cook. Flossie wondered how such an intelligent man, and so attractive, could have married such a thing, such a *Hausfrau*.

Then, explaining nothing of the telephone conversation, the irresponsible Ursula, whom her mother adored, would flop into her chair, push her plate away and . . .

"Eat your supper, Ursa. You haven't tasted that lamb, it is very good. And your potatoes, eat at least a little."

"Oh, shut up!" said the daughter. "I'm sick of you."

Flossie flushed and looked down, expecting an outburst. But Mr. Hendricks would merely shake his head, while the poor woman looked at Flossie and seemed about to cry.

"You see, you see." And to her daughter: "What must your friend think of us—all?"

Ursula looked up then, contrite, and said, "I'm sorry."

"That's the least you could say to your mother, my dear, after such an outburst."

At that the daughter burst into tears and left the table. "Then why do you try to insult me?"

"I insult you?"

"I don't mean that. But—you don't understand anything. You. Leave me alone."

Flossie remained with the mother and father, who tried to build up a little conversation about this, that and the other: "Are you in Ursula's class in school?"

"I have some subjects with her," said Flossie.

"Well, that's fine. Your sister is the one we see more often, she's a remarkable pianist. I enjoy her playing. I like to hear good music and—I hope she will influence Ursula to like it, too. You can see what a spoiled child she is. I know she doesn't mean the sort of thing she did tonight. She's so impulsive."

"Yes," said Flossie.

"Some boy or other, I suppose. Do you like the boys, Miss Stecher?" Flossie wasn't used to being called Miss Stecher.

"Yes, I like the boys," she answered.

"But you don't think of them *all* the time, as poor Ursula does."

Flossie wondered why he said "poor Ursula."

"She'll come to no good, if she goes on this way," said her mother dolefully.

"Oh, yes she will. All girls go through that stage when they're sixteen, don't you think so, Florence? You don't mind if I call you Florence, do you?"

"No, I don't mind."

"What do you think?"

"I'm only fifteen," said Flossie.

Mr. Hendricks laughed a loud, gusty laugh. "Good for you. Seek the protection of your age. Good for you." Then Ursula returned.

That night in their room, she said, "Oh, my mother's so stupid, I could die. Couldn't she see I was all upset? Arthur—" Floss had heard of the boy—"just turned me down. I invited him to . . ."

She had the most beautiful lingerie. Flossie admired and envied her it, all silk. Naturally, her father's in the silk business.

"Mother is always accusing me of thinking of the boys. Well, what else is there to think of?"

"Aren't you going to graduate from school?"

"I want to get married. How else am I going to get away from this dump? I can't stand it."

"Aren't you going to be a singer?"

"Agh, I suppose so. But there's lots of time for that. I want a man . . ."

Flossie didn't know exactly what she meant.

"I want to be in love. I want someone to love me. I don't want to keep on going to school."

"But you have so much."

"They can have it all. I don't want any of it. I'd give it up in a minute if . . ." The telephone rang again, as late as it was. Ursula rushed for the stairs, bounded down them in leaps—as if she had been chasing a ball in a game—her hand on the bannister. "Hello," she said, all out of breath.

"Yes, darling . . . I knew, I knew . . ."

And then Flossie closed the bedroom door so as not to hear and wished she had stayed home. "She must be crazy," she thought.

After a good twenty minutes—her parents hadn't even come to their door—Ursula returned and sat on her bed, her hands hanging between her knees. Then she took up her pillow, hugged it and kissed it, lay down on her back with it in her arms. She seemed entirely to have forgotten her little guest.

"Oh, I knew it, I knew it . . . Darling," she turned to Flossie, "you must think I'm an awful girl. I'm not really, but I was so hurt.

"You know I'm going to have a big party the week before Christmas—you're going to be invited—haven't I invited you yet? Well, I'm going to. And just . . . The only reason I'm going to have it is—well, anyhow, it would have been spoiled for me—you don't mind my being so frank?"

"No," said Flossie, wishing she'd put out the light and let her sleep.

"Well, *he* told me he wasn't coming. I felt terrible. I was crushed. I knew he was only doing it because of some of the others. I knew he didn't mean it, he was only doing it so it would make me unhappy, but . . . He just called me up to say he'd be here. He loves me, he loves me!"

And so, taking off her dress, and her underwear, throwing them about the room, heedless of Flossie, who wasn't used to such sloppy habits, she walked naked and indifferent to the closet, pulled out her gown of sheer gauze, and leaped into bed, switching off the light and was asleep in a moment—after sighing deeply. Gone!

The night of the party was, just her luck, a beautiful one. There must have been forty or fifty boys and girls invited, anywhere from fifteen to eighteen years of age, from both Riverdale and Passaic—mostly from the private school Lottie and her sister, together with Ursula, attended. It was to be the biggest and best party of the whole Christmas season. Ursula of the dark, olive skin was the queen, glancing up with hardly a word to anyone as they came in and climbed the stairs to the girls' or boys' room on the second floor.

"Hey, you look swell tonight."

"Thank you."

"Who are all these bums you've invited? Who are they?" his back to the others newly arrived.

"What kind of people do you let in, in this second-rate town?" was the rejoinder.

"You boys go upstairs toward the back. You'll see the room. And the girls to the front, the end room."

"Hi, Ursa!"

"Hi, Roland." A blond, curly-headed youth, rather short, cherubic, with laughing eyes of blue walked in following the others. "So you came!"

"Of course. You don't suppose I was going to let those rotters get ahead of me? Do you? Where is everybody?" For the moment, though a few were standing in the middle of the room with their backs turned, the sound of shouts and laughter showed that most of the guests were still upstairs.

The boy looked quickly right and left, and then, going boldly up to the dark girl in the yellow dress, tried to kiss her on the mouth. She turned her head aside so that he missed, hitting her on the temple instead. He laughed and went toward the stairs as she clutched his sleeve—but he broke away and left her.

Others were coming. She wondered if they had seen. First a tall girl—the door had been closed and there was a curtain across the glass. "How are you, darling?" Behind the newcomer was a lad even taller than his sister, who had preceded him, who simpered slightly and, without unbending, formally shook his hostess by the hand. His hair was brushed smoothly back from a high forehead. "How are you?" he said. Ursula seemed not to hear him. He shrugged his shoulders and slowly followed the others upstairs.

They were coming down now, meeting the late-comers going up. "Darling! What a pretty dress!" They crowded on the stairs, pink, green, blue and white—organdies and chiffons with ruffles to hide their budding breasts, their thighs encased in petticoats, only the bare arms permitted to reveal the charms otherwise unacknowledged.

The sexes, at this age, were only beginning to be differentiated, they could be rough with each other, asked and gave no quarter. One of the Riverdale gang grabbed a flower a lively little girl was holding in her hand.

"Give me that back!" She ran after him and grabbed the tail of his coat as he attempted to duck around a corner and almost pulled it off his shoulders. They had jostled the tall girl who thereupon, seeing what was going on, grabbed the flower out of the boy's hand and gave it to her sister—who tried to smooth it out, then seeing it had been broken in the struggle, she threw it violently into the boy's face. "You clown! Just what I'd expect from a person like you," and she turned her back on him.

"Won't you all sit down at the tables—sit anywhere, but pick yourselves partners—four to a table."

"May I sit at your table?" said the tall boy with the high forehead.

"I suppose so," said his hostess.

"Or would you rather have someone else?"

"Oh, no. We're going to play five hundred."

"Oh, Ursa, I thought you were going to sing."

"Later." There had been a group about the piano thumbing through a foot-high pile of popular songs. "Gee! What a collection! You've got everything."

From that time on, the overheated house rocked with the strident voices of the card players, winning and losing. Each table became a center of youthful banter—the girls in general siding against the boys. "I don't see what she sees in him."

"His people have money."

"So have her people. If she ever marries him, she'll regret it."

"You're just jealous."

"On account of him? Poo. That runt with his tight little blond curls, he's not even a good athlete, and he certainly isn't bright. Oh, I suppose his father will take him into his office."

"I understand he doesn't want to go in with his father."

"He doesn't even want to go to college. All he wants to do is marry a rich girl and spend her money for her."

"Where have they gone?"

"I don't see either of them."

"I'll bet you . . ."

"She hasn't any shame."

"Oh, there they are!"

"He's no good."

"No worse than she is herself. They're in love! Love."

"They're just kids, leave them alone. But I hate to see her get mixed up with a boy like that. My brother doesn't like him."

The talk and the clatter, alternating with periods of almost complete silence when the hands were being played, had been going on for the better part of an hour when suddenly there occurred a sound toward the back of the house, as if some heavy object had fallen. Everybody heard it, and turned to look as Ursula came flying through the kitchen door, completely absorbed in what she was doing, turned and held it closed.

As she realized what a noise she had made and that

everyone was looking at her, she turned away laughing and went to the piano as the blond boy, the resistance of the door gone, burst into the room and almost fell flat. His face was flushed, his tie awry. Seeing all eyes on him, he cast a quick glance at Ursula and, taking a comb from his breast pocket, began to smooth back his hair.

"Battle!" yelled someone.

"I hope she gave it to you good," shouted another of the boys.

Ursula had begun to sing "Egypt," her favorite song of the moment, as the play at the tables abruptly ended and some of the boys and girls gathered around the singer.

"What happened?" they asked each other.

"I didn't even see them go out. That fresh guy. She asked for it, I suppose."

"But where was her mother?"

"Where do you suppose she was? In the kitchen."

"What was he trying to do to you, Ursa? What were you up to, kid?"

"She pushed me."

"I certainly did," said the girl, breaking off her singing. "Who wins the prize? Will you gather the cards, Wilbur?"

The tall boy with the high forehead started at the sound of his name, but dutifully began to gather the cards, summed them up and announced the winner of the expensive gold cuff links and locket, in each case, boy and girl. "Oh, Ursa, they're lovely. Thanks."

"What shall we do now? Will you boys clear the tables away? Just fold them and push them out in the hall."

"Sing for us, Ursula."

"I will, if you'll join in the choruses." So she began to pull out of the pile of music anything they asked for. The only one they knew well was "In the Shade of the Old Apple Tree," which, off-key, the boys roared after her.

"Come on, sing it again."

Those who didn't sing continued to discuss the incident

just passed: "She's an awful fool. It's all right making out it was something he did, but you bet she was the one started it. All she is interested in is a man—but when she gets into trouble . . . You'll see. She has no brains."

"Did you see his face?"

"Some day she'll regret it."

"I like her. Why must we always put a bad interpretation on what goes on?"

"Because he's no good and she knows it. Would you want to go out with him? You know what they say about him? I understand he drinks a lot. He flunked out of high school. He's positively stupid."

"What's that I hear?" said Fred Hoyt, coming up. "You bunch of cats."

"I think so too," said Lottie. "Leave them alone, they were only having a little fun in the back corridor . . ."

"You've got it down pat, I see."

"No, I haven't," said Lottie.

"Well then how come you know so much about it? Come on, Lottie, let's go back there and see what it's like. Wanna?"

"Fresh. Not with you. That's sure."

"Oh you wouldn't."

"Let's play Wink," someone called out.

"Naw, not that sissy game."

"Well, I'm tired of sitting down. And I'm tired of singing. Get a platter. Let's play Spin the Platter. What say?"

So a heavy metal platter was procured. "Be careful of it," Mrs. Hendricks cautioned the boys. "I don't want it dented."

"No, ma'am, you can count on us. Here y'are," said the perpetual clown, coming into the room again, so pushing back the chairs, "Here y'are, ladies and gentlemen," and he threw the platter up to the ceiling and caught it. So they began to spin the platter, calling out a name as they began, a girl rushing out to pick up the spinning disc before it should lose its impetus and fall inert.

"What'll the forfeit be if you miss?"

"You've got to kiss the one who called your name."

"Oh, don't let's begin that!"

"Yes," insisted Fred Hoyt. "If you don't want to play, you can sit down on the sidelines. Come on, let's go. I'll spin it first. Ursula," said he, and gave the platter a vigorous spin. Ursa, although seeming indifferent enough, darted out like a flash and had the dish in her hands before anyone could catch his breath.

"Wilbur!" she called out and set the platter in motion.

The tall boy got up quietly and with apparent indifference caught the plate still spinning. He stood there glancing around, then leaning far over gave the plate a spin and called, "Florence."

Flossie, who had been a keen observer of what the older girls and boys were doing, was so startled that she almost missed the spin. She picked one of the more obscure boys, more her own age, for her turn. And then they all began to cheat— not to give it much of a spin, hoping to get someone to miss.

"Oh, that isn't fair!" Then some of them tripped and fell over in a wild attempt to retrieve the falling disc. Someone kicked it back into the arena; when someone else tried to catch it, it flew out of his hands. Someone else batted it, when— crash! the big chandelier in the middle of the room was hit and a shower of glass rained down on the heads of the players.

"Now look what you've done," said one of the girls. Mrs. Hendricks, hearing the crash, hastened into the room, poor soul. Everyone was sorry. The clown had gone to the kitchen to return with an apron around his waist, a broom and a dust pan in his hands. There was glass everywhere.

"There's a piece, Ursa," said the poor woman. "There's another piece!" she said again and again, all absorbed. "Ursa, there's a piece. Look, Ursa, there's another piece." But Ursa wasn't listening. She had detected a movement at the door as, taking advantage of the excitement, Roland had slipped out the front door and gone home.

21

"Who's that?" said Gurlie.

Flossie looked out, standing well back in the room so as not to be seen. "I don't know. An older woman. All in black. She looks like a caller."

Gurlie, blinking her eyes, came to the window just as the woman was mounting the front steps. "Oh, that's Mrs. Moore. I'd given her up entirely. I wonder what she wants. And we haven't a bit of tea in the house. One of you will have to run down and get me some."

At that moment the front door bell rang. Eva, the maid, came out of the kitchen, but Mrs. Stecher waved her back. "I'll go." Flossie disappeared upstairs.

"Why my dear, I couldn't find you. Where have you hidden yourself?"

"If it isn't my old friend, Mrs. Moore. Come in. I'm glad to see you." And Gurlie put one arm about the woman's shoulders and gave her an affectionate hug. "What are you doing here?"

"Oh, I thought I just had to come north to see my old friends in Riverdale. My! Haven't we got a fine house! How long have you been living here?"

"About a year. Take off your things. You must be tired. How is your son?"

"Edward's away at college, and I'm so lonesome without him. I can't tell you. Oh, I love your house."

"Don't you want to take off your wraps?"

"Oh, let me rest a moment first. Thank you. I've walked all over this blessed town. I'm so tired."

"Flossie!" called out her mother.

"Yes, Mother. I'm dressing."

"Well, as soon as you're through, come here a moment."

"All right."

"I'm so anxious to see her. She has always been one of my favorites. The girls nowadays! I wouldn't give you a penny for them. But your two daughters still have some respect for their elders. It's the upbringing that counts. There are so few people fit to have children nowadays. It's wonderful to sit down."

This was the first time that Mrs. Moore, Mrs. Edward Moore of Shady Springs, Maryland, had seen Gurlie since Gurlie's return from Europe, and Mrs. Moore was just a little worried about what had happened relative to her friends the Emorys.

"Oh, I *am* so glad to see you. Please tell me *all* about your trip. What an opportunity! That's one of the disadvantages of being so poor. It's terrible—terrible, my dear. You are so lucky. I haven't heard a word of the Emorys since you've been back. I wonder what became of them?"

"That's what . . ." began Gurlie.

"I saw them several times while you were away, keeping track of them for you." She laughed. "They were so happy to be in your house taking care of your sweet husband. To tell you the truth, you just about saved their lives. They were stony broke. And your husband, *your* husband! He was an angel. A veritable angel. I don't know what they would have done without him. Did they leave everything all right? Clean and . . ."

"Clean," said Gurlie.

"Because, you know, it was I who recommended them to

you. They come from the nicest people, the very best people in Maryland." Another laugh. "For years they had their place right near ours, oh for a hundred years or more. What am I talking about? Two hundred years. On Smith Creek. When you come down to visit me this fall—you know you promised! —I'll take you all over that part of the country. It's a beautiful state, Maryland, especially in the fall of the year. An aristocratic region, with beautifully rolling hills and green valleys. I do want you to see it. Because you know that I'm married again."

"You?"

"Yes, I'm married again. What could I do? George didn't leave me anything. He went through everything before he died, his last illness and all that. Your husband was so good to him. He always said, 'That man Stecher is one of the few instinctive gentlemen in this town.' He did, that's just what he always said. But you haven't told me a thing about your trip. I'm afraid I talk too much." Another laugh. "Oh, there's your sweet young daughter. Darling! How she's grown! Why, she's almost a woman. Look at her, look at her legs. Come here, darling. You've become a very attractive girl, you know. She really has."

"Just a skinny thing like her sister."

"Oh you shouldn't talk like that about your own children. I wish I had a daughter. That's the way it goes with the old families. They're all dying out. Soon there won't be a living one of us. Oh I want you to see the South before it is finally gone. Why don't you bring your daughter with you when you come to see me in the fall? She'll have a wonderful time."

"She'll be at school."

"Oh, but for a week! Do you ride?"

"No," said Flossie.

"We have friends who have a stable. It would be so nice at that time of year, while your mother and I are gossiping, visiting the Grange and meeting my friends, for the young

people—there are a few nice boys left—to be riding out around
the country. You'll enjoy them and they'll enjoy you. They'll
love entertaining a Yankee." Again the laugh. "They're so
gallant. But you mustn't expect them to marry you."

"Mother," broke in Floss. "I'm going downtown. Is there
anything else you want?"

"Your mother and I . . ."

"No. And come right back."

"Oh, isn't she sweet. How I talk! Did you really have a
good trip?"

"Who did you marry?" said Gurlie.

"Oh an old man, an old family friend—William Garvan.
But he needs me. And to tell you the truth, he offered me his
home. A widower—we've been friends all our lives. Still living
in the old house. A lovely old place, a little out of repair, but
he has money enough and we can have a life economically to-
gether—in our old age. What can a woman do? I'm very
lucky. You will come and visit us, won't you?

"Of course, people here don't have the same feeling that
we have about our forebears, ancestry is everything to us. You
hear a lot about the first families of Virginia, the FFV's, as
they call them, but Maryland! Well, there's the Carters, and
the—well, I won't bore you, there are only a few of the real
bluebloods left. The Moores are among them."

Gurlie was becoming restive.

"The recent immigrants are hardly of the same breed.
We were all English and Scotch of the purest blood. The
aristocratic tradition. And we've kept to ourselves. It isn't
good, I suppose. Of course the Nordics are our own blood."

"They're broke, most of them," said Gurlie laughing, as
in her mind she remembered one evening, at the Greers, a
group of them were being bored by this same Mrs. Moore and
her boastings about her ancestry, her talk of "recent emi-
grés," the riff-raff of Europe, the servant-girl type, when
Charlie had interrupted her.

"Listen, Margaret," he had said. (She was an old friend

of his wife's.) "I wouldn't boast about my ancestry if I were you. My people came over on the *Mayflower* the same as yours. A lot of them had good blood in their veins, good English blood. But they were mostly younger sons the family wanted to get rid of. That's why they sent them over here. Or indentured servants. Or thieves or adventurers, petty tradesmen at the best. Just the ordinary run of the farm. They didn't have an extra pair of britches to their names, and came here hoping to make a fortune. That's what your famous first families were, land hogs. They got a little bit ahead of their neighbors and that's all there was to it."

"Come on, let me show you the house," said Gurlie. "And then we'll have tea."

"But you'll promise to come stay with me?" said Mrs. Moore at the end of the afternoon. "I'd so enjoy it."

"I'd be very glad to," said Gurlie.

"When?"

"This fall. In October—if my husband will let me go. I've always wanted to see the South—where the aristocracy of America lives, there and in New England, of course."

"Oh you mustn't expect too much. We're poor. Very few of us boast fine houses today. Two of my cousins, the sweetest old ladies you'd ever want to see, last summer, do you know what they did? They were starving. Literally, they didn't have enough to eat."

"What did they do?" said Gurlie.

"It's terrible. They started a little business. They're wonderful cooks—like all Southerners. They had a family recipe for pralines . . ."

"Pralines, what's that?" said Gurlie.

"Oh a kind of candy, made with pecans. They made pounds of it. They're tall, dignified old ladies but they had to do something. They couldn't ask for charity. So they put up two orange crates with a board between them, right at the side of the road, and took turns selling what they had made. Right at the edge of the road. It was a very brave thing to do.

You know the automobiles we have nowadays? They did a good business selling pralines to the automobilists that passed."

"I should think so. Good for them."

"Well, we're not all so badly off. You'll come. I'll write you. You were *so* good to my friends, I'd like to show you how we live."

And in October, when persimmons were beginning to ripen, Gurlie arrived in the little market center of Shady Springs. "Why it looks just about the same as around New Jersey when you get back from the main roads," she said. The trees were in full process of shedding their leaves. Mrs. Moore's son, Edward, had driven their old car to the station. Gurlie got in and they headed over the rolling country, past fenced-in fields where colts and mares were grazing.

"This is wonderful," said Gurlie. "I agree with you, it's a very beautiful country. It makes me think of Norway when I was a child, on one of the biggest farms in southern Norway. You can breathe in the country. I love it."

"Oh, I'm so glad," said her hostess, doubtfully.

The farm was about a mile and a half out of town, on a macadam road, the last quarter of the way on a dirt road, with high banks on either side. Gurlie saw two or three poor farmhouses setting back in the fall foliage among the tumble-down barns and other small buildings. Then they came to a board fence that had been painted white many years before and a gate that was jammed open leading to a curving carriageway among yellow pines and walnut trees from which the leaves had already fallen.

"And here we are!" said her hostess.

There was no lawn, just ragged grass about a house standing among the half-bare trees—a medium-size house, to which a wing had been added at one time in the form of an L. It badly needed a coat of paint. A wide porch raised about a foot up from the ground completed the picture.

It looked neglected, surrounded by the old trees. But it was inviting and Gurlie liked it—she could see the barnyard in the rear, there was a well house—and what undoubtedly used to be an orchard, now full of dead wood.

When they entered the house it smelled as all old houses smell, of rotting wood and a wood fire. That was the South of it, thought Gurlie.

When Mr. Garvan came heavily forward to greet the newcomer, Gurlie saw a big man, in a comfortable, loose-fitting suit, his hair white, his manner gracious and reserved. He offered Gurlie a big, soft hand, and with a distinct Southern accent said, "I'm glad to welcome you. Come in and make yourself at home."

Everything in the place was old, and that night when Gurlie went to bed, that was old too, a big walnut bedstead with a high ornamental back board. The mattress sagged in the middle. Gurlie threw out two of the pillows and tried to sleep. There was no heat in the room.

She could not sleep. Off somewhere across the valley she could hear a baying of hounds. Yap, yap, yap, yap. One dog was leading the others, loud and clear. Then a syncopated chorus, a counterpoint of four voices, followed by an interval of silence. Once she thought she heard a man's voice commanding the dogs.

Gurlie got up, went to the long window and looked away to the west into the darkness, down a hill over the tops of some trees—at least a mile off, it seemed, to where a light mist lay close to the ground. The barking of the dogs settled down now to a slower pace, a steady yap, yap, yap of the leader with only occasional salvos from the others and—yes, she saw a light, probably a lantern, faintly, now and then moving in the trees. The barking continued—growing fainter as she stood there looking off into the night. There was a moon—must be —shining somewhere. She couldn't see it. The distance seemed infinite and unpopulated. She grew cold in her flimsy nightgown, standing there in her bare feet, so that she went back to bed. She could still hear the hounds baying as finally she drifted off into a troubled sleep.

At breakfast the next morning they had fat back and griddle cakes. They were waited on by a young barefooted colored girl, daughter of one of the old servants, Mrs. Garvan said, who used to be attached to the house.

The quaint silverware intrigued Gurlie, teaspoons worn almost to a knife's edge, the curve of the neck strongly marked. She took one of them up and examined it. "You have beautiful things," she said to her hostess. The old man had eaten earlier and gone out.

"Yes, and you should see what there is in the closets upstairs!"

"I should think some antique dealer would give you a fortune—for the old painting alone."

"He won't hear of it. No more will I."

They went for a little stroll about the premises after breakfast and Gurlie had an opportunity to taste the persimmons of which she had heard. "What was all that racket I heard last night?"

"I didn't hear anything," said her hostess.

"The dogs barking." She had dreamed of runaway slaves hiding in the swamp and bloodhounds.

"Oh, I suppose it was some of the young bloods from hereabouts on a coon hunt with their dogs."

"A coon hunt?"

"Yes, there's lots of raccoons around here. The dogs tree them and then the men chop the tree down and the dogs finish them." Some time before she fell asleep Gurlie had thought she heard a chopping, axes striking regularly into the wood.

"Today we'll give you a rest because tomorrow when the Grange meets you're to be the guest of honor. I hope you brought that paper you have written, I heard it was good. All about Norway."

"What paper? I didn't bring any paper."

224

"My dear woman! Why I told you they wanted to hear . . ."

"But you didn't tell me. That's almost a year ago. I don't even have it any more."

"But darling, I told you."

"That doesn't make any difference," said Gurlie, laughing. "I can remember everything that's in it. I'll talk to them."

"A few of my close friends will be in to tea this afternoon and then you can see what they're like. Good. I'm glad you're going to talk. They'd be so disappointed otherwise. They've been waiting for it ever since I told them at the last meeting."

"Ladies and fellow Grangers," Mrs. Moore, that is, Mrs. Garvan, began, "I'm glad to see so many of you here, in our little old meeting place here today, because I've got a treat for you."

"Yes, naked, stark naked," Mrs. Pinkney was finishing her story to her cousin, Mrs. Mouton, at the back of the room. "Just a young girl. Raleigh, yes. Her father is a surgeon there. I don't know how the young man happened to be in the house. I think his father and the doctor had gone to school together . . ."

"And so without ado, I'll ask Mrs. Joseph Stecher, my dearest friend from Riverdale, in the Garden State of New Jersey, to tell something of those famous people—the Vikings, of whom she is a proud daughter. Oh and by the way . . ."

". . . a Northerner, from Massachusetts. Oh, a boy of about eighteen. A nice enough person of a good family. She walked right into his room, during the night, sometime, naked as the palm of your hand, and got into the bed with him. What are we coming to?"

Gurlie was a little confused. She could talk, when she got started. But with all those Southern eyes looking her over—she could feel them, almost hear them talking about her, taking her apart. And all of a sudden her blood began to boil. She had no reason to resent these women, who had seemed inoffensive enough, the little she had seen of them. But their talk of cousin this and cousin that, their strange intonations, the pretension which was not really pretension . . .

". . . for the whole week he was there." "But didn't she . . . ?" "Of course. That's how I came to hear of it. She didn't even ask him to marry her. She had to go to her father. Oh, she's all right now. But did you ever *hear* of anything to beat it? And he, of course, got off scot free."

Gurlie thought to herself, Now I have my chance and I'm going to tell them the truth. Who do they think they are? There had been a little polite applause when she stood up—and then she opened her mouth, and out came the foreign accent—they were waiting for that.

There was an audible movement throughout the room as she began:

"I am not prepared to speak. I came to this wonderful country only twenty-five years ago—after my father lost his business. I was born on a big farm, south of Oslo. There were dozens of servants and farmers. We were well-to-do. Our family was one of the oldest in Norway. I can trace my ancestry five hundred years to the Vikings, to the time of Hamlet." There it was. She had let the cat out of the bag.

". . . Raleigh, or perhaps it was Roanoke. No, he didn't tell me, didn't tell my son Sherwin the name of the doctor. Believe him? Why it was from the lips of my own son. He's such a sweet boy. He tells me everything, to his little old mother, just the same as when he was a child—his roommate at Harvard. Can you believe it? Harvard! This summer, yes. Every word of it—we're so close. He was puzzled. Wanted to know what I thought, so he told me."

"You must not think," Gurlie was saying, "that because they cannot talk English that they are ignorant—or stupid. They come from very good families. They are poor, that is true, as I was when I came here, but that did not mean that I was a servant-girl. I had to work. I had to do all kinds of things that I was not used to, to earn my living. But I was proud, I can tell you. I had a good education and I could work, too. And I did work. I did all kinds of things.

"Your ancestors were immigrants, too, and many of them were poor. They had to work. Just like today, some of them were good for nothings. Some of them were even of the criminal class, and some of the worst sometimes seemed to have the best luck. Many of our financiers who are successful in business today came from the lowest classes.

"But that is the kind who when they get up in the world want to put everyone else down. Ha ha! That is the kind that want to marry their daughters into the English aristocracy. Some Irish immigrant who made a lot of money in the beef business becomes my Lady This or my Lady That.

"You will see! My Eva Anderson, who came to me three years ago, is a fine, healthy girl. Now she can speak English. She got married to a farmer in Minnesota, pretty soon her children will be the leading citizens, maybe doctors and lawyers and then you'll see. They have brains.

"But that is what America is for. That is why we come here, because there is liberty for all. We should recognize that. We cannot afford to be so proud. Because we all come from the same place and we have the same blood. The English and the Norwegians are from the same blood. The Norwegians are a pure race. When the first settlers from England came over here, the Norwegians were already a great people—and long before this country was ever discovered. So when we come here today, we bring something to this country that you should be glad to get. We don't have to bow down to anybody."

22

Flossie looked, made her choice and that was the end of it. She didn't expect to get her wish, she seldom did; her sister was the prima donna with a dozen young blades (and some older ones) flocking about her, not she. The one she had seen, in a flash, was among them. He paid no attention to her. And that was her secret and she kept it. Whether it was a good thing or not never occurred to her. Meanwhile, she was popular with a slightly younger set, and her days were anything but dull.

There were three Englishmen, born in England, who had been living in Riverdale for many years and were now middle-aged. They were all interested in the stage. It was through Lottie, the pianist, that they came into the Stecher orbit. Slightly outside the accepted circle of the local club world, perhaps from their own wishes as English, holding themselves apart, they were slightly suspect on moral grounds among their fellow townspeople.

Most prominent was S. T. Holmes, an accomplished musician, who unhappily had only recently lost the apple of his eye, a boy of sixteen who on a two-week camping trip with friends his own age had contracted appendicitis, kept his belly-ache secret, and, too late, had been operated on and died. The boy was a promising pianist in whom all the dreams of the old man's youth seemed about to flower.

He was crushed. All that was left was music, music itself. He was an agnostic, he'd quit all church affiliations, and many thought he had received only his just due in the loss of the child. The Episcopal minister refused to say the conventional service over the boy's body. Holmes was bitterly resentful. Some sort of compromise was effected, but the man was only confirmed in his unfavorable opinion of religious practices in general. From that time out he cut loose from all conventional behavior (so the town felt) and plunged instead into the organization of a group of the younger people of Riverdale who wanted to produce Gilbert and Sullivan's operas as a first venture. Lottie associated herself with the group as one of the pianists. There was no orchestra available.

The second of the three Englishmen was Bishop—not at all musical—also rather an outsider in the town, both from his absence from it often on long business trips to Europe and South America, but also from the fact that his wife, a foreigner, was unwilling or unable to find any close friends about her; rather she kept a secret and soul-consuming longing for Paris! Paris! where part of her education as a girl had been gained. She was not antagonistic to the town but felt ill at ease in it and consequently was virtually unknown in it. Bishop had two sons, both among Lottie's admirers.

The third Englishman was a brilliant, if submerged, actor. Everyone had loved him for a long time when he appeared in little skits at the Royal Arcanum benefit performances. Now at last, as Sir Joseph Porter, K.C.B., in *Pinafore*, he was perfectly cast for the first time, and his small but accurately tuned voice and cultured British accent made him a great favorite. He looked and acted the part. Without Percy Sykes there could have been no show.

Thus they had an impresario in Holmes, an accomplished stage manager in Bishop, and an actor par excellence in Sykes, about whom the young people of the town clustered with tremendous enthusiasm, giving themselves, their time and their not inconsiderable talents without stint.

The group, during the months of rehearsal, by ones or twos, was often seen at the Stechers'.

But Lottie's admirers were not limited to these. And as the years went by and *Pinafore* had been sung and applauded, and the company, augmented and better trained, had gone on to the *Mikado* and become well known one to the other, they finally began rehearsing *The Pirates of Penzance*.

Their world had by this time considerably ripened. Holmes was the ageing hero. The movies had begun to appear at the small local theater; "Our Own," as the group was called, was doomed. And Holmes, abetted by those who knew and admired him, began to look toward Hollywood.

The First World War had not even entered the minds of the people of Riverdale. Scandal was still the best topic of conversation, and there had been time during the past three years of the opera company for it to accumulate. Bishop and Sykes were exempt. But Holmes, with his passion for the human voice and his emotional dependence upon his singers, felt strange stirrings. The proximity of the young actors to each other, the consequent breakdown of inhibitions, the late hours, the borrowed atmosphere in this little suburb of the dreams of the great capitals of the world, induced in them ideas of love. Rumors spread.

Love and music! And if Lottie didn't combine them in her own person, as did old Holmes in his enthusiasms, desperately, having lost their prime objective in his darling son, who else could know them? She was just the age.

Everyone loved the dark Lottie. And she was gracious to all, indefatigable—you couldn't tire her out or abash her. She seemed to rise superior to all those about her, not because she was beautiful—she was too tall, and a little stooped, she was not voluptuous in figure—but she had a dreamy mystery about her that, while it frightened some, put her on a pedestal for others.

She was not frivolous, a man felt that at the first approach; she was not facile, even a little awkward, but you couldn't take liberties with her. She seemed older than other girls of her age. But to be near her made you breathe a little faster; to want not to touch her—that you couldn't do!—but to lose yourself in her completely. You hardly knew what you wanted. And while you were with her, you felt that you were the one who would do, that perhaps you were the chosen one. Now! But somehow you held back.

She made you feel inferior, less than the dust. Which one of the dozen men who surrounded her would get her? She was so kind to all. A man named Russel, an ex-football star, strong as an ox, a natural athlete, but a good deal of a boor, who was really not of the fascinated group about her, once met her on the way to the railroad station and asked her if she wouldn't prefer to drive with him to the city. He had an open sports car, a novelty in those days.

The old plank road across the meadows was not meant for automobiles. It was cobbled and narrow with car tracks down one side. Russel thought he'd give the tall girl a thrill. And he did. He opened the throttle and at one point was making seventy miles an hour, which in those days was something. It was breathtaking, frightening. Lottie hung on to her big hat with one hand and onto the side of the seat with the other, expecting to land in the ditch at any moment. She stared fixedly ahead as they passed a horse-drawn cart ahead of them as if it were backing up. The narrow river bridge was ahead. As they rushed upon it Russel gradually slowed down to a more reasonable speed.

Then he turned and grinned at Lottie, saying, "How do you like it?"

"Is that as fast as you can go?" she replied.

That was how she took men down. Before her, the older men, her willing slaves, merely looked and asked her to play. And she was always willing. You couldn't tell what were her thoughts.

What was it? Once she had gone canoeing with one of the Bishop boys on the upper Hackensack. The out tide was strong, and they had to paddle hard to get through a raceway under the bridge at Milford. Overhead on the little bridge was a young colored man watching them. It was slow going against the rocketing tide. Leaning on the rail, at ease, he was right above them as they started creeping through, the expression on his face one of interested detachment, waiting to see if they'd make it. Lottie looked up and winked at him.

That was the kind of girl she was. What did she want?

At the piano she was queen. Perhaps the very feeling of frustration she induced in her suitors came from that. She was really, at that time, such an accomplished pianist and there was such a mystery about her as she played her Schumann, her Debussy, her Chopin, that they were overawed. They simply did not dare.

Sometimes of an evening, in the new house (there was a sitting room upstairs from which Flossie listened) Lottie, the wonderful Lottie, would be entertaining a group of her friends, a man or two, some singer from the opera company, and someone would ask her to play. Then the room would quiet down.

"I'll play the '*Liebestraum*.'" And she would begin.

The kaleidoscopic dreams that possessed the minds, as well as bodies, to the very toe tips, of those young men, and perhaps the girls as well at such times, left them limp at the end. And after a decent pause, Henry Baker, the baritone of the company, who was pathologically self-belittling, would say, "Well, there's nothing to do after that, I suppose, but to go out and shoot myself."

"Why?" Lottie would say, turning to face the room on her piano stool. "Don't be ridiculous. Here, I'll play something else to liven you up." And she'd go into a Chopin polonaise because she could play anything from Bach to Grieg with complete ease, though few wanted her favorite, Bach.

But they knew that Bach was her music and that she played it when she was alone. That increased the legend of her profundity, the reputation for the catholicity of her tastes— and made her seem more unattainable than ever. The other

232

girls also adored her, especially Leona, of the beautiful so-
prano voice, who was her nearest friend. They did not invite
the usual chit-chat of ordinary conversation when she was
present.

Yet there's always a clown ready to step in where the
serious man hangs back—but Lottie could handle him, too.
He never could get to the point. He'd come all alone some-
times and, with his barber-shop tenor, try ineffectually to sing
to her accompaniment. She would play the willing martyr.

"I want to try these songs over, Lottie. Have you ever
heard them? They're beautiful. 'The Indian Love Lyrics.' "

Oh my God, she would say to herself! Have I ever heard
of them! As a matter of fact for a year or more, every young
man with or without a voice who was eligible to call on her
at one time or another had asked her to accompany him as he
bleated those vulgarly passionate words. She'd pound away,
almost in her sleep while he'd sing: *Pale hands I loved"* . . .

There was an insistent violinist, somewhat older than the
local boys, and with a strong Scandinavian accent, who was
wild to marry Lottie and made no bones about the proposal,
coming again and again to the point. He even pleaded with
Gurlie and, to a lesser extent, with Joe to join him in per-
suading the girl to accept him.

"I love her," he said, "and I will make a good home for
her. It is so reasonable. I with my violin and she with her
piano. We can have such happy and profitable times together.
We can have the same musical friends. It will be an ideal
marriage."

"He wants an accompanist, that's all," Lottie would say.
"Let him hire one. No, I know his kind. A wife would be
cheaper." In spite of her European parentage, Lottie did not
want that. She was an American; she could see through such a
man's designs.

"What do these young men that want to sing their senti-
mental songs to you know about true music? What do they
know? What do Americans know?" the violinist would ask.

"They know more than you think," Lottie would defend them. "Some of them have fine voices, Henry Baker, for instance."

"He sings like a cow. Poh! Poh! Poh! He has no feeling. The Americans don't know what it is all about. They are superficial. They have no deep, no philosophic understanding of what it means, to the soul. They have not read Schopenhauer. They have not suffered. Love to them is . . .''

But Lottie only laughed. He tried to embrace her. To kiss her. "Leave me alone," she said. "You dirty thing."

"That is the end!" He was furious. And muttering to himself that she would regret it, he sarcastically wished her infinite happiness with some boring businessman of a husband. "American women! Empty! All they want—all they want is money. They make fools of their stupid men, and what do they give? Nothing. Their minds are like ice cream . . .'' That made him laugh, well satisfied with himself. He was already beginning to feel that he had almost made a fool of himself. "American women are like ice cream," he said. That's wonderful. How nearly he had been caught! His violin packed carefully away, he lifted a smiling face to this young girl and bowing sharply took her hand and kissed it. "Good-bye."

Lottie couldn't imagine what had happened to him. He was gracious, smiling. The perfect gentleman.

"Miss Charlotte, I am *persona non grata* to you, I am forced to see that. I hope that I have not been boorish. You will forgive me? I will not bother you again."

Lottie was bewildered but firm.

"I will go upstairs, if I may, to say good-bye to your parents. I wish to thank them for their hospitality."

"Ma," Lottie called out at the foot of the stairs. "Can we come up?"

Joe, who was in his shirt sleeves, looked at his wife. "Sit still," she said. "Sure, come on."

So Mr. Grueher came up, made his formal apologies and, taking his violin under his arm, bowed once more at the door and left forever. Lottie sat in a rocking chair and fanned herself. "Thank God that's over."

There were also the Bishop brothers. Both were in college and during the active years of Lottie's popularity, could see her only during vacation periods or during the long summers. They both were entranced by her playing. They were both at the parties given from time to time at the Stechers' during the Christmas vacations when there would be a crowd, and Flossie, the younger sister, would be helping in the background, serving the refreshments—Lottie was always too busy—or looking silently, unnoticed, studying faces.

Sometimes one of the brothers would call up and appear alone. Fred, especially, would bring his music and sing. *"Gott!"* Herr Stecher would say to the world in general, "there it goes again."

Less than the dust!

Fred didn't have much of a voice but, as with the others, the words of the "Indian Love Lyrics" spoke to exquisite perfection what he longed to say—he felt indeed less than the dust before this enigmatic and accomplished young woman's chariot wheels. He was entered at that time in a national competition which would decide his fate—in architecture, at which he was an accomplished student. He looked at Lottie with serious eyes.

His brother, Charlie, who sang only in the ensembles, was an intern without money in a New York hospital; neither of the Bishop boys had a cent, a major deterrent to any thought of marriage. But Charlie had been observing Lottie closely for a year. He looked at her forehead, which was broad, like her father's; he looked at her flaring black hair, her shapely nose, her flat chest—surely she'd win no prize in a beauty contest—her lanky thighs as she sat at the piano, allowing him to see her without being observed; her skinny legs; her large, mysterious eyes. Surely she was no beauty, but he had to acknowledge that she was disturbing, to say the least.

He talked with her. In no way did she resemble her

mother, that fierce determination to ascend the social ant-hill, that turned-up nose, clear blue eyes. Lottie had brown eyes. Where did she get them? Joe's eyes were even bluer than his wife's. Some throwback. To Joe's brothers? Perhaps to the violinist who had remained in Europe, a teacher at the conservatory in Prague. If anything, she was her father's daughter, though she was tall and her father short. But she was too like him or his family for her own good. He looked at her and seemed to read her thoughts. And she didn't want her thoughts read. She avoided her father's glances. What she thought was none of his or any man's business.

They talked, Lottie and Charles. Slowly he got to know her and she him. He was studying her carefully. For one thing she was horribly superstitious, believed in nothing. At the first clap of a thunderstorm she'd fly for a closet and stay in it till the danger was over. Bishop himself had been terrified at thunder and lightning when he was a child and did not hold it against her—but smiled. "You're a big girl now," he told her, when she confessed her terror. "Suppose you do get killed? What of it?"

"No, no, no, no!" she said, hiding her face in her hands.

"You don't believe in an after-life, you say."

"No. But I want to live now. I want to find out a lot of things that I don't know yet, before I die. I'm young. I don't want to die, yet."

"A complete hedonist, eh?"

"I don't know what that is, but if it has anything to do with enjoying yourself, I'd like to be a great artist. I want to be admired, I want success—I've never even been in love. That's something, isn't it? Everybody says it is. I'd like . . ."

There was a blinding flash followed by a splintering crash of thunder.

"Ow!" shrieked Lottie, and dove into a corner by the couch, a pillow over her head. After a moment she looked out cautiously, quite ashamed. "Where did that hit?"

"It was pretty close," he laughed. "I guess you thought the devil had you that time."

"Do you think it'll do it again?"

"No. It's gone now. You'll live." She seemed a child at such times, hardly a woman.

Only one of her many male admirers had a real voice. That was Henry Baker, the baritone of the opera company, with whom she practiced his roles. That gave him an advantage over the others, but he was a morose fellow, terribly unsure of himself, with the sad eyes of a bloodhound, as gentle as they and with as deep a voice. He was inarticulate, submerged, never daring to think of himself as a successful lover.

Henry could laugh at himself with the same jaundiced eye as he could look at all others. He was lonely, an expert fly fisherman, but he could sing. As Lottie was an inch or so taller than he and, always alert, she had him beaten before, in his slow way, he could get to speak seriously of anything. She kept the room brightly lighted and always had another number to suggest when he wanted to rest from his singing. He, like the others, would sing the "Indian Love Lyrics"—like a frustrated bull.

"There they go again," Joe, reading his evening paper upstairs, would announce.

> *"Pale hands I loved*
> *Beside the Shalimar . . ."*

Krieger was another big fellow from out of town, a successful businessman, hail fellow well met, a fair tenor voice and a bag full of practical jokes. He was fairly popular with Joe and Gurlie, and had visited the family the summer before when they had been at a small cottage in Orange County, New York. But Lottie couldn't stand him. He was too crude. She wasn't to be rushed off her feet that way.

And then, among the others, there was the last, who seemed to be the favorite. Lottie thought so too, or so it seemed to her. When he would call, a different atmosphere pervaded the house than with any of the others—a sadness, a gentle mood that seemed as of someone listening.

Elmer Fawcett was from one of the most cultured and best thought of families in Riverdale and one of the oldest. Both his father and his mother were of that gentle old style that created an aristocratic air all about them. And Elmer loved music. He was much at home at the Stechers', but seemed always sad. For the truth was he had a bad heart, and had to be careful, especially going up and down stairs. Lottie was sorry for him, her sad eyes showing her deep sympathy for one whom death had addressed gently, saying, I may some day have to call upon you. Enjoy what you can, my dear boy. But don't expect too much.

The young man knew his possible fate. He had never before been in love. To be young, to live, to know one's self doomed. It was a hard fate.

Sometimes Charlie Bishop would read her his poems, bitterly, defiantly, in a harsh voice.

"Why do you write like that?" she would ask him, puzzled. "Your first little book was beautiful."

"It stank," he said bitterly. "I was a fool ever to have let it be printed."

"No it wasn't," said Lottie. "I loved it."

"It just shows your ignorance."

"And you wrote me such a nice sentiment in it." He ground his teeth. "But these things, you are making fun of yourself. I don't think a poem, to be a poem, should use ugly words, dirty words, vulgar . . . A poem should be beautiful. And you can write beautifully. But you seem to want to spoil everything. Why is that?"

He would laugh to himself sardonically and change the subject. "I don't understand you," she would say.

One night Elmer was very low. He'd gone to the doctor, who had been frank with him, told him he'd have to give up his studies and, in fact, all thought of an active life. "Your condition is serious."

238

"How long will I live?" the young man had asked.

"No one can say."

"A year?"

"Oh, it's not as bad as that."

"You mean it is as bad as that. Don't you?"

"Anything can happen. But you had better go away, for a month. Then we can tell."

"Oh, don't believe him," said Lottie, when he spoke of it. "If you don't overdo, you can live a long time. I betcha. Don't you want to sing?"

"Not tonight." Then with his head in his hands there was a long pause. Lottie watched him. He looked up, right into her eyes without a word—but she could feel the tears coming as she too sat there in the dim light, at the piano, with her hands folded in her lap. A thrill went up her spine, her thighs felt stiff as she became aware of the seriousness of the moment.

They looked at each other for a long minute; then he began to speak, after clearing his voice. She could see from the way it shook him how his heart was beating. She thought his lips looked blue. "It's been wonderful to have known you, Charlotte. You know, of course, that I love you. I've never been in love before. It's a wonderful experience. It's hard for me to have to give you up."

Now she was indeed crying—from happiness, from sorrow—she made no attempt to define. His entire sentimental nature was moved and if, at the back of her head, she felt a strange relief, she could not have told you the cause. "Why do you talk like that?" she said.

"Darling, may I call you that?"

She nodded her head dumbly, but didn't move.

"It's wonderful to call you that! My darling . . . My own." Now she was sobbing openly. "What a world of happiness . . . Look, Charlotte," he braced himself and went on in a more practical tone. "I won't propose to you, you might accept me. And that I don't want. I love you with every ounce of strength I have in me. But my dear, I'm a sick man.

I won't live long and I'm not going to ask you to be my nurse. I know what happiness is. Now I'm going home."

"Oh, no."

"Oh, yes. And I'm going to go to bed. The old doc wanted me to go to bed today, but I had to come here first. Now he can have me and if—if after the next six weeks are over . . ." He coughed and straightened himself. "No. I'm crazy. I'm a sick man," he said, fiercely, "a hopelessly sick man. Good-bye, Charlotte. It's been wonderful knowing you. Say good-bye to your parents. I'm going home to die."

"Oh, come on, darling, sing one more song. I don't think it's as serious as you say."

"All right."

"Pale hands I loved . . . "

"Oh, my God," said Joe, upstairs. "Here we go again."

He went to Bermuda and came back at the end of a month wonderfully relieved, so much so that he gave a party one night to celebrate his recovery, and the next morning was found dead in bed.

23

Those were the days! By dint of her native energy, her drive, popularity and Joe's continuing business success Gurlie had arrived at the top of the heap. You heard her name wherever the social affairs of the town were discussed. Everyone knew her, and she knew everyone. Her house, largely because of Lottie's abilities, was the musical center of the town.

Joe, an astute politician, when he wanted to exercise his talent, was her one stumbling block. If he had been willing to give in to her, she'd have made him a senator.

There isn't one of them that has your head, she would alternately taunt and coax him. She wanted him to go into county politics. But he said no, and he said it so vehemently that even Gurlie had finally to leave him alone. All politicians are crooks was his positive and unshakable conviction.

Sometimes one of the girls would bring home an *Evening Journal* for the feature story, some lurid and improbable love tangle illustrated with pale color prints of a seminaked female on a divan with a drooling and blank-eyed lover leaning over her. On the front page would be the three-inch headlines in black and red playing up the usual Hearst pattern. If by chance Joe saw it a veritable hell would break loose.

"Haven't I told you never to bring that dirty sheet into this house?" And you knew what he implied by "sheet." If there were a fire in the grate, he'd tear the paper up and throw it in. Whoever was responsible would run into her room and close the door. Hearst and crooked politics were synonyms to him. "If we ever have serious trouble in this country, that sort of yellow journalism will be at the base of it." The *World* was the only paper fit to read.

Gurlie had induced him to join the German *Liederkranz*, though not as a singing member, or even an active participant in its social activities of any sort. They did, however, go to its annual or semiannual concerts and would sometimes take guests. One year the girls had invited the Bishop brothers for a New Year's supper and dance. Champagne was king; no other wine was served. It was wild. One pompous male across the table from the Stecher party, a big fellow with a vari-colored ribbon across his chest, was making himself objection-able. At midnight, when confetti and serpentines were being thrown and disorder was rife, one of the young men rolled up a wad of bread into a solid dough pellet and hit the offensive Heinie a whack in the cheek. He went crazy, spotting one of the boys as the offender—but when he came around the table to face them, they stared him down.

Gurlie, besides, became a member of the executive com-mittee of the Scandinavian-American club. In those days there was great excitement over the race for discovery of the North and South Poles. Stecher, for some reason, distrusting Peary's pompous assertiveness, backed Dr. Cook and his claims to have been the first at the North Pole, and only after the reve-lation of the falsity of his claims to having scaled Mt. Mc-Kinley did Joe give up his belief in him. But Roald Amundsen had been a schoolmate of Gurlie's brothers in Sarpsborg, and when he had been successful at the South Pole, her exultation knew no bounds. Fremstad, also, making her debut at the Metropolitan Opera, Olive Fremstad, whom she had known as a child, confirmed her in her good opinion of herself. And when the tall and lean Amundsen one night stalked onto the stage at Carnegie Hall for a lecture on his exploits, sponsored by the Scandinavian American Society, Gurlie's spirit found itself finally justified.

Amundsen did not like Peary. He stood on the stage, a pointer such as a schoolteacher uses in his hand. A committee walked out to him and presented him with a gold medal similar to the one Peary had received from the National Geographic Society with which he, Amundsen, had no patience. As the chairman was making his speech, the great man stood impatiently but obediently waiting. Immediately thereafter, the medal in its case in his hand, the audience expectant before him, he looked up and said, "I thank you for dis *niise* medal." And, walking to the wings, put the medal, in its case, down on the floor. Then, going back to the center of the stage and taking up his pointer, he called out in a tremendous voice to the men in charge of the controls at the back of the auditorium, "Switch off die lights!"

The audience roared with laughter. After which he gave an account, with stereopticon views, of his experience aboard *"die Fram,"* on his marvelous voyages.

He was entertained later at a formal supper at the Scandinavian-American Club, with great gaiety. But in the middle of it he made his excuses and, giant as he was, following a beautiful young American matron whose queenly appearance and manifest pride at carrying off the hero of the occasion was apparent, he strode from the room, his long legs fairly twitching with half-suppressed excitement and agility. The Scandinavians were incensed. He seemed to be shaking himself free from their parochial implications.

"He's become too good for us." Gurlie didn't like it. "Some American floozie," she said. "Men are fools to a pretty face." Everybody laughed. "He belongs on a ship."

So Gurlie entertained herself and advanced her prestige.

The Fletchers, of the Fortnightly Reading Club, became the Stechers' closest pals. It was a turnabout arrangement. Andrew Fletcher was to his own family what Gurlie was to the Stecher ménage. He was the gay, though calculating, inciter, in a modest way, as Gurlie was to her family. And his wife, Elizabeth, with her little, twitching nose through which, whenever she was nervous, she sniffed vigorously while she cleared her throat with a little nervous cough, was the unwilling foil.

Joe, in his way, was only dragged against his will out of the house nights. "Fortnightly tonight," Gurlie would announce toward seven o'clock every two weeks when he'd be looking forward to a nice, quiet evening at home.

"God damn it! God damn it to hell! Why don't you leave me alone?" But she would have already laid out his dress clothes, his stiff shirt, and he would have to get into them. He'd be fit to be tied as he struggled with his studs and black bow tie and made the air fairly blue with his curses. The girls would hear him and snigger—but he would go. Perhaps his backing of Dr. Cook as the true discoverer of the North Pole was merely the unconscious protest he was registering against the smug acceptances of his world. His logical mind would bring up all kinds of arguments to support the adventurer's claims. It was something to say, something to stir up the resentments of his associates, whom he secretly despised.

"Those fools," he'd laugh to himself. But he'd lend money on occasion to an impecunious artist, one of the club members, and talk, when he had to, pleasantly enough.

Gurlie and Andrew Fletcher, who was very successful in his ribbon business, which took him often abroad, became the active leading spirits among the younger members of the club. Stecher, while in no way the counterpart of Liz, and for very different reasons, merely followed their leads. The acquisition of personal property and an intense rivalry became a game between the friends, mounting hotter and hotter for those climactic years before the fateful outbreak of the First World War.

As Gurlie thought back to her ancient lineage, now broken, she felt herself predestined to re-establish it. To win, to acquire possessions was her mad dream, some day to own an estate which should have the stability of he ancestral home. She would found it for the family, forever, and it should be called Alverheim! All this was still cloudy in her spirit—you can't call it her mind, for, in a way, she had no mind, she had only a blind drive, inarticulate but dominant, which gave her the impetus to despise her own brothers and sisters who were willing to accept a subordinate social status. She broke with them, as she broke with her own mother, who attempted to subdue her.

But she liked Andrew Fletcher, him she could understand. He had the same impulses as she did—but he couldn't patronize *her*, nor she him. So the rivalry was let loose.

At Christmas and birthdays the two families began by giving each other modest presents. At the next occasion each would cap the other's gift with something more expensive. Neither would allow the other to put him down. And if Liz had a new dress, Gurlie had to have a better one at the next meeting of the club. Until on one such occasion Gurlie appeared with a magnificent diamond ring. Lizzie, within a month, came up with a lavaliere featuring a diamond of notable proportions.

Not that Gurlie wished to make a vulgar show; that was too easy. But diamonds, aside from the opal, her birthstone, were the sole jewels she cared to possess. And by the end of that winter Joe, who was happy to give his wife whatever she desired, came up with a diamond necklace and pendant with a stone so beautiful that, upon her broad breast, it shone like a sun in the sky.

Whatever it was that Liz next acquired, perhaps the large house into which she had moved, or the new car—Joe would not have a car—Gurlie next bewildered her club members, some of whom, the remnants of the old literary set, were poor as church mice, with a crescent, worn in her hair and set with diamonds of graduated sizes, twenty or more, that no one in their set could equal.

But for all that, though one or the other would be challenged and annoyed by turns, the families remained good friends even when, at a later date, on the occasion of the marriage of the Fletchers' older daughter, Gurlie, with Joe's consent, presented them with a huge grandfather's clock to their total surprise and dismay.

The meetings of the Fortnightly Reading Club became gayer now than they had ever before been, and the music, which was always an essential part of the program, much better in quality. Violinists and vocalists of Lottie's acquaintance were often heard, and Lottie herself became the favorite with all the members. They felt very lucky and even the Arentses, who were regular operagoers during the season and thoroughly sophisticated music lovers, had to acknowledge that at her best the accomplished Charlotte was well worth listening to.

But Gurlie was a devil—aside from all this. Her high spirits prodded her to all sorts of pranks. One Halloween she grabbed her elder daughter. The two of them dressed themselves in ragged clothes and outlandish hats and went to sit in the office of one of their club members, a very staid physician, whom they knew well. Gurlie had never forgotten her early days, when, on arrival in the United States, she had had a job for a while in Macy's basement. Her experiences there with the then ubiquitous Irish immigrant never left her mind. Being a perfect monkey, she had learned their lingo in jig time and when she wanted could make herself sound as if she was no more than weeks from the "auld sod." This time, when the doctor looked out into his waiting room, he was completely taken in.

"I want for you to look at me daughter? I think she's a little weak in the chest," said Gurlie to the good man.

"Well, bring her in." And so it went with Gurlie jabbering away at a great rate until the doctor became annoyed with her interruptions. But when the two women began to laugh at him he was at first angry and then: "Mrs. Stecher!" he cried out. "And Charlotte!" he could scarcely believe his eyes and had to call his wife to see. They laughed together, hardly able to control their amazement.

"We're going to the Fletchers' now," Gurlie told them. "Let me use your phone. I want to ask first if Mary is at home." Mary was the Fletchers' Irish maid, a heavy woman who had been long with the family. "I'm looking for a woman named Mary Foley," said Gurlie, when she got Andrew Fletcher on the phone. "Does she live with you?"

"Yes," said Fletcher doubtfully, "but she's not in now."

"Well, I'm her mother's only sister, fresh over from the other side, and I'm coming to see her."

"But I tell you . . ."

Gurlie had hung up and was already giggling at Fletcher's probable state of mind. When she arrived there with the disguised Lottie, whom she had enjoined not so much as to open her mouth, in tow, Fletcher tried to turn her away at the door, but she insisted and finally got in. And there she gave them a good story, how she had come out from the city an old woman, hoping to see her niece—she was poor and . . .

Fletcher could sense a touch, and completely forgetting that it was Halloween, became fussed. Lizzie was nervously keeping in the background, half-frightened at the woman's importunity. "Why doesn't he put her out!" she kept saying to herself. "She's an obvious impostor."

"Do you mind if I sit down and rest meself a while?" said Gurlie. "Maybe me niece has gone to mass and'll be back soon. I don't want to go back that long way without seeing her."

At last Fletcher got rid of them, crowding them to the door until they were out, virtually slamming the door in their faces, but not before Gurlie admonished him, "Tell Mary that Mrs. O'Toole called!"

The two women called next at the Bishops', three houses below. But there after talking for a while unrecognized both to Bishop and his son, the medical student, she couldn't refrain from telling them who they were and what had happened

247

at the Fletchers'. Everyone laughed his head off at the way she had shown up their neighbor. So Gurlie had her witnesses and for weeks afterward the joke was at her rivals' expense.

"I never saw anybody so mean," she taunted them. "You could see I was an old woman in distress and you never even so much as offered us a drink. Shame on you! What do you think of that?" she'd say to those about her. "They didn't even ask us to sit down."

Gurlie in fact, demoralized the whole club. Once at a musicale, serious and successful, she distributed to each member a toy, a noisemaker of whatever sort, whether flute, drum, trumpet or bell, "And now," she said, after her always delicious and profuse refreshments had been served and consumed at the end of the evening, "we are going to put that classical stuff in its proper place. Take the souvenirs that have been distributed to you and at the sign I shall give you, fall in while my daughter plays the accompaniment."

The noise was deafening. The Millses, the most staid of the club's members, the idols of Mrs. Covell, who made a living as the lady's companion and the one responsible for her cultured sobriety—Mrs. Mills especially—howled with delight. It had never been dared to do such things in the club before. To the frowns of some of the others Lottie kept pounding out the tune, da da te da, da! until all were exhausted.

24

When little Paul was nine years old he was a beautiful child; his scowl was magnificent. His matted poll of wavy blond hair, his long, straight and powerful legs, his erect bearing and defiant look often tempted Gurlie to dress him in neatly ironed shirts and suits for which he showed the same disrespect that his father did for dress togs. He was a good kid too, and though no teacher's pet at school, did well enough in his work. He was not loud, but unassuming, and loved at times to be alone, to go into the patch of woodland bordering to the rear on the Stecher property. As young as he was, he once, with a homemade figure-four trap, came in with a sixteen-pound opossum which he had caught and killed there. Never in the history of the locality had anyone even seen such an animal in the vicinity.

Often Gurlie would put on the gloves with him, kneeling on the rug before him, and let him slug her as hard as he might. She'd battle back, breaking all the rules of the game, to his disgust, pinning his arms to his side with a bear hug from which he'd struggle to escape until she'd get him down and conquer him with a big excited kiss. He'd fight loose, give her one final bat from which she'd protect herself with her arms in front of her face, take off his gloves and refuse to go on—until the next time. Joe never could do that. That he was proud of the boy would be to put it mildly, but he had no way of showing it.

Every summer there were days when the house was closed and the family would go away either to the mountains or the seashore. At first, before Einar went to live there permanently, the old farm in Vermont had been the chosen place. It was perfect for the growing children. But it was inconvenient for Joe and as the years passed Gurlie would have nothing of it. It was, besides, too poor for her; she would not put up with her mother's domination, and she was through with that old-world atmosphere and her sisters' simple habits. She had visions, bred of Joe's increasing achievements in the business world, which warned her not to get stuck in that backwater.

Not that there had not been the time when they had gone all together, little Paul and all, on a day-long trip up Haystack, the local mountain peak, old Charlie plodding along to its foot, where Einar would unbridle him, take him out of the shafts and tie him under a tree for a long rest. Then up the path they'd go, Auntie Olga along with the rest, laboriously climbing the woodsy path to the spring. That was the halfway point where Auntie was left with the lunch baskets while the rest of the party would, after a breather, go on to the summit.

Even now they'd often speak of it: the day clear, the view on all sides unobstructed until the eye lost itself in the distant mists and obstructing peaks in the distance all the way to Monadnock. The last part of the way had been precipitous, the rocks sharp, the steps over the projecting shoulder high and slippery—and then to arrive!

Here we are! The rocks studded with crumbling garnets, low blueberry shrubs, the fruit small and hard, wind-bent scrub pines, the branches all to the south and east, distorted and broken. Your lungs felt clean and you struggled pleasantly with your breath.

"I'll be a wreck tomorrow!" Gurlie would say. And, "*Du du!*" to the little boy. "Look at you! You're a mountaineer. Look at him! Isn't he wonderful to climb all those rocks?" Everyone admired the little fellow.

The young ladies, though their boots were quite improper for the rugged terrain, seemed to enjoy it as much as the others. They had one or two scares over turned ankles. "Do you remember," said Hilda as they arrived at the top and sat down a little out of the wind to rest a moment—it was really cold at the top—"do you remember the first time we came up here how little you were? Just little girls."

"Yes," said Flossie, "that was the year you made the Norwegian costumes for us."

"I remember that, yes. It was for Old Home Week. I think I still have those costumes at home."

"Yes, they were pretty. We sat in the big carriage."

"In the surrey, yes."

"And we were in costume, like Norwegian peasants. And you tied four little flags, two Norwegian and two American, to the four corners of the carriage. Then, with us sitting up front, we drove in the parade. Didn't we have fun?"

"Yes, those were happy days when we were all together."

And so the young people explored the spiny bushes, found a few harebells in a sheltered corner. "Oh, look!" Lottie called out. "Look how delicate they are. I wonder what their name is."

Nobody knew.

Little hanging bells with ferny leaves. A half-frightened or subdued bird with a red head kept a rotten tree trunk between himself and their eyes. A woodpecker; they could tell that, at least, because they heard him tap tap tap with his beak.

And so, reluctantly, they turned their backs on the scene and began to descend, quite different from the climb and no less difficult, down to Olga and the spring again. There on the beautiful green grass the fat auntie had laid everything out and, as they came up, flushed and ravenously hungry, was in the act of shooing away a bothersome yellow jacket which was attacking the food.

But those days were long past now and did not interest Gurlie. "You can go if you want to," she told her daughters. "I'll stay home." She was glad to get rid of them.

First after that she tried the seashore. "Let's take a cottage!" the girls shouted, when what they'd do for the summer was being discussed, thinking of the freedom, the sea, the light and, in their bathing suits, to find companions—to find adventure.

So one year they had taken a cottage at a resort, a barren and wild stretch of sand on the outer coastline near Westerly, Rhode Island. They had even induced Joe, whose sole use for the out of doors was a mountain stream with trout to go with it, to go with them. Weakfish washed in by a storm tide and stranded on the beach gave the Finnish girl, wide-eyed at the bounty, a chance to show her prowess to select and pickle them. That was all that the shore meant to him. And pickled mussels. But for the rest, he stood it for a few days and then, "Sahara!" he said, and went home, taking one of the girls with him to keep house for him on alternate weeks while he went back to the office.

Already Gurlie was looking about for something else, some place, nearer home perhaps, because, after all, Joe could be troublesome and obstinate. She decided to go once more to the sea to please the girls and because she herself still had a residuum in her of what all Norwegians have, mountains, yes, as fine as any in Switzerland or the Harz Mountains which recalled to him Joe's boyhood in Silesia, but in addition for a Norwegian, there were the fjords! And that meant the sea! All the way from the Lofoten Islands down past Oslo, the sea which enlarged the soul.

In spite of Joe she'd go to Westerly one more year. The girls had their companions there—had they not been looking at the snapshots all winter?—and even Inga, the maid, wanted to go back. Joe could make the best of his "Sahara desert" for one more season. Little Paul longed to play in the sand. Even Joe, for the short time he'd spend there, enjoyed the seafood, and the girls could alternate taking care of him at home a week or two as formerly. It was agreed.

But that was no answer. Joe had heard rumors of a region in lower New York State, in Sullivan County, which was ideal for fishing. "Oh my God," said Lottie, when she first heard of it. "Are you going to stick us up there?" But the fishing was superb, on the upper waters of the Delaware— and they knew that some day . . . "Oh, they could at least *try* it."

"You mean a *boarding* house?"

"Why not? Other people have a good time there."

"But Father, I'd rather . . ."

"That'll do."

"Then we shan't go anywhere."

So Gurlie knew that sooner or later, now that Vermont was abandoned—Joe refused to have anything to do with the New Jersey beaches—Gurlie knew that something in the back country within perhaps about fifty miles of New York City would finally be the place they would choose. Her objective was still a farm, though she had no idea what the upkeep of a farm would mean in this country. She was thinking in terms of Norway fifty to a hundred years ago.

It was all in her dreams. But one day, she was absolutely determined about this, she would find such a place, with a stream and a romantic forest. There she would have cattle— cattle are always so picturesque grazing about on the hills on a fine day; besides, she was practical. If you don't have cattle, where are you going to get the manure for your fields and garden—and fruit trees? You must have cattle, a herd to begin with of at least twelve head. You can sell the milk which would help to keep them and grow their fodder right on the place.

There'd be pigs, too, and chickens for fresh eggs. Gurlie sighed to think of it. Joe, too, got it a little into his blood. He loved to hunt. A partridge or two, a few pheasants—they were getting fairly plentiful in New York State in recent years.

He'd have the place posted, of course. And rabbits. He wanted little Paul to become a good shot when he grew up. It made Joe think of his own boyhood, though he'd had little opportunity to shoot; his father had been a forester on one of the big estates. He was a good shot. But the small boys were not allowed to handle a gun and, by the time they might have followed the father's profession, he was dead and gone. Joe's mother was also dead. There had been nothing left and the other sons had been forced to go into the army—there was the Franco-Prussian war in the offing . . . But Joe, a printer, had been commissioned by a publishing house to come to this country and start them off in the color-lithography skills. Little Paul would have to go through nothing of that. At last Gurlie could begin to see her way ahead now for several years.

There, when she finally found the right place, she would build a solid stone mansion as the seat where her blood should establish itself in America. There is no better place for a boy to grow up than on a farm. Little Paul might even become a farmer. He should get to know animals. They would keep a dog, a real dog, not like that little trollop they now had. What a dirty little thing *she* was, that little Skye terrier. She bit people when they came to call. Why only yesterday, when Charlie Bishop came to see Lottie, the little bitch had seized him by the pants leg and ripped his trousers. In spite of everything they could say she wouldn't let go. Of course she had pups, that was the reason. You can't blame a female if she has pups; she is defending them. What a little slut!

The girls giggled at her and often were amused. They found Gurlie laughing at the window one day. "Look at that scandalous little thing! What is she doing?"

Somehow the animal had taken her one little female offspring out on the front terrace to give it an airing, when up came a dog, interested in the mother. You'd expect her to go for him! Not at all. She took her little bitch of a puppy and with her own nose rolled it over on its back for the big dog to smell it all over.

"What do you think of that?" Gurlie howled. "Did you see what she did, with her own little daughter? Gave her to any dog that comes along to teach her what to do."

"Oh, Mother," Lottie had objected.

"Hurry up, go on out and bring them both in. Disgraceful."

But on the farm they'd have big dogs. And these scrawny girls of hers— "Why don't you eat? Girls in Norway are not skinny and flat-chested the way you are. Look at you." Flossie's legs were well-shaped enough, but Lottie's were like bean stalks.

Gurlie for years thought of the farm, or, rather, the estate she would found. Joe smiled and let her dream.

This was still five years before the First World War; "Our Own" that spring had produced the *Pirates of Penzance*, in which Flossie had appeared with the rest of the young ladies, that part of them that could put up with the questionable morals of the group—Flossie had appeared in an interpolated number with others of the chorus in lace nightgowns.

It was at that time, seeing her on the street walking away from him one day that Charlie Bishop had first noticed her straight and well-rounded legs.

Love was in the air. Old man Holmes of the opera company felt it when the contralto, Mrs. M., would let go in one of her arias. Ursula Hendricks had been engaged for the part, and with her distinguished voice had practiced with the group a few times. But either she had forgotten the role and had to begin it all over again wherever she did appear or, simply, she would not show up. And finally, to her annoyance, she was dropped. Mrs. M., rather out of the fashionable set in town, had taken her place. They had tried her in gingerly fashion —but once she had begun to sing, first Mr. Holmes and then everyone in the company began to prick up their ears.

There was something dark, unknown about Mrs. M. Her husband, a teller in one of the local banks, who had been, innocently, of course, but none the less seriously, involved in the disappearance of a packet of large-denomination paper money, seldom or never called for her after the evening practice sessions. It gave her an air of irresponsibility. Someone usually accompanied her home afterward, sometimes it was Mr. Holmes or his son—or whoever it might be.

"Good night, my child, you sing divinely."

"Good night."

"Is your husband home?"

"Yes, he had to go to a bank meeting tonight. He must be in bed asleep long ago.

"He's a nice fellow."

"Yes, he's a nice fellow. Good night." And she'd be gone.

How do such things get noised about? It must be the stars. It interested Lottie, but she was not one to ask questions. As she sat patient at her piano while Holmes would be trying over a certain passage which the chorus was rehearsing for the twentieth time, she'd look around at the faces of the singers, at the soprano, at little Gannon, the tenor, and at Mrs. M., and try to guess what they were thinking. It offered wonderful opportunities, these rehearsals, for any two to get away together wrapped about in an atmosphere of music. How really beneficent such a person as Mr. Holmes really was to give his time, his energy to afford everyone so much pleasure.

She'd sit there and half-guess what was going on. Why doesn't something like that ever happen to me? she would think; she who never, until that time, had known a kiss full on the lips. Never! She wondered what it would be like to have a lover.

It was in the air. From one and another it moved through the group of singers, these wives and husbands, buoyed up by the interchanges of musical sequences until they began to wonder if perhaps they too might not themselves dare, as how many have dared before them, to enjoy! Lottie, sweating there at the piano, weary from sitting, hearing the tiresome repetitiousness of the rehearsals—envying Mrs. M. her voice. Oh to have a voice like that! Poor thing, I wouldn't blame her for anything she did, Lottie would find herself confessing. "I hope she does."

"Does what?"

She started awake. Mr. Holmes had been speaking to her several times.

"What? What did you say?"

"In love, Lottie?" someone called out.

"Oh no," Mr. Holmes would chaff her, "not Charlotte. She's just a dreamer. She was way off." And she would smile her enigmatic smile. "When *she* falls in love," Mr. Holmes, who took all sorts of liberties, would say, "she'll fall heavy."

Love was in the air. Fred Bishop was competing for a prize in architecture, the Prix de Rome itself, and it looked as though he would get it. His father, his strange but talented mother and his brother, the young intern and poet, were all rooting for him to make good. It was early spring, the world was on its way to the greatest triumphs for peace and for plenty it had ever known. All a young man needed was to get his start, to marry, perhaps—and paradise, as near an earthly paradise as one could wish for, would be opened to him. Fred believed that, too.

He had determined, if he won the Prix de Rome, that there was only one thing that would complete his happiness and that would be to have a woman like Charlotte Stecher to share it, if she would. Why not ask her?

The only drawback: his brother. They had discussed Lottie together, close companions as they had been all their lives, and though neither had broached to the other a word of his true feelings, each sensed that the other, admiring this girl so openly, was a rival. Each suspected the other of perhaps deeper motives than he showed. Holy and pure, as their natures demanded their thoughts to be, buoyed aloft on wings of song, nevertheless they were practical enough to find themselves on the brink of action.

Love was in the air. Mr. Bishop had said, and his wife had seconded it, that if Fred won the Prix de Rome he'd send

257

the older son along with him to Europe for a year in Germany to complete his medical education. The tension as the weeks passed was intense. Few knew of it outside the family, but at home the atmosphere was breathless. The week of the final problems, when their drawings were finally exhibited and the contestants waited for the judges to make their decision, hardly a soul in the household could sleep.

Then the news burst forth. Fred had won! He had won! He had achieved the highest honor accorded to any architectural student in the United States. By his own long years of effort he had capped the family striving, begun when his parents, saving every free penny that they owned, had sent him to school. And he, because it was what in a man should be expected, had applied himself and worked. Not that he didn't have the original talent—but he had painstakingly and persistently applied himself and won. He had won the prize! He would go to Rome, to Rome, think of it! To Rome to study and his brother would go to Europe likewise!

His mother kissed him and promised that she would go to see him at least once during those three long years; they would take a trip over, she and his father. His father put his arms around him and congratulated him. Even kissed him on the cheek. And Charlie, his brother, was fairly beside himself with joy. You might think that it was he who had won the prize, he was so proud and happy.

The next morning, a beautiful June morning, as the two young men were talking together in the back yard, Fred turned to his brother and said, "Will you go to Charlotte?" His brother looked at him sullenly, knowing well what was about to be said. "Tell her each of us wants to marry her. Tell her to choose between us. One of us will have to do it, because if you won't go, I will. Will you ask her?"

"No."

"Then I'll go."

"Go ahead."

Always, if you're going to ask a woman to marry you, a

cynical old friend had once advised Charlie, do it before noon, because you want to have your wits about you. Fred had done it before noon.

Charlie didn't see his brother to speak to for the rest of the day, either one or the other being out of the house when the other was there. They did see each other at supper, but Fred disappeared soon after and Charlie went to bed early.

Next morning, meeting Fred again in the back yard, Charlie said to him, "Well, how did you make out?"

"She accepted me," said Fred.

"Fine," said Charlie and then, disgracefully, he flung his arms about his brother's neck and went mad. Fred was embarrassed, loosened himself from his brother's hold and fled.

Charlie thought the earth had dissolved under his feet. He hadn't foreseen the sweep of his emotional reaction or the wreckage it would cause. Had Fred been decent enough about it? He had. He had done everything one man could do for another, under the circumstances. In fact the perfection of his behavior only added to the effect. And yet something had come to an end. It was a deeper wound than he should ever thereafter in his life be able to sound. It was bottomless.

At last Lottie had found her mate. Charlie congratulated the two lovers and—really he was ashamed of himself—when alone sobbed and sobbed, uncontrollably. He ground his teeth, he fought back his unreasoning tears. And then it left him. Like a flash. He made up his mind and was determined to act upon it.

25

More than once during the preceding months when she observed the long train of suitors who had been flocking to pay homage to her elder daughter—and little Flossie was beginning to come along as well with her kiddish admirers—Gurlie had singled out the elder Bishop boy for her attention. They didn't any of them add up to much; most of them she rejected forthwith. But that boy, the young doctor, had particularly irritated her.

"That boy!" she would say in the hearing of her daughters. "He's a selfish one. All *he* wants to do is sit in the house and write poems all day long. He says so himself. He isn't the slightest interested in money. That's what he says. He'll be poor, just a poor doctor—who writes poems. Poo!"

That was all for him. He insulted her idea of what a man should be.

Neither of the girls ever replied. But Flossie knew, at least, that her father liked the young man. That gave her a little comfort. Not that the Bishop boy had ever addressed more than a passing word to her, but she had not given up hope. She loved him. It was unreasonable. Nothing would ever come of it. But she liked his nose. What a silly thing! But there it was, she loved him, secretly. It was no one's business but her own; she never even mentioned his name aloud. His nose fascinated her.

The day after Fred's engagement to Charlotte, the elder brother disappeared. He remained at home looking out the window or lying on his bed. He ate nothing at all. His mother admonished him, telling him that he would make himself ill, that he would get over it and . . .

"Over what?" he barked back at her savagely.

"Well, over your grief," the poor woman said. It was that perhaps that brought him about. For after all, what else was she to call it? He felt sorry for her, helpless as she was, and smiled. And took a little plate of soup she had prepared for him the second day and on the third day went out of doors again. After all, the world goes on as usual no matter how we feel about it, he said to himself. No, I'll be damned if it will this time. It's going my way.

It was still no more than ten o'clock in the morning. He went back into the house, called Flossie on the phone and by luck got her in person.

"Are you in? I want to come down and see you."

"Yes."

Again, fortunately, when he arrived at the familiar residence no one else was about.

"Let's sit on the porch awhile."

"Sure. What is it?"

"Florence," he said, "will you marry me?"

Though she must have been more than a little startled, she didn't show it—it was so unemotionally put that she may not have realized the full significance of the words. He was obviously in a disturbed mental state. Perhaps her heart sank. But all she said was, "You don't love me. You love my sister."

"I do not love your sister."

"But you don't love me."

He looked down. Then he looked up, straight into her eyes. "I don't love anyone," he said, "but I want to marry you. I think we can be happy."

That was a stumper for a young girl. She had been in love for a year, perhaps two years, with the man and somehow he knew it—and counted on it. He presumed, insolently presumed, on it to seize her. He wanted her, but refused to lie to get her. Either she would take him as he was and they together would make a go of it or what you will.

He himself was without love—for the time being—but if she loved him and would have him, here he was at her feet.

She at least shall have her way, that will be a beginning. "I'll make a go of it no matter what anyone else says or does. I will. I refuse to go under. I refuse to be licked. Meanwhile, here is this girl, there is love about her." He couldn't say that he saw it shining in her eyes, he didn't. But he had been conscious for some time, he realized now, of her presence in his environment. He felt her now as love itself. He couldn't have recognized it sooner, he hadn't been able to. It had taken a cataclysm to bring it to a head, but, as he looked back now, it had always been there. It had always been rejected, as he himself now had been rejected. He did love her, he had a fellow feeling for her. Together they, having found out what love is, having been rejected, and what it could do, with their eyes open, could and would face it together.

One thing was certain, he was not going to start over again what he had in this tragic experience already been through. Finis. Full stop. From now on, having gone through that, he was done with it—whether she would have him or not. But if she said yes, even without florid declarations of love, they could, she loving him and therefore willing to take his lead, they could—for he would teach her what comes after love—they two could make a life of it. They might even conceivably make a superb life of it.

He would never go back. Never. There is a sort of love, not romantic love, but a love that with daring can be made difficultly to blossom. It is founded on passion, a dark sort of passion, but it is founded on passion, a passion of despair, as all life is despair.

She, young, in love, would add her portion, and he, wiser, would add his. And it would never come to an end. It would be a marriage that would be founded on human understanding that would be difficult but passionate, passionate as one says of a saint—those saints that were womanly, or, like St. Francis, full of compassion. It could be like no other love that had been conceived between a man and a woman.

How could he explain that to her? He couldn't. She wouldn't know what he was saying except by pure instinct. But it was valid, it was a real thing, it was not an adulteration, not a leftover from her sister's bouquet. It was a vivid, living thing—of a new sort.

Whatever his genius, right or wrong, he had had the drive to get her to commit herself in downright fashion, with the belief that she, knowing the circumstances as no one else could, would know how to decide. It was tough on a young girl, but with uncompromising cruelty, as to one who would be his wife, he proposed the question and watched, fascinated, to see what would result.

"I don't know." The young girl, who, after all, had never faced a problem of such seriousness in her life, wanted to think. He respected her decision and went off. He knew she would not tell her mother, certainly not her sister. She, a woman, would not go to her father, a man. This was her affair. She spent the whole day upon the problem.

He had said that he would call that night for an answer. She loved him, of that she was sure, and now—after the humiliation she had suffered from his neglects, the off-hand way he had always treated her—the prize had fallen into her lap. She should be angry, not pleased. He had not even said he loved her. He had not said anything other than that "Will you marry me?" and in a few weeks (she must keep it secret) he was going away to Europe. Even their good-byes would have to be secret and—for a year! Anything can happen in a year. Maybe he'd grow tired of her. Maybe she'd tire of him. She was young, hardly more than a child. What's a year? She'd be unhappy for awhile and then everything would all go on as before. Why not? Why not say I'll marry him? But she knew, if she said yes, it would be the end for her. And she knew that he knew it too. If she said yes, that would be the end.

All day long she tossed the ball about, one way, then the other, and that evening when he came to call she said, "Let's take a walk." Protected by the darkness, they headed around the old farm that still occupied the center of the town.

She would not let him touch her. They walked apart. She began, as rightly she should have done, to object to his coldness. She was not used to men so much older than herself, perhaps it was their way, she was in her own mind still a child and did not know exactly how to proceed. You don't know what a man's intentions may be. It was tough.

Finally, at the far side of a field, in the darkness she paused and, hanging her head, said very doubtfully to him, "Yes, I'll marry you."

He put his arms about her body, holding her close, and attempted to kiss her. She was scared at her own temerity and half-turned away her face so that he touched only half her mouth with his lips. But it was enough. He took her hand and they continued around the block together. The next day the family was going off for the summer—he would not see her again for another year.

But they would write. And so, with strange misgivings, more torment than happiness, they parted. And he sailed away for a year and a day—and Gurlie saw the letters coming regularly and surmised enough so that she gave her young daughter the devil. "You're making a fool of yourself." Her sister, too, looked at her as if she had caught her stealing her stockings.

"Are you engaged to Charlie Bishop?"

"What do you care?"

"I don't care. My God, the children nowadays! He'll never marry you."

Flossie wanted to get a job now that she had graduated from her precious finishing school. She was accredited for her sophomore year at Vassar, where Gurlie would have liked to send her to break up this silly infatuation. She refused to go.

Her father frowned on a business career. And when she suggested becoming a nurse, the whole family fairly howled. "You a nurse? You're not husky enough," though in a fragile way she was strong as a filly.

So she remained at home waiting, and that summer at the shore again, whatever it was that had changed about her, she suddenly became a woman, and her boyfriends with whom she had grown up began to propose marriage to her. She had, with misgivings, to refuse them all even when, in the bay in a cat-boat, one vigorous youth so lost his temper when he discovered the true situation that he stamped on the boat bottom knocking the bung out and the water rushed in glub glub glub! So that he had to replug it with rags and whatever else he could find. She loved the waves and was a good yachtswoman.

Within a year Lottie and Fred, with two years of his absence still to go, had broken off their engagement as intolerable. Charlie had returned after his year of study and travel. On the ship he had been pursued by an importunate young woman who had begged him to marry her. She was wealthy and would set him up in practice outside of Pittsburgh.

"I am expecting my fiancée to meet me at the dock."

"She won't be there."

"Nevertheless . . ." And Flossie was not there.

He had been at times an insulting lover, impossible for a girl to put up with. Toward the end she had refused to reply to his letters. Nevertheless, he would not give up till he had talked to her, which he did immediately after he had deposited his luggage at his parents' home and greeted them.

She was cold and distant. He had hurt her by his taunts and indifference. She had at one time sent him a photo, a formal picture of herself done by a fashionable New York photographer: her hair was fixed in a great bulging mass above her forehead, held in place as it was in those days. It infuriated him. But when he saw that the awkward, young-girl's curve of her neck had been retouched, her shoulders smoothed over by the "skill" of that God-damned photographer he was infuriated—at her for permitting such contemptible practices.

He took the blade of a knife and, by scraping the surface of the photo away, restored the normal, the actual, not beautiful contours of the neckline. That was better. But he could do nothing with the hair. And so he had put the picture on his chiffonier in his narrow room in Leipzig and wrote his bitter letters.

They were not all such. Sometimes, as when he was in Italy, he was so carried away by the beauties and antiquities of the scene that he filled his letters with love for her. Once at Fiesole, above Florence, he had watched an early airplane try to get up off the ground, watched from a temple ruin and saw it fail. Then back to the hotel to fill page after page with his descriptions.

Toward the last, she had given him back his freedom—as he apparently had wanted it. And now here he was again. What was this thing: to be married? Certainly it did not appear to be a happy thing. It was not so for her, at any rate. She held him off. But he was so insistent that after a few days she melted and, against her better judgment, gave in once more.

Gurlie was more or less aware of what was going on and she more or less accepted it. This young man was not her choosing. And, after all, what could he see in that skinny thing, her younger daughter? He'd never amount to much with his lack of ambition, but she liked him, in a way.

Lottie had taken up her music again more seriously than ever, she was constantly practicing, perfecting herself in her techniques. The summer after her younger sister's fiancé's return, the family took a small cottage at Monroe, New York. It was not too far away—a flourishing community of dairy farms—and the orchards, the scenery and air were superb.

They had heard of a Revolutionary farmhouse, very small

but very picturesque. It had near it a spring in an old-fashioned well house, a crystal brook on the premises and a half-broken-down old barn near the road where they could keep a horse. This, at last, was getting close to the real thing. It looked as though here or hereabouts Gurlie would find her bastion, her satisfaction. Everyone liked it—even Joe. There was an ancient forge on the property, and, to make them laugh, the people who owned it kept a little jackass in the old orchard, called Sonje.

Here Flossie could be visited by her doctor lover, here little Paul could grow up, here Lottie could plan her winter concerts and here Gurlie could dream. The community was convenient enough to New York City for Stecher's daily train trip if necessary.

26

The spring, not ten feet from the kitchen door, must have determined the location of the house in the first place. It was the source for more than the mere water it gave. And though the farm had been abandoned long since for higher ground, the old house still stood. It attracted Gurlie with her sense of the primitive, the elemental. It was a source, a rebeginning. Water is the source of everything. She had rented the place for the summer.

And what water! The well house, built into the side of a bank, was made of boards that by being constantly soaked had become as hard as iron. It was a cavity facing north, into which the sun never reached, protecting its coolness in the semidark. But if you waited a moment for your eyes to grow used to the shadow you could see the movement of the white sand at the bottom, a live thing, where the icy water was profusely bubbling up.

On hot summer days when you'd go there for a pitcher of water you'd stand a moment or two under the well-house roof to watch that ceaseless stream gushing from the earth. It refreshed the mind as it promised to refresh the body. You waited, almost enjoying the dryness of your throat, prolonging the anticipation of the delight which relief would afford. And the mind, too, drank of the idea of that spring.

That it was a dying pleasure in no way reduced its effectiveness. The Stechers were no more than city folks. Like all such people, they didn't know much about the country. They loved the place. The natives didn't think much of it.

Therefore it was on its last legs. A couple years more and the roof would fall in. That would be the end of it. But to Lottie and to Gurlie, especially, it was romantic, and for the moment completely satisfying. Little Paul loved to play in the brook; the steep dirt road up the hill eastward, a side road, was used by no one; the little donkey nodded half-asleep among the rotting apple trees. It was more to Gurlie than just a place to spend the summer; it was the beginning of the realization of an ambition. She had found her objective in this idyllic spot. They hung their hammocks under the old broken willows by the brook's edge, Lottie rented a piano while apple blossoms were still on the trees, and the whole family settled down to rest at their ease waiting for what would come next.

On rainy days there was the old colonial fireplace, an authentic reminder of other days. It had a broad hearth, wide and deep, and the forged-iron crane was still in place. Lottie chortled with glee when she first saw it. Built in to the right was the primitive oven where bread had been baked. They planned some day, when they could gather enough wood, to use it at least once during the summer. It had the authentic feeling that took Gurlie back to her family's farmstead in Norway.

"We've got to have a horse," said Gurlie.

"Get one," said her husband. "Do you think one of these farmers is going to give it to you?"

It just happened that a doctor back in Riverdale was at that time switching to his first automobile and told them he'd sell his mare to them cheap.

"Cheap!" said Joe. "I can imagine."

"Charlie and Floss can drive her up for us."

"And who's going to take care of her?"

"We can do it," Lottie offered. "It isn't much trouble."

"And I suppose the harness and the carriage goes with the deal?" said Joe.

"Of course."

"And who's going to feed her, buy oats, hay and fix the roof of the barn and put her out to . . . ?" He didn't know himself much about the details of taking care of a horse.

"Agh, you!" said his wife. And so it was arranged to have Floss and Charlie drive the little mare the forty miles to the farm. Which she willingly enough accomplished except for the last hill, at which she balked, and the young doctor had to get out and lead her. But she did it at last and was none the worse for it once they had stabled her, rested her, watered her and fed her.

Now indeed they were established. A nearby farmer named George Nash, and a shrewd and able one, became their advisor and protector.

"You like the place, do you?"

"We love it," Charlotte had said.

"Take you around soon's I get a little time and show you the whole section. There are some nice estates out around here in the hills. Quite a lot of money has been coming into these parts in recent years."

"Is that so?" said Gurlie, pricking up her ears.

"Yes, it wasn't two or three years ago you could pick up these farms for a song. House and barns, the whole thing for a few hundred dollars. No more."

"Why was that?"

"No money in farming around here now, it's good dairy country and some makes a go of it, but it's hard work. And nobody wants to work like that today. Real estate's the thing. I'll drive you around some time and show you the place."

"But your own place looks prosperous," said Gurlie. It was the nearest farm; you could see it through the trees, off the narrow dirt road, a large clapboard building painted white with neat lawns and well-trimmed hedges around it. It faced a pasture sloping down to the same little stream that continued past the Stechers' cottage. The fences about it were in first-rate order and at the pasture bottom where the ground was inclined to be swampy, Joe had noticed some newly cut ditches with tile pipe laid along each of them to be put in for drainage. Altogether it looked to be a well-kept farm.

"You look as if you were making money," said Gurlie in her downright way.

"Got to keep things up," said George Nash. "But I'm getting too old for the work. If I didn't have this real-estate business—a sale once in a while . . ."

"Oh go on," said Gurlie, "I'll bet you've got a pile of money in the bank." And she laughed her raucous laugh. "You must be making money. That apple orchard you have by the house is the most healthy-looking I've ever seen, loaded with fruit. I've been waiting to see your daughters. I hear they're pretty."

"Nice girls, Inez and Hattie are nice girls. Their mother's downright proud of them. Well, have a good summer. I suppose we'll be seeing you once in awhile. Come up to the house and meet Mrs. Nash. I think you'll get along."

"And the milk and eggs—and vegetables? Can we get them from you?"

"The girls'll leave what you order every morning right by the fence post at the corner of the lot there every morning when they drive to town. A dozen eggs. All right. Come up and see us any time you like."

When the two girls finally appeared a day or two later, Joe, who was there, blinked. He had, literally, never in his life seen anything like it. They were tall, beautifully made in their simple farm dresses. They didn't look like farm girls at all but more as if they were made up for a Broadway show. Except that they were not made up, they were real—and they were able.

"Where did *you* come from?" Gurlie said, when she first saw them.

"We are Mr. Nash's daughters, with the milk," the dark one said, and her blond sister smiled.

"Come here, Lottie, yoohoo!" Gurlie called. "Look."

"Oh," Charlotte uttered amazed. "Who are *you?*" She couldn't believe her eyes.

"They are our neighbors," said Gurlie. "Why, you're beautiful. Sit down here a minute." She pointed to the chairs on the low porch in front of the cottage. "I want to look at you. Are all the young ladies up here as pretty as you? Now, that's what I call a healthy girl," she said to her daughter, who, in an old dress, her hair awry had been lounging about the house. "That's the way *you* should look."

"Are you staying all summer?" said the older girl, quite at ease. "It's so nice to have a neighbor."

"Do you like it here?" said her sister.

And that's the way the summer had begun. Up the hill beyond the little brook where the road crossed it, out of sight, was the neglected house of the old lady who owned the little cottage, the aristocrat of the region. She never went out, the fields were overgrown—an eccentric. But she was glad to see Gurlie when she called and seemed to liven up quite a bit. Her son was a physician, as his father had been also, and lived elsewhere. The old lady, aside from occasional visitors in summer, was quite alone.

It was *her* little donkey that wandered the old orchard. The girls tried to pet him as he would stand there half-asleep under a tree hourlong, but when you tried to go up to him he'd move off, at a leisurely gait, but effectively for all that. His coat was heavy and matted. Nobody from the old house came near him.

"He has a corner, up the hill beyond the barn," they said. "He stays out of doors the year round. He's old. He used to belong to the little grandchildren when they lived here years ago. They're grown up now. They don't come any more. We call him the philosopher. He gets along."

Hee haw! Hee haw! You could hear him bray now and again. "There goes the old philosopher!" said Joe once, on hearing it. He liked the little fellow. "He's telling you what he thinks of you."

They were a scant mile and a half from the town. Very few wagons and no carriages ever passed that way. So that in the little valley their isolation was complete. Birds, the oriole and the tanager, the indigo bunting, thrushes, and in the little patch of cattails where there was standing water, red-winged blackbirds were never disturbed.

In the earlier part of the summer the girls found several patches of wild strawberries growing profusely in the grass, so much so that they preserved more than a dozen jars of them to take home for the winter.

But most of the time they merely wandered about the fields or read books, did a minimum of cooking, went to town on simple errands. It was an easy walk, past the ruined lime-kiln, past the Jones farm, that looked very well tended atop its high bank, past the race track where later on they were to witness the nearby trotting races, and so to the stores, the post office, where, around the curve, right through the street, you might say, the Chicago Express would roar, shaking the ground, setting the dust flying and occasionally killing some-one too little cautious, who had strayed too far and too late onto the tracks.

After such a trip along the hot roads, what a relief it was to get back, a little footsore, to the cottage by the spring! It became home to them as the summer wore on, a real home where Lottie practiced patiently; and once in a while the Nash girls, so fresh and wholesome-looking, came to sit unseen, if they could arrange it that way, to hear her. To them Lottie was a world away. They thought of her as something miraculous. Though they were intelligent, exceptionally so, they felt lost beside her.

It was a lazy time. Lottie had acquired a two-months-old Irish setter pup. He was lovely, but after the first day she had him, he yipped all night long keeping her awake. So the next day she spent her entire time keeping *him* awake. Never for a moment did she let him rest. If he flopped down and closed his eyes, as a pup will, she was after him. She prodded him, she made him run, she made him play with her finger. She took him for several long walks, though he balked and pulled against his leash. That night he slept the sleep of the dead.

On week-ends sometimes they'd have visitors. Charlie would come up to spend the day with his wife to be. They'd go off for long walks alone, lie together under an apple tree, out of sight side by side and talk or whatever it is that young lovers do. One tree whose branches arched over to touch the ground all around them was their private bower.

Lottie, too, had her callers again. Krieger was there one Sunday during a veritable mushroom bounty. The well-grazed pastures and under the trees of the old orchard were literally peppered with them. There were thousands. The family had eaten them stewed, fried with butter, on toast, on steak, in every way imaginable—and on top of that, besides the pasture mushroom, there were hundreds of puff balls, some half as big as your head.

No one knew that these too, sliced and fried while they were young, were as delicious as any other form of the fungus. The four of them, Lottie, Flossie, Krieger and Charlie were walking up the hill when it occured to one of the boys to throw these fragile but heavy balls of fluff first against a tree, then playfully at one of the girls, then more seriously at each other. It developed into a regular war. They'd pick them from the ground as though they were snowballs, running right and left to find some bigger ones, then letting fly, smash them on each other's backs, legs.

Krieger at one time sent the family a crate of live lobsters from one of his salesman's trips to Maine.

Far in the distance was Sugar Loaf, which they planned one day to climb. But in general, through sunny days, first decorating the house with wild crab-apple blossoms, then dogwood, blue flags and daisies to goldenrod and purple asters as it got toward fall, the summer passed happily enough.

"What do you do with yourselves all the year round?" Gurlie would say to the Nash girls.

"Oh we go to high school now. We have a good high school here. And summers we work on the farm. There's a lot to do. We milk and cultivate the garden, and help Mother in the house. When there is haying we drive the team or take over the rake."

"That's what makes you so healthy."

"Don't get any ideas," Lottie would say to her mother, "that when you get *your* farm I'm going to do any of that. Not on your life."

27

It was a broad, barren hilltop with a fine view over the entire surrounding country—several acres, with a breast-high wall of fieldstone crawling like a snake to close in the area.

"You can't grow anything here," said Gurlie.

"But look at the view," said the powerful young man sitting in the carriage beside her. Lottie and a young woman named Dora, the man's wife, holding a little girl on her lap, another, older girl at her side, occupied the rear seat. The black horse, who was puffing from the winding hill road up which he had just dragged them, paused as the place first came into view.

"Marvelous!" said Lottie. "What a site!"

"Do you think so?" said the man, turning about. "Yes, I think it pretty fine myself."

"You get tired of it," said Dora, the wife.

"Are you tired of it, darling?"

"After a year or two you do feel as if a change wouldn't do any harm."

Gurlie looked around. She hadn't yet got used to the Oxford accent. Lottie, too, glanced at the young woman; her expression as she spoke hadn't in the least altered. The horse started up again approaching a gap in the wall, the entrance gateway.

"And that's the house we saw in the distance all last summer. We often wondered who lived there."

"Yes," said the man. "What a pity we've wasted so much time."

When the Stechers had arrived at their little bird's nest of a cottage the second year, prepared for another lazy and profitable time, the *Monroe Gazette* had run a notice of the event in the local news column:

The Joseph Stechers of Riverdale, N. J., have taken the Genou cottage for another season, their second in our midst. Miss Charlotte Stecher, the distinguished concert pianist, is here for a rest after her last successful season.

Lottie laughed!

We are happy to have the Stechers with us. Monroe is getting to be a popular summer resort for many New York artists.

A day or two later, Gurlie had received a note, on blue paper with a crest, from a Gregory Ives—"Who's he?"— saying that he was their neighbor—"I never heard of him"— that he had read the notice in the paper, that he had a concert grand Steinway in his studio which he would be happy to put at the disposal of Miss Stecher, and that, with Mrs. Stecher's permission, he with his wife and children would like to call.

Lottie was frozen to the spot, wondering what her mother would say. Gurlie hesitated a moment then said to her daughter, "Write him a note."

"Me?"

"Yes, I don't want to bother with it. Write to his wife and ask them to call." That was how it started.

Two days later they arrived, a strapping fellow with straight, straw-colored hair and what appeared to be weak eyes, a man in his middle thirties, a long jaw and the wrists and forearms of a heavyweight prize fighter. With one of his little girls beside him he filled the front seat of the carriage. His much younger, dark-haired wife, with the other little girl, seemed frail beside him. He got down, leaving his wife to shift for herself and, fastening his animal, came up to introduce himself.

Now as the carriage ground slowly over the graveled driveway, Gurlie looked right and left. It was not one of those manicured places of the usual city dweller come to establish himself in the country. There was a vague attempt at flowers, but in general, due to the lack of water on this hilltop, the grass was scanty with rock outcroppings evident all about what would otherwise have been a lawn.

"Do you want to get out here?" he asked the ladies. "Or shall we drive down to the barn and walk around a bit first?"

"I and the children will get out here," said the British wife. "You can go on if you like."

"I'll get out, too," said Lottie.

"Oh, don't you want to look at the view?" asked Mr. Ives.

"No. I'll go in with your wife and the children."

"But I want to look around," said Gurlie.

So the younger women and the children alighted. They were good little girls, rather shy and subdued. They didn't say anything, but ran to the house as soon as their feet touched the ground and were admitted by a maid. Lottie and the young mother followed while the carriage proceeded to the barn where Ives unharnessed the horse himself and put him in his stall.

"Do you take care of him yourself?" asked Gurlie.

"No, the farmer does that, but when he's not around I do what is necessary. Let's go out this way. Around behind the barn is a good place to start." Gurlie, who was not too sure afoot, followed with her short steps over the stony path. It was a clear, sunny day with scarcely any mist. You could see twenty miles or more westward over a wooded valley with a few white farmhouses scattered about in the distance. At the back was Sugar Loaf projecting above the scene.

Gurlie looked but was not interested. "Is this your land here?" she said. "This is no good to grow anything."

"My property line is the other side of that pasture. Where, you see, the stone wall ends. But we have a garden. I'll show you." And they came down from the little lift in the ground where they were standing and began to circle the house.

"Did you build the house yourself?" asked Gurlie. It rose before them now, a square three-storied pile made of field-stone.

"Yes, I designed it."

"You are an architect?" asked Gurlie.

"I am an artist. That's why this place appealed to me. The light. There is nothing to obstruct the light here."

"Hum," said Gurlie, "but there are no trees. I can't imagine a home in the country without trees."

"Trees won't grow here."

"So I see. But you said you were going to show the garden. You have to have a garden."

"There it is, across the road."

And there in a dip under the summit of the hill Gurlie did see a patch of corn sprouting in rows and the tilled soil assigned to what would later be the other vegetables. "Hm," she said again, and shook her head. "It must be hot here in the middle of summer."

"The house is very comfortable. The studio takes in the whole three stories, right to the roof, and it is on the north side, so that the sun never beats into it. It's always cool there. Shall we go in now?"

"No, no, no, no," said Gurlie. "Do you have any cows?"

"No, it isn't worth it in this dairy country. We're only two miles out of town."

"And what is that?" asked Gurlie, seeing a low, monumentlike building to the north of the house in the center of a field.

"That is my father's tomb."

Gurlie looked at the man incredulously. "Do you mean that?"

"Yes."

"Why is that?"

"I wanted him here."

"But isn't that a strange thing, to have a tomb like that in the middle of a bare field? Why did you do that? I should think . . ." It was a new-looking heap of blue granite of no particular distinction right out of the field, as bare of planting or lawn as the rest of the grounds. They went up to it. Gurlie looked for some legend, some lettering. There was none.

"Who was your father?"

"General Jonathan Ives."

"Where do your people come from?" asked Gurlie in her usual blunt manner.

"Did you ever hear of Mme. Jumel?"

"Yes," said Gurlie. "She was a bad woman."

Ives smiled. "Well, she was my great-grandmother."

"Oh," said Gurlie, "you shouldn't tell anybody that. She lived with a lot of different men during the Revolutionary War. Shocking."

"My great-grandmother was a brilliant woman. The morals of the time were such that she got a bad reputation. She was merely ahead of her generation. There are always women like that during periods of great stress. She understood what was going on and—profited by it."

"Yes, I have visited the Jumel Mansion in New York."

"Have you? Then you know. My father was her son's son."

"She was rich. Huh! She knew how. Did your father have money?"

Ives was willing to talk.

"What was his business?"

"The hotel business. The family owns the Hotel Ives and the Hotel Picardy on Fifth Avenue. And some other hotels."

"Then you must be rich," said Gurlie. "That explains it.

If you weren't rich, you wouldn't want to stay in a place like this. This is just a plaything for you. Other people have to have more comfort. This is too bare. I suppose you paint to amuse yourself. Do you sell your paintings?"

"I have sold a few paintings."

"Oh, well. You don't know much about how the other half lives," she said with her insane laugh. "Rich people don't know anything."

"I'm not rich," said Ives.

"Agh!" said Gurlie slapping him on the arm and laughing. As much as to say, Who do you think you're talking to? "What do you do with yourself all day long with two little girls like that up here? And your wife, I wonder what she thinks of it? I bet she wishes she was back in England sometimes."

"Maybe she does," said Ives.

"Does she like it? I wouldn't. Not even a flower to look at. Are those weeds?" she said pointing to a clump of blue flowers beside the path. "They're pretty. I should think you'd pick some and take them in the house. What are they? I'm going to pick some and take them in to your wife. Haven't you got a flower book with illustrations? I want to know what they are." And she tried to pick a spray of the showy blue stalks, but they were too tough. "Here, pick me some." He crouched down, his heavy thighs flexed, the muscles bulging as he did so, and ripped a bunch of the weed up by the root.

"You shouldn't have done that. You are too strong."

So they went along a poorly marked path, she clutching the weed in her grip, around to the front of the house. He opened the door and they went in.

"How dark it is!" said Gurlie rubbing her eyes.

"Just the change of light." They listened, but could hear no voices, so he led her directly through the entry hall into the studio itself. She immediately looked up, three stories, to the roof above. "Well," said Gurlie.

It was obviously the center of interest to the interior of the house, the other rooms being merely applied about it.

And featured in it, a little to the left of the big north window, where an easel stood, was a concert grand piano to which Gurlie went at once, after sweeping her eyes about the four walls, to read the lettering over the keyboard.

"A Steinway, no less. Well everything is certainly in the grand style."

Ives was fidgeting about, wondering where the others had gone to, but Gurlie kept his attention, a little to his beginning annoyance, by plying him with questions.

"You told me you had a nature book. Look up this flower. I want to know what it is."

"Yes," he said absently, going to the bookcase, the books all helter-skelter in an unlighted corner, coming up after a moment with a flower book into which he looked rapidly, comparing the flower in Gurlie's hand. "Here it is. Bugloss."

But just at that moment a door opened and the voices of the young women could be heard as they entered the room. Ives was relieved. Gurlie, without hesitation, called out to her daughter, "What do you think? He has his father's tomb right there outside the window."

"Mother!" said Lottie. "Oh isn't this a fine room!"

"You must be a regular artist. It's just like the pictures you see of a studio. A regular Bohemian atmosphere," said Gurlie.

"You should see the rest of the house. It's charming."

"Not now. I want to rest."

"Have you seen this?"

"No, what's that? A pile of waste paper?"

The other three laughed. In the middle of the studio was indeed a pile of paper, an enormous pile, a veritable mountain made up of envelopes, large and small, white and pink and blue. If you looked closer you saw that many of them bore special-delivery stamps. All had been opened and lay helter-skelter there piled up without order.

"What is that?" asked Gurlie.

"Poems."

"What kind of poems? Are they yours?"

"A contest. They have been pouring in from all over the United States."

"And Canada," added Dora.

"My sister's fiancé is a poet," said Lottie. "Would he know about the contest?"

"Oh," said Ives, "it's not too late. Tell him to submit one. I call it the *Lyric Year*. There is a prize of a thousand dollars and there will be a book later. You should see some of them!"

"Are you a poet, too?" asked Gurlie.

"Oh yes," said his wife, "my husband does a bit of everything." Greg looked at her sharply, but made no rejoinder. He changed the subject. "Won't you play for us, Miss Stecher? I'd love to have you try the piano."

"Maybe your wife will play for us. You play, don't you?"

"Oh scarcely at all any more," said Dora.

"No," broke in her husband, "she never played seriously. And now she never touches the piano. It's just there gathering dust."

"He doesn't let me touch anything in this room," said the young woman quickly.

"Do *you* play then?" asked Lottie of their host.

"No, not a note. Come on." He went over to her as if he were about to lift her out of her chair. Lottie got up slowly, she was tall, she caught her skirt in her shoe, freed it after a moment, and walked with her slight stoop, her skirt sweeping the floor, to the keyboard, sat down and gently wrung her hands, avoiding the man's look.

"What shall I play?" she asked Mrs. Ives.

"Anything you like, my dear."

"Do you like Bach?"

"I adore him."

Lottie struck a few chords. The room came alive. "Oh, this is a good instrument, really magnificent. You keep it in tune, I see."

"Oh, he had it tuned when he knew you were coming."

"Don't let's have so much talk," said Ives sharply. "We want to hear Miss Stecher play."

"I'm sorry," said his wife. "Aren't we rather pushing her?"

The acoustics were superb. Lottie had been practicing a toccata, a work she frequently played at the beginning of a concert to loosen up her fingers. She waited a moment and in the absolute silence of that isolated spot some wasps could be heard buzzing in the high ceiling. She played well, extremely well. The lively music filled the room, its precisions making the ornate vases and drapings seem strangely out of place.

One of the little girls came to the studio door and looked in, but when she saw her father she quickly vanished.

When Lottie had finished, Ives got up and went toward her.

"That's very beautiful," said his wife. "We used to have such music at my home in Oxford, England. It takes me back. Bach," she smiled to herself, "takes me back to those blessed days."

"It sounds very good in this room," was Gurlie's comment. "You're lucky to have a piano like that here."

"I wish your daughter would come here and make use of it. Tell her we'd like her to come here and make use of it as often as she likes. You tell her," said the man to his wife.

"Yes, of course. I should like it so much. Any time you like. Just come when you want to. We're always here," she added with a smile.

"There you are," said Gurlie.

"Play something else," said Greg. "Do you know the 'Liebestraum'?"

Mrs. Ives coughed and, getting up, asked to be excused for a moment, she wanted to speak to the maid about the children. Lottie said she hadn't played the "Liebestraum" for some time and that she'd rather not. Instead she struck quite spontaneously into "Anitra's Dance" from the Peer Gynt Suite. Gurlie had gotten up and wandered to the big window.

Ives remained leaning on the piano, his chin in his hand, looking at Lottie as she played, looking straight at her eyes which were downcast. When she finished, she got up quickly and went to her mother.

"Mother, you haven't seen the house," she said. "You should see how cleverly it has been designed."

"Yes," said Gurlie. "I'd like to see it." So Ives took the lady in tow. Lottie, having already been the rounds, did not go with them, but asked if she might not look at some of the poems from the heap in the center of the floor while they were gone.

"Here's a cushion, sit down and help yourself. It's pathetic. Imagine the emotional backwaters that that heap of manuscripts represents—terrible. Horrible! But we have found a few good ones, one or two really outstanding poems."

"I'm glad of that," said Lottie. "They can't all be that bad, it can't be that there isn't even one. Go on now and leave me alone." And she sat down taking one poem after another out of the envelopes, reading them and shaking her head. After a moment her hostess returned. "Where have they gone?"

"He's showing Mother around the house."

"I hope he doesn't take her out on that top balcony. It has no railing. I'm frightened to death of the beastly place. And he's always taking visitors out there. You play beautifully."

"Thank you," said Lottie.

"No, but you do. Beautifully. Quite the professional touch. Do you think you'll be coming here to make use of the piano?"

"It would be an imposition. I couldn't. Besides it's rather far from where we are staying."

"Oh, I'm certain he'd adore fetching you. We live such a humdrum life. It would be—a great relief. May I call you Charlotte? My name is Dora. It would be really a pleasure, Charlotte. Come when you can, whenever you like. He's often busy and we should be quite alone here. It would be a comfort to me." Then out of a clear sky: "I think I'll be going to England, for a visit, in another year. It's so nice to have you as a neighbor this summer. We ought to have a pleasant time of it. Do you think your mother would like some tea?"

"I'm sure she would."

At that moment the voyagers returned. "You go so fast," Gurlie was saying. "You don't let me get my breath."

"Do you like it?" said Dora.

Gurlie was always downright. "Well," she said . . .

Dora laughed with a slight touch of bitterness and defiance in her voice. "Neither do I," she said. "I think it's horrible."

"Now, my dear," said Ives. "You've always said . . ."

But she broke in on him, apparently enjoying herself at his expense. "I always said that I could stand it, for a while. It's a very barren place really—unless you're an artist." He obviously squirmed, but clamped his jaws shut and went toward Lottie, who was just getting up from before the pile of poems.

"What do you think of them?"

"I haven't had time . . ."

"You'll have tea?" Dora put in.

"Yes, I'd like some," said Gurlie. "It's plain to see you're English. In Norway we drink coffee."

"Would you prefer coffee?"

"No, give me some tea. Thank you." Then, as Dora left the room Gurlie said to Greg, "Bring me some of those poems, I want to see them." He picked up a handful and put them in her lap. "Oh, I don't want to see these," she suddenly changed her mind. "You are an artist," she said, "show us some of your paintings. You must have some over there against the wall."

"No, I'm not working on anything just now. What I'm most interested in is the portrait. Do you know the work of Seurat?"

"Who is that?"

"A French artist. He calls himself a pointillist. I'm very much interested in his theory of color presentation. He uses pure colors, tiny points of pure color placed one beside the other from the tip of a brush. When the canvas is covered by them the eye blends them all together to make the design. I should like to paint a portrait of your daughter. She has a beautiful profile."

"Now look at that," said Gurlie. "He wants to paint your portrait. I bet he's good. Show me what you can do."

With that Ives drew out a small seascape, a misty sea of running waves in a light mist. It was well done, an opalescent canvas of considerable charm. "But that is not a portrait," objected Gurlie. "My, you can paint! He can paint," said she to her daughter.

"It's beautiful," said Lottie.

"I see you've been showing them your paintings," said Dora, re-entering with the maid who was carrying the tea things. "We're not losing much time, are we? What do you think of them?"

"He's an artist, all right," said Gurlie. "And to think you were here all last summer and we saw the house there on the top of the hill. It just looked like a square barn—and we didn't know who lived there. Well, now."

"Can't we see more?"

"After tea, my dear. Shan't we? I don't know how you Americans prefer it. Will you have Russian tea or would you prefer cream and sugar?" Dora had prepared some delicate little sandwiches which she passed about. Gurlie noticed that Ives was not joining them, and remarked upon it.

"Oh you don't know my husband. He never takes tea or coffee."

"What?"

"Tell them, my dear. He's a very particular eater. He never eats meat. We have foods from a place called Battle Creek, Michigan, wherever that may be. Nuts and breakfast foods. Don't we, darling?"

Ives had engaged Lottie in private conversation and seemed not to hear.

"Does he drink any *schnapps?*" asked Gurlie.

"Any what?"

"*Schnapps.*"

"Darling," she asked her husband, "what are *schnapps?*"

"Brandy," said Gurlie. "It's good for you."

And so the afternoon wore on until it was getting time for them to go. The tea things had been cleared away, but before his guests should leave, Ives asked Charlotte to play once more.

"Yes, do," said Dora. So that Charlotte, obliging as always, went to the piano and sat down with her hands in her lap.

"Now this time," insisted her host, "you must play the '*Liebestraum.*'"

"You can play it perfectly well," said Gurlie. "Come on, we've got to go home." So Lottie began to play the "*Liebestraum,*" while this time Ives went to the far part of the room and watched from there. Dora looked at him once or twice, while Gurlie in the center of the room sat with half-closed eyes as was her wont.

A purple wasp was crawling, its body pulsating slowly up and down over the tabouret where the sandwiches had rested. Now he got up and flew toward the piano. Lottie was the first to see it. Crying out "Oh!" she abruptly stopped playing and stood up.

Everyone jumped. "A wasp," she said.

Dora said, "Oh, we're quite used to them. They have their nests on the ceiling."

But Ives got up and went toward the table to which the thing had returned. Lottie said "Oh, oh," cowering as the insect took off and flew toward her again pursued by the man. But now it continued rising toward the windows and went off.

Lottie played no more.

"It's been a wonderful afternoon," said she walking from the piano.

"Oh, won't you finish? You must come often," said Dora, carried away.

"Yes," said Ives, seconding his wife. "I'll pick you up and you can spend the day here whenever you like. I want to paint your portrait."

"Paint a portrait of my little son, too," said Gurlie.

"I'll do that. A good idea. He can come with his sister."

"How was it?" said Floss when they got home.

"Mother, you were terrible," said Lottie. "You practically asked him . . ."

"Agh," said Gurlie. "I know what I'm doing."

"What was he like? What I saw of him, his pants were too tight," said Flossie.

"The pig. I hate him," Lottie replied, "and I refuse to go there again. His poor wife."

"You ought to be ashamed of yourself," Gurlie came back at her. "He's a perfect gentleman. And a wonderful painter. We're lucky."

28

Astrid was a good little mare. She liked nothing better than to run to town for the marketing. The Welch Brothers' butcher shop, on the curve of the road next to the drug store, could be counted on for excellent cuts of meat. They knew Gurlie there, and liked her. She was a good buyer, not easy to fool. "What'll it be this morning Mrs. Stecher? We have some nice legs of lamb, well hung. The best. About eight pounds. What do you say?"

But Gurlie wasn't looking. "That last one you sold me was tough, and you know it was tough. If you can't do better than that . . ." The farm people came in and just stood around, silent, or talked privately to the elder brother. Their orders were sometimes as much as they could carry. The boarding-house orders were even bigger, ten-pound roasts, two or three hams, a dozen chickens. Saturday-morning shopping was a big event.

From the butcher, leaving Astrid hitched to a post at the high curb, Gurlie would go to Mr. Miller, the grocer, while Lottie might call for the mail or wander up the street looking in at one of the dry-goods store windows at the farm dresses and hats displayed there. She knew her mother would be slow, so often she'd wander several blocks or even go beyond the Congregational church, round the memorial boulder at the corner of the little park, get even as far as the abandoned entrance to the half-mile trotting track—where in the early summer violets still were blossoming in the heavy grass.

"Good morning, Mrs. Stecher," the white-aproned Mr. Miller would say as Gurlie came busting in. "How are you this morning?"

"I feel fine. Where is everybody?"

"Oh they'll be along after while. What can I do for you?"

"Let me sit down," said Gurlie.

"Take your time. Have you met any of our new people yet this year? We seem to have quite a few new faces around."

"What do you know about Mr. Ives, the artist? He lives up on the hill past . . ."

"You don't need to tell me about that man. You mean 'Affinity Ives'? I've known him since before he was married the first time. He grew up around here. Used to run with Sadie Brower's daughter. But she turned him down. They say he's all right with a paint brush. Comes of a fine family. Lots of money. But he's sort of the black sheep of the litter. How'd you meet him?"

"Don't let me forget," said Gurlie. "I want a pound of that sharp cheese. American cheese you call it, crumbles . . ."

"I know just what you mean. Excuse me a minute." And he went to the front of the store. Gurlie got up and, wandering over to the vegetable stalls, began picking up what she wanted and putting it on the counter. "I want a dozen of your best eggs," she said, when Mr. Miller came back to her.

"Yes, that man's had quite a career—I guess he's been all over the world. He turns up here, though, every so often. Pretty little girl he's married this time. Maybe this'll settle him down. I'll never forget the beating he got a couple of years back. Seems he got a little ahead of himself one night with a fellow who was bigger than he was."

"What happened?" said Gurlie.

"Oh he was coming—you take care of Mrs. Jones, will you, George?—he was coming out from the city here one night, during the racing season, and the train was crowded. Wasn't a seat to be had and there was a young lady standing in the aisle he thought ought not to be there."

"Well, I'm glad to see that there are *some* gentlemen left in the world."

"Well sir, there was a fellow sitting there reading a paper that Mr. Ives thought ought to give up his seat to the lady. So he spoke to him and told him to get up and give the lady his place."

"Hm," said Gurlie.

"But when the man wouldn't do it, Ives grabbed him by the collar and pulled him out—and you know that Ives is powerful. Why he came in here just a month ago with a sprained hand from taking hold of his horse by the mane when he went to catch him. He pulled a handful of the hair out, he got such a heavy grip on it, but the horse got away. You can't hold a horse that way."

"What happened on the train?" said Gurlie.

"Well, I hate to tell you. They had to help young Mr. Ives off it, he was beat up so bad. He was a mess. He really got it that time. That fellow pounded him to a jelly."

"Oh," said Gurlie, "wrap up those things I laid out on the counter. And the cheese . . ."

"All right, ma'am. I'll put them in the back of the carriage. The usual place?"

"It's standing right in front of the drug store. And don't you overcharge me. What are eggs now?"

"Twenty cents a dozen, fresh laid. The finest that can be bought. That Ives is a great fellow. But you gotta watch him. You gotta watch him. He's not as young as he was, though. Maybe he's settled down now for good."

Gurlie left the store. She wandered into the Spirits and Wine Emporium where an old fellow in his shirt sleeves, his feet up on the counter, sat half-asleep with a newspaper across his belly. He took his feet down when Gurlie woke him. He didn't know her and looked at her quizzically, without a word.

"Have you got any Old Crow Whiskey?"

"Yes, ma'am," said the man, "we have."

"Well, I want a bottle," said Gurlie.

"That's just what you'll have then," he said, getting slowly to his feet and going to the shelves behind where Gurlie was standing. He reached up, got the bottle down and, placing it on the counter, asked her if there was anything else he could do for her.

"No, that's all," said Gurlie.

"It's a fine day, ma'am. You're one of the summer people," he said as he proceeded to wrap the bottle. "I haven't seen you around."

"My husband prints the labels for Old Crow," said Gurlie. "He says it's a good whiskey."

"He likes it, eh? Yes, it's a good whiskey. Come in again some time. We've got a lot of it here if you need it."

A long freight train made the next five minutes before the station an arena of flying dust and dancing papers while the pounding at the rail ends, and the clatter of the loaded cars caused the nags tethered along Main Street curb to dance nervously back and jerk ahead to the limit of their halters. Standing before the store, Gurlie turned her back, gathered her skirts about her and bowed her head before the artificial gale. "Pugh!" she said as she stood against the wall to let the fury pass.

Lottie came down the street just when Gurlie was beginning to look for her. "Yoohoo! Here I am." Their purchases were stored in the back of the carriage, some under their feet, and the mile-and-a-half drive back to the cottage lay before them.

"I was talking to Mr. Miller," said Gurlie, "about our friend Mr. Ives."

"Were you? What did he say?"

"He has a name, 'Affinity Ives,' they call him. It seems he's been married five or six times."

"Well?"

"That's awful. What kind of man is that?"

"A marrying man."

The road went south through the village under the elms and maples that met over it, past the old blacksmith shop and the bakery. "Isn't it quiet and beautiful?" said Lottie. "Such simple flowers as geraniums are charming here. They seem to grow better than at home. Their colors are more intense. I don't see why anyone lives in the city when they can have this. It's so beautiful."

When they had crossed the highway which circled the town and started up the long hill past the Jones farm, the valley opened out to the east, well-kept fields beyond the idle grandstand of the race track, the telegraph wires following the railroad throughout the center of it all to rolling hills in the middle distance. "We must drive out that way some time," said Gurlie. "It looks interesting."

Beyond, rose the low mountains. On the top of the highest sat the mansion of the railroad tycoon who had built it for his old age, but he died soon after. The cut for the inclined railroad which led to it from the valley below was clearly discernible. "I wonder what it's like up there," said Gurlie.

"Why don't you go and see?" said Lottie. "You can get passes from someone in the village to visit it when the family isn't there."

"It must be marvelous to have so much money."

The little mare slowed to a walk as the road wound past the golf course on the left. There were several couples on the greens, mostly women, scattered here and there over the course. "I wonder how old he is?" Lottie did not answer. "What can a man like that . . ." She changed her line of thought. "I wonder what he's doing in a place like this, with such a reputation."

"Who have you been talking to?"

"They say he's been married three times."

"Four," said Lottie.

"How do you know? You've never heard of him before."

"I've heard of him."

"Who have *you* been talking to? Who told you he was married four times?"

"Hattie Nash."

"When?"

"Last evening. She says he's a horrible person."

"So that's what you were talking about last night there in front of the cottage."

"She doesn't like him. She runs when she sees him coming in the village. She's funny."

"She's just a country girl. What does she know? He doesn't want *her*. Besides, he's married. His children are very charming. When is he coming to get you?"

"I'm not going."

"But you said you would go. You're not a child. If everyone acted that way we'd sit here all summer and never get to know anyone. He's a gentleman."

"You go," said Lottie. "You always wanted to get your picture painted."

That nettled Gurlie.

"Are you afraid of him?" she replied to her daughter. "Like these farm girls? You are supposed to be somebody. He is an artist. He can perhaps help you. If I were your age . . ."

At last the little mare reached the top of the long hill where a side road to the cottage branched off. Far to the right, on the very last ridge visible, but at no great distance really, high above the lake, which you could not see, stood the now familiar square stone house, all alone, not a tree near it, outlined on the summer sky. Both women glanced instinctively toward it as the little mare, sensing home, started out at a lively trot down the hill.

"How different it looks now when you know what's in it," said Lottie. "All last year it didn't mean a thing to us. It was there but I never even thought of it."

"Now I remember reading about him somewhere. Wasn't he married the first time to a French woman named . . . ?"

"Yes, I remember that too. Then it was someone from Chicago. I wonder how many children he has?"

Suddenly her mother turned to the girl. "You're a selfish woman." Lottie was taken aback and said, "What are you talking about?"

"You take, take, take everything that is given you and you never give anything in return."

"What have I done now?" said Lottie.

"You've always been that way and it's about time somebody told you."

The little mare slowed down to a walk, shying a little, as she always did when they were passing the ruins of a thirty-foot-high lime kiln, so incongruously standing beside the road in the open fields.

"You'll never be a concert pianist. You're too lazy."

"And now I'm lazy," said Lottie.

"What have you done since you came back from Germany? I thought you were going to make a name for yourself."

"What do you think I am? I'm no genius. I can't go up to an agent and say, 'I'm a concert pianist. Get me a booking.' Maybe I'll never get a booking. How do I know? Just because I've been to Germany doesn't mean anything."

"Of course it means something."

"There are hundreds of young artists drifting around New York. Many of them are gifted. Does that get them in a concert hall? The agencies are filled with them. I'm just a beginner. You have to become known."

"How are you going to become known?"

"Well, you have to be good. Then you have to have a backer. Somebody with money."

"You can't find a backer if you never go anywhere. And you can't get a backer by refusing your opportunities. You have to be aggressive. It doesn't matter if you don't happen to like a man, you can't afford to be so fussy. When he wants to have you use his piano . . ."

"Oh, so that's it? He's a nobody. I never heard of him as a painter."

"How do you know? Go and investigate. One thing leads to another. You will meet other people, people will get to know you, they will hear you play, they'll talk about you. But you . . ."

"Oh, you make me tired."

"Look at you. Gawky, hollow eyes, skinny legs. You look sick. You don't take after my family. You don't eat properly. Look at these farm girls, they have some stamina in them. But you . . ."

"Oh Mother, why don't you leave me alone?"

"That's what I've done. I thought you had some sense. We give you opportunities and what do you do with them? Nothing. You don't know how lucky you are. You don't know how to improve yourself. What do you expect the world to do? Fall at your feet? You've got to be ready. You've got to be alert. When a famous artist wants to paint your portrait you should say, 'Yes, of course.' But you act like a silly girl. No! No! Agh, you make me sick."

"All right, if he wants to paint my portrait he can paint it. Is that what you want? I'll be waiting for him tomorrow morning on the porch in a pretty dress as if he was going to take me to a party. I just can't wait for him. Is that what you want me to say?"

"Well, it's about time you got some sense."

By then they were in front of the cottage where Gurlie got out and, taking her market purchases from the carriage, laid them on the porch. Lottie helped her. Flossie, who was in the hammock by the brook with her little brother, came up to help also, but there was nothing to do, as Lottie drove the horse into the stable to unharness her.

The brook was low just then and the little boy, barefooted, had been attempting to dam it where it was no more than an inch deep at the ford. With a small shovel he had piled up the sand between two flat stones until the water, which had more of a head than he knew, spreading out back of the obstruction, began to trickle off through the weeds into the stream again. There was an old fence rail with which he half-succeeded in blocking the weakness of his design there. But then the water had gone off in the opposite direction.

His sister had helped him move two stones, which he was not able to roll over without her assistance, getting her shoes wet in the process. A frog jumped out from beside one of them and after two leaps buried itself again in the mud at the stream bottom. Now the dam was completed, making a broad pool where, with a piece of broken shingle for a boat, the little fellow was playing.

"What were you two so excited about?" asked Floss, when her sister returned from the barn. "I could hear you from the corner of the lot."

"Ma got on her high horse about something I said and was giving me the devil."

"It sounded like it."

But since Lottie offered no further explanation, and went into the house to change her dress, Floss returned to her book in the hammock under the willows where heavy clouds piled up in the sky from the west and a chilly breeze began to sway the long green tendrils of the old trees. The little boy was delighted, as his ship, on which his sister had improvised a small sail with a bit of paper and hairpin, dashed madly across the ocean and was wrecked in the weeds beyond.

29

Joe was furious the following Saturday when he heard what had been going on during the week. Nor was he pacified when Ives, his wife and the two little girls drove over on Sunday to make his acquaintance.

"Do you know what you've done?" said he to his wife, when they were alone that night in the small cottage. The girls could hear them talking heatedly and surmised what it was about, though their words came indistinctly through the thin walls. Then he said something in German. "Any fool who calls himself an artist or lives in a big house." Then, as Gurlie shushed him, his voice dropped to a lower pitch.

After breakfast the following day when the livery man came to drive him to the early train, he went off without a word. Poor Joe.

He was even more furious the following week when he returned to the cottage, having made inquiries about his artist neighbor, and found the record even worse than he thought. "Why he's a notorious blackguard, no better than a crook. *Ein Schwein*. A good for nothing." But by that time the damage had been done. Lottie had already sat for her portrait three times, had even taken little Paul with her for the last time, for a preliminary sketch, and the pattern of the summer was established.

Meanwhile Flossie had announced that she and her doctor friend were finally to be married late that fall. So the days wore on happily enough and even Joe at last accepted, with resignation, his wife's machinations.

Lottie admired Dora, who in her turn accepted her as a frequent guest. For hours there would be complete silence from the studio as by the artist's painstaking method the portrait slowly progressed, and no one could say that it wasn't an outstanding piece of work. When Gurlie saw it for the first time: "Did you have to make the neck so low?" she said. But aside from that she acknowledged that it was masterly.

"Lottie has such a beautiful neck," Ives had protested. "You can't cover that up." He had in fact insisted, when Lottie had first come to sit for him, that she unfasten her dress and wear it low in front, to which she had only mildly objected. But he had come and pushed it down over her breasts so that their full beauty would be at least indicated.

"Yes, it is well done," said Gurlie. "Now, when you have finished that you must do one of my little boy."

As the summer wore on Lottie came regularly to pose or play by the hour upon the piano which was at her disposal. Little Paul's portrait was being built simultaneously with her own: his blue eyes, his direct, proud look, high forehead and abundant mass of wavy blond hair, his straight little nose, full empurpled lips, highly colored cheeks and round chin. He was an exceptionally beautiful child whom Ives faithfully put down on the canvas with great skill and devotion until you melted to the man because of his patient abilities. Joe had to admit that he was an artist and a good one—and as a consequence relaxed his instinctive opposition.

When little Paul's portrait was completed after the first month, it was presented to Gurlie by the artist and became her prized possession. But the picture of Lottie never left the studio.

Ives acknowledged that portrait to be the best he'd painted to date. "You're positively inspired," Dora would say to him when, on Lottie's arrival in the morning, they'd be inspecting the previous day's progress preliminary to what lay ahead. Lottie would beg her to stay and talk to her to relieve the monotony of posing and sometimes she'd do it, often bringing with her the children's hose to darn or alternating with a little dress from which the buttons had been lost, she'd sit there watching her husband at his work.

They talked of many things, of the future of the artist's life in America and the misunderstandings with which, in a Puritan culture, it was still surrounded. Neither Dora nor Lottie had ever seen Paris. How wonderful it would be if they could see it together! The French know the right value to put upon the apparent immorality of the artist's way of thought. To know the profundities of life, at some point in one's career one must let go, one must abandon one's self completely to the full range of emotional shock. Only by ceasing to hold back, denying one's self what is plainly there to be known, *could* one fully grasp what is to be learned from the artist's canvas or sonata or poem. America is a maimed environment out of which nothing wide and broad enough in the artist's experience could come to stand up against time. With this Lottie instinctively agreed.

"You should know Oxford, England, where I was born and grew up," Dora would say. And she'd laugh. Ives, too, would laugh, but made no comment.

"When he first dawned on my horizon it was to me like young Lochinvar come out of the West!" She laughed again. "I would have followed him to the ends of the earth—and did, didn't I, darling? He swept me right off my feet."

Ives would be painting doggedly as she rambled on while Lottie would be trying to hold a pose. "I knew all about him. My mother thought him a terrible person. My father was dead, you know. And nothing I could say could convince her. But I was in love, I suppose. And I was fed up with Oxford. It's really a beastly place for a girl to grow up in. She senses, of course, that she is surrounded by what are probably the most brilliant minds of tomorrow but—you can't imagine how dull it is there for a young woman. They're interested in each other, not in her. But there's an atmosphere, for all that. It drove me to want to get away. So here I am."

Then she'd put her sewing down at the call of one of her children and perhaps not return for the rest of the day. When Lottie would tire of posing she'd play, play anything that came into her head while Ives would lie on the couch, place his hands back of his head and listen or suggest a new number; get up, stand at the window or even at moments leave the studio while Lottie was still playing and let her have the place to herself.

Afternoons, tea regularly would be served except on the days when little Paul would come. As it was always somewhat of a fight to get him there, she'd have to go home earlier. Sometimes Ives would take the whole family for a long drive through the back roads of the region and the ladies would put up a picnic lunch which they'd eat at some beautiful vantage among the hills in the open fields or under broad trees.

Lazy days! The surface of events was hardly ruffled while Dora spoke of her coming visit to England the following year and Lottie dreamed of Europe again, saying how much she would like to go for another year of piano coaching in Berlin— Teresa Carreño, the great woman teacher, was her present choice. Time was passing, and if she was ever to make anything of herself she would have to begin pretty soon. Altogether the acquaintance which had blossomed into their friendship and filled the summer for her so beautifully had been a most rewarding experience.

"It has been very pleasant to have had you for a friend this summer. I can't tell you how much it has meant to me," Dora had told her when the Stechers were about to leave their beloved cottage on Labor Day and return home. "It has meant so much to me—in more ways than I can say."

Well, you don't need to put on so about it, Lottie had thought. I've had a good time too.

fish pond. A small stream came out of the woods to the north and, in the spring, ran pleasantly enough along to the small river in the far distance.

It was called the old Smith farm and had about it the smell of dirt and poverty, of old rags and dampness in the cellar under the hand-hewn beams. But this in no way interfered with Gurlie's roseate view of a future homestead.

The squatters who occupied the place would be cleaned out at once and carpenters brought in to make the roof tight for the winter; the floors would be cleaned and scraped. What wonderful broad boards! A toilet would be installed and in the spring they would move in. Ives, who had seen the farm and approved of its purchase, even went so far as to design for them a practical barn of fieldstone—which would be their first construction—beside a giant white oak back of the future garden in a dip of the land below the rear hill; it was all hill! Gurlie was delighted. She wanted stanchions for a herd of twelve cows as a minimum, stalls for three horses also. She would have pigs, chickens—a chicken coop would have to be built. A hundred and fifty acres! Joe paced off the boundaries with the authorities, walking through thickets and brambles northward to the highest point of the land. It continued to rise at the back through heavily wooded area belonging to the next farm, then came back down across the saddle where the road lay, then up again to a stone wall faced by scraggly hedge to the extreme south where there were ten acre fields, side by side on the road, graced by a copse of white birches in the one farthest west.

Joe liked the place. It had no frank brook, but it was surrounded by water on all sides. What he particularly enjoyed was the woods and the isolation. There was no one around except on the farm of old Weigant, a Dutch descendant of better times, over the hill to the west. Joe went down and made the acquaintance of the old Dutchman, who obviously had seen better days, and met his two silent sons who looked at him as much as to ask, What the hell do you want up in

"Your portrait is lovely," Dora continued. "I'm sure Gregory must be very satisfied with it."

"You speak as if we were saying good-bye forever. I'm sure we'll see you sometime during the winter. I insist."

"My husband, no doubt, but not me. It's very difficult for me to get out of here in the winter. After that, England. England again!"

"Oh, but you're coming back."

"Yes, but perhaps not here. It's not very satisfactory a place for children. After they are of school age it will be worse. It's a lovely place, though, isn't it? I wonder often what will become of it."

"Don't talk that way," said Lottie. "I'm sure we'll all be together again next summer."

Prompted by his wife, Stecher had decided to purchase, for a bare three hundred dollars, an abandoned farm on the opposite side of town, to the east. It was on a narrow dirt road two or three miles out among steeply rolling hills which effectively shut it in from all view save that of a shanty below it occupied by a disreputable parcel of typical mountain white trash. The small, low building, dating from Revolutionary times, was badly run down and occupied by two shabby families living in indescribable filth. There was a well house, a tumble-down barn and fields hardly a foot of which showed any level ground. They hadn't been cultivated for years and were covered with a thin stand of fox grass.

The chestnut trees that had once dignified the area, filling the woods in the hollow and the "grove" back of the farm buildings, were all blighted and doomed. Half of them were already gone and the rest would follow shortly. The narrow road went off to the east through a deep cut, steeply down over a culvert draining the swamp at the bottom. One of the things that had sold Joe the idea of purchasing the run-down place was that there, at the bottom of the hill, it would be quite easy to construct a dam by which to flood the three acres of swamp and make a lake of it for a swimming pool and this country? Joe told Weigant he'd bought the Smith place for a summer residence and that one way or another he might want to build a house there some day.

Weigant said he'd been a stonemason when he was younger, and though he'd gained a lot of weight as he'd come along and had a weak back, he thought that he could still do a day's work if it came right down to it.

Joe had flushed a few pheasants on his walk around the place, and found some old apple trees full of fruit, a Northern Spy and a Baldwin, together with the usual sweet summer apple at the corner of the kitchen garden. He made up his mind that fruit and game would be plentiful. The die was cast—Gurlie would at last have a place in the country, not more than fifty miles from New York and in a beautiful spot and although, it is true, little of the land lay in such a way that it would be fit for cultivation, it was picturesque, and the soil, where you could find a few level acres, was of the richest.

A farmer of the neighborhood, one Charlie Carpenter, was forthwith hired to come for the summer, the barn was commissioned, carpenters and plumbers were loosed on the old building, and when the Stechers had returned and settled down in Riverdale again all their friends began to hear about it.

But the wedding of Flossie to her doctor was first to be attended to. It was September now. In December they planned to take the big leap and already were beginning to draw up a list of the guests to be invited.

A disagreement occurred at the start. Lottie wanted to invite Ives. Flossie said no. "It is my wedding and I'll have whom I please." But Gurlie highhandedly went over her head and Ives was invited. Dora couldn't leave the children. Nothing could be done about it. It was about at this time that Lottie rented a private box at the local post office for her business mail as a potential concert pianist.

The preparations for the wedding occupied the whole fall season. The young doctor, naturally, took no part in them, being mere accessory before the fact. As far as he was concerned, it was of little significance other than that in three years, or two years, really, he had got to the point where he had saved enough cash to make it seem possible for him to begin to support a wife. In the two years since he had returned from Germany (where he had witnessed the first zeppelin flights in the mists above Leipzig) Floss and he had got to know each other pretty thoroughly.

All but every night of the week they had grown more and more intimate in the small, darkened parlor of her parents' house—escape as they were able from the persistent attentions of the small brother. He liked the "doc" and the "doc" liked him. Sometimes they'd let him stay in their downstairs hideaway and for a change devote the evening to him rather than to their own affairs. It was a harrowing time in all, but the young couple were devoted to each other. And it was an exhausting time. They were both drawn, pale and hollow-eyed as the engagement drew at last to a close.

It was a cold, clear evening in December. Floss, whose father trusted her, had put everything into her hands. The coaches were engaged; a list of those to be called for was placed in the liveryman's hands; the bridal party was ready to be taken to the church when it was discovered that at the last minute Joe, fearing that Floss might have been too busy to look after the details, had countermanded everything and given new orders for the disposition of the coaches. Result, complete confusion, everyone running in the wrong direction and worst of all, one of the ministers—there were to be two taking part in the ceremony—was forgotten.

The groom, contemptuous of the whole ceremony, was behind the scenes. The bridal party was in the portico of the church. The minister had not arrived. Knowing that the ceremony could not go on without him, the groom absented himself from his place until the minister finding herself—it was a woman—waiting for the coach, called a cab and got to the church at the last minute.

Floss, pale as a ghost, walked up the aisle on her father's arm, as the young physician, full of sympathy for what he knew must be her state of mind, smilingly waited. Thus they were married.

The Stecher household was ablaze with lights. Champagne was the sole drink. The champagne punch was particularly strong and, by the time the bride and groom were about to leave, the party had become wild. Some of the girls were dizzy to a point of drunkenness and long afterward remembered the event as the highlight of the season, if not their lives. Ives and Charlotte were forgotten in the mêlée, but when, in a shower of serpentines, rice and confetti the couple tried to leave through the front door, they found it roped against them. It had been Ives's idea. But in a moment Charlie's friends rallied to his rescue, cut the ropes, and let the couple go.

30

All during the summer Flossie was carrying her first child. There were rumors of war, though no one believed it really possible. Gurlie's dream of an estate to be named Alverheim after the ancestral home of her forebears was taking shape and Dora Ives was getting ready to quit her Monroe home for England to visit her parents. She didn't think she would ever return to that particular location in the American hinterland; it was too lonesome. Ives had decided to put it on the market. Gurlie bought his wild black horse and various miscellaneous kitchen items as well as a tall Normandy clock, with the proviso that he could buy it back from her at some future time should he want it.

A great argument went on about the small house on the Smith farm, whether to keep its classic American lines, merely enlarging it at the back by a masked central wing and putting in modern conveniences or to rebuild it from cellar to roof. Whenever Flossie and her husband come up for a week-end, the argument would become especially heated. He stood out for keeping the old building intact—save for making it habitable—until Gurlie one day lost her temper and flew at him on the pretext of his suggesting a row of whitewashed stones to mark the carriage entrance for night use.

Gurlie let him have it, "What do you think I am?" she

said. "This is no poor farm. I am proud, I am. We don't want to live like these white trash of the mountains."

"If it comes to that," he lashed back at her, "I'm proud, too. But not about the things you are."

When the barn was finished, twelve head of cattle were installed there under Charlie Carpenter, who had already plowed one of the fields of the west hill. He planted it with corn, which, when he was ready to cut it that fall, measured fourteen feet from root to tassel. He took an armful of the stalks and stood them against the front of the house for all passers-by to witness.

The garden wall to the left of the house was rebuilt, steps were re-established leading to the area above it, and a dozen hybrid lilacs were planted along its crest, a fifty-foot hedge that took hold in the rich soil and grew phenomenally. Back of that, and the house itself, lay the kitchen garden, a hundred feet long and fifty wide. An asparagus bed was laid out and planted, thirty rhubarb roots were put in, that, within a single season, produced enough juicy stalks to supply a regiment. A strawberry bed and a raspberry patch were installed and also loganberries. Of the annuals such as eggplant, carrots, beets and three sorts of lettuce, parsley—whatever could be thought of—there was enough for a family ten times the size of the one it supplied. What soil!

A bathroom with all modern conveniences added greatly to the comfort of the summer. Gurlie made dandelion wine from the succulent and overwhelming masses of that golden-flowered weed which grew on every side. In the old orchard across the road, part of the purchase, the grass was thick with wild strawberry. Quarts and quarts were picked and preserved. Once the young doctor and Flossie, roaming the far fields back of the woods above the eastward low ground, came upon a patch better than any they had found heretofore. They noted it and went back the next day with pails, but someone had been there before them. The grass was trampled and the berries were gone.

It was probably the mountain people who had moved into a filthy shack which Weigant let them occupy on the road across from the Stechers' low ground. Their sore-eyed, ragged children, never speaking, were often to be seen furtively lurking about their trampled domain.

The twelve tuberculin-tested Holsteins meant the installation of new fences. One of the Weigant boys was engaged to help with the milking. He was a gangling, long-jawed youth not too bright in the head who nevertheless was fairly reliable. There was a good market for the milk at the local cheese factory, which gave a certain authority to Gurlie's plans. The manure began to pile up in the barnyard. This, too, was encouraging; it was just what the fields needed in the spring. But the state inspectors weren't long in putting in an appearance recommending the screening of the stable windows, the installation of a cooling system and better facilities for the care of the milker's cleanliness. This made Gurlie mad.

Joe hated the cows. From the first they would break out of their enclosure and go trooping across the lawn. Two little English walnut trees that he had planted either side in front of the cottage had to be especially protected when one day they all but disappeared down one of the beasts' gullet. The doctor again rashly suggested that they connect the lower field, where the cows mostly were set out, with the upper yard by way of a lane, a narrow fenced-in approach across the front of the property, so that by lowering the bars at the bottom of the hill, the cows could by themselves come up near the barn for the milking instead of having to be driven along the road— with all the attendant wandering about, getting into the garden or running clean away. But Gurlie again opposed herself. She wanted the front field to be beautiful. Ultimately it would front the mansion. She didn't want to turn it into a runway for cattle. And when Gurlie was opposed to any common-sense suggestion, she was so violent, so insulting, that everyone began to hate her.

Once she caught Charlie Carpenter, at the end of the day,

with a two-quart can of milk in his hand just as he was leaving. "Where are you going with that milk?" she asked him.

"Taking it to my cousin."

"Who told you to do that?"

"Nobody. They haven't got any cow now and with all their younguns they can use it. You got more here than's needed."

"Put that down. That's stealing," said Gurlie.

"No ma'am. That ain't stealing," said Charlie. "Everybody hereabouts lets the help have all the milk they want."

"Well you can't do it to me," said Gurlie.

"All right ma'am, I ain't coming back," said Charlie. And he didn't. And then Gurlie really found herself in a bad way, dependent on the Weigant boy until she could hire another farmer.

She did get a good farmer, though, a Magyar, a very cocky one, who spoke with a strong foreign accent. One day after he'd been there a few weeks the colored cook whom Gurlie had brought up for the summer baked him some delicious corn muffins. Joe, the farmer, ate one and enjoyed it.

Julia was doing the ironing while he was at breakfast. "What are those little cakes you gave me? They're good," said Joe.

"Those are corn muffins," Julia told him.

"What? Those are made from corn?"

"Yes," said Julia.

"Fit for pigs," cried Joe. And he spit out what he had in his mouth onto the floor.

Julia picked up the hot iron and flew at him. "You get out of my kitchen," she yelled at him, "or I'll sear your face!"

The man got up as if the devil was after him and flew out the door, Julia after him. He wouldn't come into the house from that time on until he had looked to see that the coast was clear. He cooked and ate his own meals outdoors from then on.

The new heating system with its big hot-air furnace nearly filled the old cellar under its low hand-hewn beams. It was an enormous affair with one top vent which came out through the floor of the large front room so that when the heat was on you could hardly stand it. But it kept the place livable in the cold weather.

All the hillsides about the house, and back of where the final mansion would stand, were planted with young fruit trees, peaches, plums, pears and apples of four or five kinds, hundreds of them.

"What in God's name are you doing?" Gurlie was asked. "You'll have more fruit out here than you can ever harvest."

"There's always a good market for fruit in New York State."

"But who's going to spray them and pick them?"

"Agh, what do you know about farming?" was her reply, and like as not the answer would have to be, "Nothing." That Gurlie herself knew little about farming never seemed to occur to her. She had a complicated, turreted pig-pen of sharp stone pieces built at a distance from the buildings at the bottom of the hill in the edge of the woods.

"But who's going to bring them their slops?"

As Joe once said to a friend, "Do you know how to make money out of a farm?"

"No, tell me."

"Sell it!" confided Joe, speaking in a loud guttural stage whisper back of his hand.

But Gurlie had them build a stone smoke house at the edge of the isolated grove which was Joe's favorite spot. A chicken coop and fenced-in yard where a hundred hens had to be fed was another feature. More than once the young doctor had to drive into town in the buggy where the grain merchant dumped a bag of cracked corn into the back. It was gone in a week. The merchants of the town were only too glad, finding Joe a prompt payer, to give him all the credit he wanted.

He planted young fir trees of all sorts about the hillsides, larches, balsams, white pine and spruce, and all of them took hold and grew like mad. It promised in a measurable time to be one of the show places of the region, as Gurlie boasted it would be, as long as Joe was able and willing to foot the bills.

Water, as on all farms, was one of the primary requisites. The old well was inadequate, the water, besides, not safe to use. You could see the surface of it far down. Charlie Carpenter had daily lowered the milk cans into it to chill them at the beginning of his tenure, but you couldn't keep that up. There was even a sort of cupboard there for butter and other perishables and it served well, too, but in the end something more serviceable had to be provided.

So the drillers appeared in mid-summer and began their operations. First they went down under the hump of the hill back of the barn and the big oak where gravity would carry what they found into the buildings which lay all below. They got some water, too, close to the surface but it wasn't good water, and there wasn't much of it. So they had to go deeper, beyond the five hundred-foot mark and there they found a good supply, but it was too strongly alkaline, unsuited for domestic use.

Finally, abandoning that site altogether, they dug a cistern twenty feet across, thirty feet deep, at the very bottom of the hill approaching the bottomland, walled it in with loose stone, installed an electric pump and solved the problem. It was an expensive operation, but inescapable. The cows were at least properly supplied.

Then there was the ice house, under the hill near the old house. The site had been used for the same purpose in former years, but the buildings had gone to rot. The ice from a nearby pond could be hauled in and up a short incline to the top of the ridge where the ice blocks could be slid in from the top until the virtually underground cubicle was packed full to the roof. But at the front, facing the barn and the house, the ice house presented at the base a bolted door out of which the sawdust-covered ice hunks could be drawn as needed. The ice lasted all summer. The young doctor, who knew nothing of farms, was impressed.

Young Paul, while all this was going on, who would have been at a loss to find any companions in that isolated spot, had been sent away to a boys' camp.

As that first summer advanced, it became apparent to everyone that the location was ideal as a place to which a New York businessman and his family could retire for relaxation and the enjoyment of the beauties of nature in summer. Joe was perfectly happy there week-ends. On Sundays he'd sit on the narrow little porch, facing the old orchard, smoke his cigar and note with perfect tranquillity how the phoebe, unfrightened under the edge of the porch roof, continued to feed her fledgling within six feet of his idle hand. He had planted clematis, which from the first had grown luxuriantly, twining itself up the lattice columns to his right and his left. He had acquired a mongrel pup that as it grew became his staunch friend and companion, a typical short-tailed yellow dog, powerful in build, and death to the woodchucks that infested the stone walls on every side.

Those stone walls interested Gurlie for their antiquity and for the fossils she found in them. Joe would often bring home a shell-incrusted piece of rock which would be put aside for the building of future fireplaces.

But the grove above the barn was Joe's particular retreat. When of a Sunday after he had explored the acreage to its remotest corner with Mike at his side, he'd come to the grove where a hammock had been swung, light up a cigar, and, his dog at his feet, doze off, for a delicious hour.

He had cleaned up the grove, grown over with huckleberry and wild azalea, largely by his own hand, and enjoyed it, gradually picking up the stones lying about, as many as he could move, and making a neat pile of them. This "fortress" he named, after the legendary resting place of the Prussian State Treasurer, Spandau. Everyone knew that that pile of rocks was his private keep. It got to be ten feet around and as high as your head, neatly piled, as he would do it, the stones fitted all about like the exterior of a Gothic cathedral. "Spandau!" he'd say, with his ironic smile and one never knew quite what he meant.

From all parts of the farm, the front porch, the grove, the high field back of the orchard, you had a view of the ridge of low mountains upon the peak of which stood the low-lying stone mansion of the late railroad tycoon who within a year of building it had died. As the farm faced due south the Scorpion on clear nights was the outstanding constellation visible in the summer sky. The whole valley with this high limiting ridge capped by the sight of wealth in the distant background seemed to give Joe a peculiar satisfaction and it was evident that he enjoyed it.

The four little attic rooms, with angled ceilings to conform to the slope of the roof on either side, were seldom unoccupied that summer. They were hot, summer nights, and unquestionably the few mosquitoes there could be very annoying. The beds were still primitive, though all that would be corrected later, but a steady stream of guests came and went for all that. All were enthusiastic about the site, the wonderful view down the valley to the southward and the rolling fields with patches of forest to right and to left.

At the end of August, little Paul, now grown to be a strong young fellow of thirteen, returned from his camp, brown and healthy. He, like his father, liked to roam the woods and fields and often, like his father, he'd take a gun with him, either a light-weight rifle or the twelve-gauge shotgun which was always standing back of the kitchen door. He was a good shot and had been taught to handle a gun so that he had free use of it.

His favorite spot was the stand of white birches at the western corner of the farm where the road came in from the town. There were plenty of rabbits there and the birds seemed to like it. He was pretty good. Once he came home with a woodcock, a bird not easy to bring down.

The family hated to leave the place when at last fall had come. "It's the finest time of the year," Gurlie protested, "and we have to go home! Well, it won't be for long. As soon as we get the house built and everything organized, we're going to move up here permanently," she said to her husband, "and live here. I've met some fine people already—and there are lots more. Rich people, too. You never hear of them, but they're the best people in the country."

Joe had no objection, except he always added, "Yes, if we don't go broke first." But Gurlie would laugh, and that, to all intents and purposes, would settle it.

But it was beautiful! The maples before the house were all crimson and the two hickory trees above the cut in the road were pure gold while a tupelo in the stone wall at the edge of the old orchard was the most brilliant of all, its enameled leaves alternately green and highest crimson. The underbrush of the blackberry and alder with goldenrod in the fields in the foreground seemed veritably speaking with pathos, inanimate things that they were, turned vocal with the end of the year.

Apples hung unpicked in the trees, red and russet. The ground was covered with them. What can you do? There was a cider press, but little use was made of it; the old white horse had eaten all the apples that were good for him; the rest just had to rot. The broken-down utility house across the road just below the farm, its roof stove in, its stone walls down on three sides, the rest overgrown with poison ivy so that no one went near it, was just one year closer to final collapse.

Joe, the farmer, was left alone in charge at last for the winter. The family was driven to the station and that year was at an end.

31

All during the latter days of December they waited for the pains to begin. On Christmas Day they started. All morning they continued at about half-hour intervals and then just when Dr. Borden was about to be called, they subsided and the Christmas festivities took over. "So we're not to have a little Christ child after all."

On New Year's Day it was the same routine: at dawn the cramps, Flossie thought that this time the baby would surely come, but again everything quieted down. "He's an accommodating little bastard," said the young doc, "he doesn't want to interfere with the festivities. More power to him."

There had been no snow that year. "He'll come with the first snowfall," said Floss. Sure enough, she was awakened by the now familiar pains at dawn on the seventh of January of the fateful year 1914: it was gently snowing. This time she knew it would go through. Dr. Borden was summoned, arrived promptly, and laid out his kit. Now the pains were severe. Her husband was to give Flossie the chloroform, but when they went to look, Borden hadn't any in his bag, neither did the young doctor have any more than ten or fifteen drops in the bottom of his last remaining one-ounce bottle. It was five in the morning; no pharmacy was open. What to do?

"You might know it," said Floss. "The doctor's wife al-

317

ways has to get the worst of it. How could you be so careless?"

A drop at a time, he nursed the precious liquid, giving her the barest minimum in the failing attempt to make her comfortable while both he and she sweated it out. Finally, distracted, he was down to the last drop. He glanced up at the older man. Then he heard a cry, a new cry! He dropped the empty chloroform bottle.

"What is it?"

"A boy," said the older man casually.

"A boy!"

"A boy?" said Floss drunkenly.

The new father wanted to make sure he had heard right. Yes, a boy! Tears came to his eyes as he caressed his wife cautiously, kissing her eyes and her hair. For the next exciting minutes the two doctors were silently occupied in their competent maneuvers, properly disposing of the infant and caring for the new mother to insure her safety and comfort.

Thus the new year started, with a male firstborn to the two sets of grandparents. Lottie and little Paul came and looked at the baby and approved. Joe came and presented Floss with a check for a hundred dollars to start a bank account in the baby's name. Gurlie came and took the baby in her arms to inspect it carefully to see if it was a worthy descendant of Vikings and, having approved, put it down and forgot it.

But Lottie was restless. She was not getting on as fast as she thought she should with her concerts, and though she played well, there was lacking that final distinction which she knew—she best of all—she must have to be a stand-out performer in her field.

She had talked to her mother. "I need a year's coaching under someone with a name. I need to be the pupil of someone with the prestige to get me heard, someone like Teresa Carreño."

"Where is she?"

"In Berlin."

"In Berlin? I don't know whether your father will consent to let you do that."

"For a year, just one year," pleaded Lottie. "In a year I'll know whether I can do it or not. But I want a chance. If I could go to Germany for a year and study under a master, and I think I'd like it to be a woman—if I could get Father to pay my expenses for one year—if I don't show signs of becoming a successful pianist in that time I'd be willing to quit."

"Then what will you do?"

"Teach. Please, please talk to Father for me. It won't cost much. And I'll work like the devil. I can't do it here. I have to go abroad, the atmosphere is different there. You have to go to someone important, someone with a name."

"Ask him yourself," said Gurlie. "He'll just yell at me. Why can't you work here? But you ask your father."

"I'm afraid," said Lottie.

And Gurlie did ask her husband for this final gesture for his eldest, his unmarried child's establishment in a career. The result was an explosive "No!" Nevertheless Lottie had been encouraged by her mother's breaking the ice.

"Oh, Papa," she pleaded, "let me go. I'll work as no one ever did before. Prices in Europe are not like they are here. Give me one last chance. I'll pay it all back to you as soon as I get working, every cent of it. It is desperately important to me now."

"Why don't you quit all this nonsense?" was her father's reply. "You'll never be a great artist. How old are you?"

"Twenty-five."

"You know that's too late. You've been loafing around playing for these nincompoops in a little town like this ever since you came back from Leipzig. You're not serious, not the way a great artist is serious."

"That's not true."

"Of course it's true. In Germany when a man wants to be a world-beater, he eats his profession, he sleeps it, makes himself a slave to it—for years, he begins when he is a baby. But you Americans! Loafers! You'd rather go to little parties and eat ice cream. You don't know how to work, to *work!* How do you think a man gets to be an outstanding performer? Work! That's what it takes, devotion to his craft. You don't know what that means. To you the piano is just a plaything."

Nevertheless, as the months passed, perhaps out of disgust, if not from the innate optimism of a spring season, business still being excellent, his son more and more filling his paternal expectations, the "farm" constantly in his thoughts —he consented.

Lottie was elated. She was a new girl, excited, blossoming as if she were going to the arms of a bridegroom. Her whole life was transformed. Berlin! was the refrain that carried her, Berlin! Berlin! You might think it was heaven. One month more, she dreamed! At the end of March, rumors or no of the warlike state of international affairs, she would be gone. She promised anything and everything—that it would not be for long, that as soon as she saw how things were shaping up, what progress she was able to make, if it were not good, that if she had not succeeded in a year she'd throw the whole thing up. She swore on her immortal soul that in such a case she would toss the whole thing overboard and return home. That would be the end, come what may, her father would have no further expense to bear from her.

So on the eve of the sailing from Hoboken on the *Kaiser Wilhelm der Grosse* they had a big party for her—at some smörgåsbord in New York. It was a wonderful party. Everyone was there, all her girlfriends, all her old lovers who were still unattached and able to say good-bye to the charming young woman, Flossie and her husband, everyone. And when Joe threw a party it was a party, everything of the best and everyone was happy, in a hilarious mood wishing the young woman bon voyage.

"See you next year!"

"Yop."

"Going to get married over there, to some Heinie?"

"What? Don't be ridiculous!"

"I'll bet it'll be some American you meet on the boat! I'll bet you a hundred to one."

Lottie didn't have time to reply, but turned to speak to one of the girls who pretended to be sniffling. "I wish you all the luck in the world, darling, I really do."

And on the next day, the day of departure, as her father handed her the check on which she was to live for the first months, holding it by one end, she the other, he said, "Well, Charlotte, work hard."

"I will."

He hesitated a moment, "Are you going to see that sucker Ives while you are in Europe?" She returned his look, straight in the eye and said to him, "Of course not. Don't be ridiculous." A week later when the vessel docked at Hamburg, she walked straight into Ives's arms and he carried her off to bed. That was the end of her plans.

As soon as it was practicable they were married. Oh happy, happy pair! They decided that for the moment they would not return to America. It was his fourth or fifth marriage, and of course her first.

When the news reached America, Joe, who had considerable influence in New York business circles, tried to keep it out of the newspapers. But it was too rich for suppression: "'Affinity Ives' does it again. Daughter of prominent New York businessman," etc. In spite of all Joe could do it came out, anyway, and everyone knew it.

Joe was beside himself. He raved at Gurlie for her part in the affair, blamed her for the whole thing, and since something had to be said to the reporters who thronged their home even to the point of being found roaming unbid in the upstairs rooms in search of a photo of Lottie, wild with anger that he had been so duped he branded Ives a "moral leper"—and that hurt. That, too, was broadcast. Even the newly wedded couple in Germany heard of it. A "moral leper," that's how he stigmatized him. His daughter he disowned, said she was not his daughter, never had been; that he had adopted her when she was an infant—and indeed she did not resemble either Gurlie or himself; threw her out. He said she had reverted to type, had become what he had always feared she would become, married a New York degenerate, known for his degeneracy. He did a thorough job.

Poor Joe, he didn't bow his head, but looked defiantly at his friends, as though daring them to accuse him. But his heart was lower than his shoes. Pride kept Gurlie alert.

"Maybe your own daughter will do it some day. Don't talk to me," she said to them. In her own mind she had the consolation of knowing that Ives had money and could take good care of his women.

"She can look after herself," she assured some of the most persistent inquirers. "You don't have to worry about her." But Gurlie now began to talk seriously of getting out of Riverdale, of selling the attractive little house she had lived in for those last happy years and moving bag and baggage to the country. How attractive it seemed there now with the opening season!

Joe's friends, who had a great affection for him, at the last meeting of their beloved Fortnightly Reading Club, elected him president for the coming year. He tried to refuse, but no one would hear of it. "I don't want anyone to feel sorry for me," he protested to his wife. "I'll resign. I refuse." But in the end he thought better of it and let them make him their president.

Early in June the family moved to the farm where the new life was to begin. Reminders of the elder daughter's romance were all about him, the final indignity being that Ives, when he had broken up his own home the year before to go abroad again, had sold Gurlie many of his lesser possessions.

"Oh well, that was ended now."

Little Paul went back to his camp of the year before, both for his own happiness in the companionship of boys his own age and the convenience of having him out of the way while the work of constructing at the farm was going forward. There was much to do. The place was a godsend now to Gurlie and her husband.

How everything had thrived! It was a veritable miracle, the eternal miracle of the soil. When they first went up there that spring, near the southeast wall of the house close against the boards, a row of dwarf purple iris was in full bloom.

"What can you do before such beauty but let your heart be softened?"

The dandelions were luxuriant, the individual blossoms two inches across made a thick carpet that crept in everywhere even to the very stones of the farmhouse steps. Violets! It was as if nothing had occurred to ruffle the spirit of a man. It was a new, a flaming new world. The cherry trees, a small orchard of a dozen trees on the sharp slope beside the ice house were a mass of blossoms purply white, a solid mass upon the trees. The apple trees, the peach trees, the plums were leaping with the forces of fertility within them. But the lilacs—why, they were only planted yesterday!—were blooming, white and purple, of three shades, single and double, while the odor of them was overwhelming to the senses. Gurlie forgot herself in that odor which she loved as she loved no other benefice of the year.

Joe, alone with his thoughts, whatever they were, took his long walks as usual about the property. He would come back, his boots muddy, his cheeks aglow, have his Sunday dinner, eat well, then doze in the sunshine on the small front porch. He measured the growth of the clematis that grew up the lattice pillars each side of him and seemed to be forgetting his recent discomfiture completely.

Typical of him, he engaged his son-in-law's brother, the architect, to design the new house. That it was to be a pretentious one soon became evident. For when Fred presented to him the preliminary sketch of a rustic Black Forest lodge, thinking that that would be in keeping with the taste of the owner and fit as well the hilltop to which it would conform itself, Gurlie threw it out without even a thought.

"No! I don't want a peasant's house built of logs! I want a stone house, something solid that will last for years." She laughed scornfully at the idea. "What do you think I am? I don't want that!" And Joe agreed with her.

So the architect was packed off to try again.

Flossie and her husband brought the baby up week-ends. It afforded wonderful siestas for her, a rest from the busy life a doctor's wife must lead, a perfect place where she could park herself with a small baby and enjoy it.

And then in the middle of it all came the news that Germany had invaded Belgium and a shocked world realized that the famous *Pax Brittanica* was at an end at last. In the very truth, as Lord Grey phrased it, "The lights were going out all over Europe."

It was something that at first you could not believe, Joe couldn't believe it. He could not believe that Germany had not been driven to it by British importunateness. He did not believe that his own *Vaterland*, close to his heart, had been the aggressor. He loved his fatherland despite the fact that he had renounced it, willingly, to take his place beside the rest of those who had come here across the seas to dedicate themselves to a better, a more democratic country.

England was the culprit, England had forced Germany's hand. Must that enlightened country, leader of the world in philosophic thought, in music, in medical research, chemical advance, must they be forced to ask England every morning for their very cup of breakfast coffee? Unthinkable.

Joe blamed England for it all and so long as the United States was neutral, he stoutly and openly voiced his opinions. "Germany will win," he said, and with the success of its arms in the early months it looked as if Paris would soon be overrun.

But he was not a subject of the Kaiser, he was a United States citizen. He scorned disloyalty to his adopted country.

He did object however when a British publisher tried to bribe him into giving up the entire floor that his printing establishment occupied on Hudson Street for English propaganda purposes. His lease protected him there, and the Britisher had to seek another location.

But he was heartbroken over the events taking place, as was every sane man in the world. He refused to speak of the war with his friends, and deeply resented the implication that by favoring Germany he was in any way disloyal to the United States.

He wandered his acres as usual, in fact, the farm became more and more the focus of his thoughts. With him the powerful Mike, the English sheep dog Tip, followed by little Tootsie the dachshund, its stumps of legs trying to keep up with its longer-legged companions, wandered over the fields of a weekend planning a time when he could move bag and baggage to his place in the country and there, when he could retire from business, pass the final years of his life in comfort and peace.

Threat of war or no, the summer passed happily for them all and as that fateful August drew to a close, little Paul, now not so little, but approaching his fourteenth birthday, his camp having ended its season, came to the farm for a last fling before returning to Riverdale and school. He was a big boy now, in the pink of health, sunburned from his summer long outdoor life, his very hair sunburned. Full-blooded and eager to get out from under the more or less confining camp restrictions, his gun on his shoulder, he wandered the fields in search of a woodcock, partridge, pheasant or rabbit.

His favorite place was across the road, into the hollow, among the beeches and oaks where a little stream ran full of water cress among the summer-worn skunk cabbages and scrubby willows. A covey of half-grown partridges had been more than once flushed in that undergrowth and rabbits, seldom giving you a decent shot, were known to inhabit it.

That day he had been gone for a good part of the morning. Returning toward noon he went around the old orchard, through Weigant's young peach trees and came out at the top of the cut opposite which the cows were usually pastured. All the old fences, that side of the road, had long since been down and the grass was long as he came to the edge of the embankment and was about to descend. His gun in his hand, he could not have noticed the strand of old rusty wire hidden there close to the ground. It tripped him and he fell headlong down the sharp slope dropping his gun which started to slide muzzle forward over the rubble behind him.

32

Robert, Julia's boy, was the first to hear it, a shotgun blast not a hundred feet away from where he was sitting idling on the kitchen steps, followed by a shout, "I'm shot!"

Robert yelled to his mother in the house as he sprinted toward the sounds. When the women got there little Paul was on his feet at the roadside, but it was apparent that something serious had happened. The gun sliding down the embankment behind him had discharged, its barrel pointing down, right between his legs. He was bleeding profusely.

No use to speak of safety catches, of the wisdom of allowing children to be free with firearms. The two women and the boy Robert carried the poor child to the house as best they could and, not daring to touch him, laid him, clothes and all, upon blankets and a clean sheet on the floor of the living room. He was conscious and silent.

They were a mile and a half from the next farm where there was a telephone. Weigant had none. The old white horse was the only means of communication. Robert, bareback, though he did not know how to ride, headed downhill to the west as fast as he could urge his mount to go.

Finally, getting to the Bull farm, he told them what had occurred. Mrs. Bull, an intelligent woman, summoned an ambulance, heavens knows where, but not nearby and, calling her husband from the barn, got into her car and went to the Stecher farm as fast as she could to see what she could do.

The first thing that Flossie and Charlie knew of it was when in the early afternoon they received a phone call from Gurlie that little Paul had been accidentally shot; to call Joe in New York and to come up to the farm as fast as they could. The baby was disposed of and the young couple, getting into their Ford runabout, forced it to its top speed over the pitted roads on the forty-mile run. No details had been given. They only knew that the boy had been injured and badly. They called Joe at once and told him to come along by train without delay.

When they had gone past Tuxedo, thirty miles on their way, Charlie saw Gurlie in a car going in the opposite direction. She was beckoning wildly for them to turn about and follow her. He guessed they were bound for the hospital at Tuxedo, an excellent one, where the young doctor knew there was a capable surgeon in attendance. Gurlie had by then disappeared.

His guess was right, and he lost no time when he got to the hospital in leaping out of his car, Flossie behind him, and going up the stairs to the operating-room floor where he knew the boy must be.

They had just finished the emergency job. The boy was back in his bed, recovering from the ether. "Hello, Doc," he said weakly to his brother-in-law. Charlie patted him gently on the head and told him to go to sleep.

In the dressing room the surgeon was just taking off his gown.

"How is he?"

The old man shook his head. "Better if he dies," he said. "He's terribly hurt. If he lives, he'll be a cripple. Boys that age should never be trusted with guns." And he turned his back and finished taking off his operating clothes.

But Charlie could not stay for that. The women, who

had not been admitted to the operating suite, were waiting outside. They eagerly accosted him, "Is he all right?" Charlie shook his head. "No. But he's still alive. Let him rest."

Then they thought of Joe coming on the express from New York. It was due in Tuxedo in a matter of minutes. Charlie ran for it just as it was coming into the station. Stecher, of course, did not know that his son was at that place, so the young doctor had to board the front car and run through hoping to see him, if indeed he had caught the train and was aboard.

He found him in the last car, got him quickly to his feet and off the train before it started again, and up to the hospital which was close at hand, and to the boy's bed as fast as it could be done.

The boy was awake and as his father came up to him, smiled and said, "Hello, Pop." "Hello, son," said the unhappy man. Then Charlie beckoned him away and took him out to the women. Returning to the bedside, Charlie was just in time to see the nurse put her fingers to her lips. He was dead.

The young doctor walked wearily into the presence of the waiting relatives and told them without hesitation, "He's gone."

Stecher's shoulders collapsed, he shrank together, bowed his head, and you could see that all the fight had gone out of him. He was a beaten man.

The funeral was a pathetic affair. Fortunately, it was the end of summer so that it was a simple matter to close the farm and move back to Riverdale. That, at least, following the familiar pattern, made it a little easier to bear. But he was gone, that energetic, that intelligent, that handsome young boy, so admired by all and so loved and planned for by Gurlie and his father. He had been wiped out, had vanished from their lives just at the moment when it seemed as if every promise that a child could show was to be realized.

But the war was there, life went on much as before and day followed day much as it had always done. Except for the unexpected suddenness of it, perhaps just for the suddenness of it—it seemed as if the tragedy had never occurred.

"It can't be," said Gurlie to herself. But it was and it must be said that whatever she felt, she was no crybaby.

In October when the first meeting of the Fortnightly Reading Club came due, though Joe would gladly have resigned the presidency, he took his place much as usual.

It was a long winter and a bitter one for German-Americans all over the United States. The *furor Teutonicus* that destroyed the library at Louvain, the sinking of neutral ships by submarines, the *spurlos versenkt* policy of Admiral von Tirpitz, and the organization of the Bund, with picnics at the New Jersey lake resorts, in the mountains, wherever the Kaiser's sympathizers, their wives and children could gather, marked the ensuing spring and early summer. But Joe had no part in it.

For all that, he felt himself to be a marked man. Bad luck had implied in the public mind a flagrant guilt of some sort. "You ain't living right," is always the popular verdict when our stars are overcast; "if you was, you wouldn't be that unlucky." He was suspect. He was, in short, a disloyal citizen in spite of all you could say. It went so far even as to the digging up of his past, his early connections with the American Federation of Labor when he had first come to America and used to make speeches at Cooper Union in favor of the workers. True, there came a time when in his opinion the workers had gone too far—but his hands had already been soiled; in the minds of his white-collared friends he would never be clean again.

"It always catches up with you." When he had left his old firm to compete against them for the United States money order contract, which he had won—the original basis of his success and "wealth"—there had been whisperings about him. "Crooked business," though nothing could have been more open. Certainly there had been crookedness in the awarding of the money order contracts in the past. To compete for them, true enough, his approach had to be secret, he could not have revealed his hand too soon or the older firm would have underbid him, even if they lost money on the deal. There had been crookedness involving the whole Post Office Department —but everything that he, Joe Stecher, had done had been absolutely above board.

His friends, middle-aged and obvious amateurs at the job, stood in the rhododendrons and from the dark looked through the front windows of former mayor Arents' house to see what might be going on there. Before them on the far wall of the large front room was the full length portrait of a man in semimilitary costume, on his head a felt hat bearing a feather, in his arms a gun, his legs were encased in leather leggings.

"The Kaiser! What do you know about that?"

The rumor spread about town that the former mayor had a portrait of the Kaiser in his front room. A full-length portrait. "Ain't that sumpin'?" Joe himself caught a glimpse one night of one of his most intimate friends among the shrubbery on his own front lawn. Incredible! His heart sank.

His son-in-law, the doctor, who tremendously pitied the man for all he recently had gone through, as always admired him and refused to be taken in.

"Why they got a machine-gun company," they said, "training up in Kronstadt," the neighboring suburb largely German-American, the town in fact from which their loved and trusted nurse "Wee Wee" had originated and with whose admirable brothers the young doctor was intimate.

He, without a drop of German blood in his veins, was furious and at once joined the *Turnverein* of that place and began to go there twice a week to attend gymnastic classes. He needed it anyhow to keep himself fit. He wasn't much of a gymnast, but he enjoyed it—he had done the same in Leipzig when he had been there earlier in his career as a medical student.

But his half-French mother was furious at him. "You are not natural," she blazed at him. "You are half-English and half-French," though that was not quite true. "Why do you do such things? You are not a *Boche*. Do you like to see them attack the French? *They* started the war. They are beasts! I hate them."

He paid no attention to her.

But when, anonymously, one of the local doctors had a letter published in the local paper saying that he was pro-German and advising people to give him a wide berth, he did get mad and write to the papers reminding the townsmen that the United States was neutral and that he was not going to turn against his friends for hearsay.

Former mayor Arents, having found out what was being spoken about him, that he had the picture of the Kaiser in his front room, invited his impugners in to inspect it and had the laugh on them when they found it to be only a portrait of himself in hunting costume. He could laugh, but Stecher could not.

The world was indeed a sad place from which it would be best to resign. The seasons were like the sea that kept beating upon a shore, now it was ice-clogged, unpeopled, but presently the sun would come back again, a pleasant surf would race in childlike and fall with a burst of laughter, white flowers—a tumble. Flossie was expecting her second child.

But when the submarines became more and more menacing, sinking everything encountered at the very shores of the United States; when the oil and wreckage began to be washed up on even the New Jersey and Long Island beaches; and President Wilson had finally withdrawn our diplomatic representatives in Berlin, some decision had to be made.

It was the winter of 1916. Social organizations all over the country were adopting resolutions backing the President in his determination to force the Germans to abandon the ruthless tactics or face the possibility of adding the United States to her enemies. We were in no way prepared for a war, our navy was insignificant, our army nonexistent. When the

Fortnightly Reading Club voted to back President Wilson in his policy, Joe voted, "No."

"I think he is wrong," argued Joe. "We are nominally neutral, but we are in fact supplying the English with arms, with fuel, with food, with everything that she needs to carry on her attacks. We should not do that."

"But if Germany could trade with us, as she did when she sent over the mercantile submarine the *Deutschland*, we would trade with her, too. But she can't. The fortunes of war are not under our control. England has the better navy; therefore she is able to trade with us. Germany is out of luck, that's all."

Joe would not accept that. "As a matter of fact, we are helping England. We are helping them at our own risk. Germany is at war. She is forced to do what she can to win. If we are England's friends, then she must attack our shipping." When the club asked that the vote be made unanimous Joe still voted, "No." At that moment many of his club members turned against him.

Not many months later the *Lusitania* was sunk in the North Atlantic and the fat was in the fire. War with Germany was declared by the United States. Joe and Gurlie resigned as members of the Fortnightly Reading Club shortly after.

"That's the end," said Joe to his wife.

"Not at all," said Gurlie.

"I'm going to sell the house. I don't want to live in the God-damned place any more."

"All right, let's go to the farm and make that our home."

"Sell that, too. Get rid of everything. It's brought us nothing but disaster."

"It's beautiful," said Gurlie. "It's the only place I want to be now. Build the house, a solid house. We can be comfortable there. And I will have my garden. You know yourself you enjoy it."

"No more." But, as always, Gurlie prevailed again.

"All right then," he said in his despairing mood, "we'll build a house. We'll build it of stone, the biggest God-damned house we can afford. A house to last two hundred years. Tell the architect we want the finest house money can buy. That's what it will be."

And so it was decided. Emotionally Joe was at the lowest ebb that he had ever known. For that reason his abandon was complete. You never knew what he was thinking; he had more than once dropped in others' hearing disparaging remarks upon his wife's intelligence. But at the moment he became emotionally entirely dependent on her, he resigned to her completely. Nothing, for the first time in his life, had to be guarded against. He had no more dependents. Lottie was gone, good riddance. Paul was dead. Perhaps that's the happiest thing that could have happened to him, dead in his happiest youth. Who would not envy him? As far as the other one was concerned—well, he'd see that she was taken care of, though there was no need of it. The doc was doing all right.

There was in fact, nothing to think of but himself—now that it was too late. A spirit of bravado, an intoxicating spirit of release made him laugh outright (am I going *verrückt?*) made him look at himself in the glass over the wash basin that morning when he realized that he was free! A free man for the first time, he had never experienced such a moment for as long as he could remember. Thoughts came to his mind of picnics in the Harz Mountains in Germany, when they'd taken a rag dipped in oil and folded it over their bare toes before placing them in the shoe. He couldn't at first understand what had come about. But what difference did it make? (when had he ever said that before—and meant it?) What difference to anyone?

So they had Fred, the architect, in, told him what they wanted, a big stone house of native-cut stone, four bedrooms on the second floor, with an open fireplace in each of them— and a place at the back where another wing could be added if they wanted it. Downstairs an apartment for the servants. The family would sleep under the gables on the third floor. A practicable heating system, refrigeration, a pool and billiard room in the basement . . .

Let her have it! She wants it—for all it's worth. Let her have it. I've got the money, I made it, I made it by the sweat of my brow. It's mine. Now she can take over. I made it. I enjoyed making it. Now let her spend it. That's what she enjoys and I'm the man to let her do it. To hell with it all.

The excavators started their work and ran into granite hard as flint after the first scoopfuls of topsoil!

"No matter. Blast! Blast it out!" said Joe. "Blow the damned rock to hell and gone. We're going to have a house like nothing in the neighborhood. Like nothing," said he looking up toward the mansion of the tycoon on the mountain in plain view to the southward, "like nothing in the neighborhood. Expense be damned."